SAN DIEGO PUBLIC LIBRARY

3 1336 03161 3350

LIT√

SAN DIEGO PUBLIC LIBRARY

ALWAYS BRING YOUR
CARD WITH YOU.

N 15 1993

GAYLORD

D1010522

THE SOUTHERN CONNECTION

OTHER BOOKS BY ROBERT BECHTOLD HEILMAN

America in English Fiction, 1760–1800 (1937)

This Great Stage: Image and Structure in King Lear (1948)

Magic in the Web: Action and Language in Othello (1956)
(Explicator Prize)

Tragedy and Melodrama: Versions of Experience (1968)

*The Iceman, the Arsonist, and the Troubled Agent:
Tragedy and Melodrama on the Modern Stage* (1973)

*The Ghost on the Ramparts and Other Essays in the
Humanities* (1974)

The Ways of the World: Comedy and Society (1978)
(Christian Gauss Prize of Phi Beta Kappa)

THE

SOUTHERN

Essays by Robert Bechtold Heilman

CONNECTION

LOUISIANA STATE UNIVERSITY PRESS
Baton Rouge and London

SAN DIEGO PUBLIC LIBRARY

3 1336 03161 3350

JUN 15 1993

Copyright © 1970, 1980, 1983, 1985 by Robert Bechtold Heilman.
New material copyright © 1991 by Louisiana State University Press
All rights reserved
Manufactured in the United States of America
First printing
00 99 98 97 96 95 94 93 92 91   5 4 3 2 1

Designer: *Laura Roubique Gleason*
Typeface: *Sabon*
Typesetter: *G & S Typesetters, Inc.*
Printer and binder: *Thomson-Shore, Inc.*

LIBRARY OF CONGRESS CATALOGING-IN-PUBLICATION DATA
Heilman, Robert Bechtold, 1906—
     The southern connection : essays / by Robert Bechtold Heilman.
        p.   cm.
     Includes bibliographical references and index.
     ISBN 0-8071-1631-9 (cloth : alk. paper)
        1. American literature—Southern States—History and criticism.
     2. Southern States—Intellectual life.   3. Southern States in
     literature.   I. Title.
     PS261.H37   1990
     810.9'975—dc20   90-40452
                                                              CIP

The paper in this book meets the guidelines for permanence and durability
of the Committee on Production Guidelines for Book Longevity of the
Council on Library Resources. ∞

To

Alex B. Daspit
Thomas and Josie Kirby
Lissy Voegelin

Friends from LSU days to the present

Contents

Preface

Though the materials in this volume deal mostly with the past, they in no way purport to be formal history. With an obvious exception or two (for example, the account of the contributors to the original *Southern Review*, 1935–1942, in I.2), my essays are not based on the research among archives that is the normal basis of professional history, and hence they do not advance the supported arguments that mark professional work. What I offer, instead, is the recollections and impressions of an amateur who was occasionally a participant and more often an observer. Though the world described is mainly academic, my account of it may fairly be called journalistic rather than scholarly. Perhaps a personal report of this kind may be of some use to formal historians.

In general I am presenting, for what it is worth, the point of view of a certain kind of observer. In the 1930s I was a newcomer in the South, I carried the usual baggage of prejudgments, and I had a good deal of learning to do during my twelve years in Louisiana. A few autobiographical passages will partly define my role. Starting as a complete outsider, I came to feel very much an insider (thanks to kindly southerners who let me enjoy this feeling), and I have continued to feel so, not self-deceptively I hope, while living elsewhere. Actually I have done most of my writing about southern subjects since leaving Louisiana early in 1948. Of the seventeen full-length essays and reviews that make up this volume, eight were published in the 1980s, three in the 1970s, two in the 1960s, two in the 1950s, and two in the 1940s.

Since situations change over the years, some of the earlier pieces may picture a past that seems quite different from the present, perhaps one not wholly recognizable. But a portrayal of that past may be both interesting in itself and even useful in the placing of subsequent developments. Hence I have let stand some earlier descriptions instead of trying to update them. Over the years one's style—that medley of perceptions, attitudes, and formulations—changes too, and now I would say, and perhaps see, some things differently. But I have retained most of my statements in their original form, and have made only a few local changes, mainly of phrasings that in 1989 seemed too pat, too simple, wrong in tone, or too hasty in that placing of blame that comes easily in early years. I have made no effort at major revisions. Through such revisions one might seek to reduce one's vulnerability and to produce a greater overall uniformity of manner, but in the end they would only bring things into line with a latter-day sensibility and a now current idiom that will also date.

Aside from changes in the objective situation that observers see, and in one's own intellectual and verbal style, there are changes in the atmosphere in which one writes. One responds to the current atmosphere in various ways, perhaps most perceptibly by obiter dicta and parenthetical allusions that suggest a timely knowingness held jointly by writer and reader. In the latter 1960s, for instance, it was easy to slip in covert references to demonstrations, street leaders, etc., ones that might be almost meaningless in later times. I have tried to eliminate references that in later decades might seem sadly dated or even puzzling. I hope that no entire essay appears to reflect only long-gone atmospheric conditions.

Writing long after events depicted, one has the benefit of hindsight, and one may fall into interpretations that perhaps were not possible at the time. One may read into the past something that belongs to later times; the tone of the survivor is different from that of the participant. Conversely, one's imaginative reengagement with a past may restore something of the feelings that one had then. One may actually recover a kind of energy and zest that belong to earlier times. With passing years, too, one may filter out the unease and uncertainties that belong to any whole past, and thus let reminiscences take on a special glow.

Finally, some of the parts in this collection were originally talks tailored to special occasions. Since the style meant for listeners is not easily made over into a style meant for readers, I have pretty much let the original forms stand. However, in the hope of forestalling a sense of stylistic discrepancy that a reader might feel, I have used initial footnotes to identify those sections of the book that had platform origins. (Otherwise I have tried to cut the use of footnotes to an inconspicuous minimum.) Actually, even in writing for readers rather than listeners, one unconsciously alters his manner as he imagines different audiences. In discussing a novel, for instance, I tend to think of its author as my "ideal reader"—the one whom I would especially like to believe that I am on the right track. Maybe this shortchanges other readers; I hope not.

The volume includes most of my essays on southern subjects, and of my reviews of books by southern writers. However, I have excluded discussions of such people as Ty Cobb and Tennessee Williams, who belong to other worlds than the South on which the present essays center—the South in which Baton Rouge was a significant scene, the *Southern Review* a significant event, agrarianism and the New Criticism significant centers of interest, and various writers in these or neighboring fields significant figures. In one way or another Eudora Welty and William Faulkner belonged to that South.

In writing about that South at different times and on different occasions and from different points of view, I have inevitably introduced some subjects (persons, events) more than once. In revision I have sought to eliminate repetitions that might seem due to simple forgetfulness or absentmindedness. On the other hand I have let stand an occasional repetition when the repeated matter seemed especially significant in a different context from that in which it first appeared. Thus what individuals are and do may be very significant in the discussion of an institution, and in turn institutional matters and events may be revelatory about an individual whom one is endeavoring to place. But I hope that the apparently justifiable repetitions are innocuously infrequent.

In arranging the materials I considered a chronological order, but I decided that this would result in rather a hodgepodge of diverse matters, each insufficiently related to what preceded and followed. Hence I have used a subject-matter order which I hope makes sense, with "Place," "Person," and "Thing," a familiar triad, as reasonably applicable captions for types of contents. One hopes not to have been too arbitrary in the placement of individual essays, and one is certainly aware of overlaps which deprive each division of logical perfection. And if I rejected chronology, oddly enough it sneaks back into an arrangement based on another principle: the placement by subject matter happens, quite accidentally, to represent a generally reverse chronology.

The acknowledgments to the original publishers of these essays and reviews appear after the essays.

I

PLACE: The University

I. 1

LSU in the 1930s and 1940s: First Impressions and Later Views

(1985)

i

Looking back fifty years comes easier than looking ahead fifty years. In 1935 looking ahead fifty years, even if one had thought of doing it, would have smacked of hubris. The main task was not going under in a not-very-comfortable present; aside from the usual vague hopes one did not imagine much of an existence beyond that present. For we were still in *the* Depression. Few will remember that one today. But then it seemed, if not terminal, at least interminable. Universities were generally cutting back, and some of my graduate-school contemporaries in the humanities were anticipating the 1970s by doing what we have come to call "exploring alternative career options." One was lucky to have an academic job, any job. I got my Ph.D. in 1935, but what in advance seemed to be an open door to the profession opened only one door for me—the door to LSU. At the time I did not know what a fortunate door it was.

My having only one door, and then finding that door opening on a richer world than one could expect, sets the tone for a glance at LSU fifty years ago. The door did not look promising to one using it for the first time, just as LSU would doubtless have seemed, to a detached observer, a hardly promising spot for the remarkable developments that were to occur. As a general rule, populist dictatorships do not lead to the establishment of elite quarterlies or push local military schools

Based on a paper read at a conference (at Louisiana State University in October, 1985) observing the fiftieth anniversary of the founding of the *Southern Review*.

3

toward national university status. My theme is, for the most part, such contrasts or even contradictions—not only the contrast between the probable and the actual but also, and more basically, a continuing doubleness, as I shall call it, within LSU. The initial impressions of a newcomer should serve as a convenient and suitable entry into a tale of two cities within the university.

My own life has some small parallels to the public occasion of 1985—the fiftieth anniversary of the founding of the *Southern Review*. I got my degree fifty years ago, as I have noted, and came to LSU fifty years ago. I also got married fifty years ago, and my wife's and my trip from the Northeast to Louisiana was in effect our honeymoon. We were finding ourselves in a strange, often difficult, and at times even intimidating world. A 1500-mile car trip was no joyride. There were no four-lane highways. When state and national highways were paved, they had an uneven blacktop surface with a high crown in the middle. Often they were just gravel roads. Detours could wind for many miles over wagon-track back roads; one of these, in north Georgia, made cars ford a stream. Roadside gas stations and eateries had a beat-up look. Dust-swathed and pitted-windshield cars were commonplace. Motels were not yet; we stayed in old hotels, usually with the bath down the hall, or in private residences that displayed signs saying "Rooms for Tourists." Nothing in the experience of the traveler intimated a brave new world that would offer new excitement and light. If one's reading had suggested a description, it might have been "Yoknapatawpha without Faulkner."

We drove along the coast from Mobile. Nighttime introduced us to the most varied, long-lasting, and vehement outpouring of sounds from nature that we had ever heard, from mosquitoes at one frequency to frogs at the opposite one. The lushness of growth everywhere seemed a little frightening. We drove through our first swarms of what we learned were called lovebugs, were virtually blacked in, and wondered whether all life would mean a stop every fifty miles for a windshield cleanup. Daytime temperatures were a stern probation. We watched heavy rain showers around the gulf, welcomed brief downpours, and found that they only steamed things up. The *State-Times* assured us that LSU football practices were going well on "these snappy fall afternoons." Since thermometers were reaching into the nineties every day, we shuddered at the thought of what unsnappy afternoons would be.

The Baton Rouge in which we arrived—on Labor Day, 1935—was nothing like today's urban center, often striking, often handsome, generally well-to-do in appearance. The population was 35,000, but the place looked and felt rural rather than urban. No freeways or Mississippi bridges provided easy access to other worlds; on the old Airline Highway to New Orleans one had repeatedly to dodge, or brake violently for, roving cattle. Baton Rouge streets were often badly paved or unpaved. The rich foliage of the present campus did not exist; what are now great old trees hadn't been put in or had just been put in. The university area looked bare and a little hard. It was more brash new than brave new. Nothing suggested a rich imaginative life.

We found a two-room apartment on the second story of a house overlooking the grounds just south of the Capitol. Our refrigerator was an icebox for which a block of ice was delivered each day. The melt dripped out through a pipe that ended in open air, and roaches used it as an entryway into the icebox and the food. Ants and mosquitoes were likewise in good supply. I do not believe that we had a portable electric fan then. In 1935 the only air cooling available was by means of a fan permanently installed in a window; it would suck in night air and bring down the inside temperature a little. We finally acquired one of these about 1941 or 1942, when we had our own house. Our experiences were representative, I believe; people who were going to write, edit, and think beyond the ordinary demands of life were not much coddled by creature comforts.

So much for the general scene, which hardly suggested large intellectual and literary happenings. Then there were forbidding events. On our seventh day in Baton Rouge, Sunday, we walked the block or two to the Capitol to look in on a meeting of the state legislature which, it had been announced, United States Senator Long would attend. We had already toured the imposing skyscraper Capitol, spacious in its public areas, handsomely marbled, the whole in contrast with a city then not very impressive architecturally. We found our way to the visitors' gallery at the rear of the lower-house chamber. In time Huey appeared on the floor, and we saw him in operation—chatting with members at various desks, striding from spot to spot, gesturing, sitting on the speaker's dais, summoning and sending. It was my one experience of seeing a single political leader wholly in command—dispensing, almost magically it seemed, what T. Harry Williams has called the "power in himself," exuding charisma; smiling, easy, almost urbane, yet falling a little short of it by a certain abruptness and thrust of nervous energy; tense, perhaps, but to the eye confident and even nonchalant; pressing, as we now know, ruthlessly toward political goals, and yet somehow managing to suggest a degree of aloof amusement at the show he was stage-managing. Before too long (twenty minutes? forty-five minutes? our recollections vary) Huey strode out, passing underneath our gallery; my memory is of many henchmen running along or following, and of a chamber still formally at business but now semi-empty, all but dead. A few seconds later there was a strange outburst of sounds in a rapid but irregular sequence. Firecrackers, I thought, puzzled. Then men came running back into the chamber below us and ducking behind desks. It had to be gunfire, though to a new young Ph.D., fresh out of Harvard, this was unbelievable. We were hearing the shots that killed Dr. Carl Weiss and fatally wounded Senator Long, who died a day and a half later.

We wondered, Is this the way they always settle political differences in Louisiana? How would it be in higher education? The shock was followed by the surprise of seeing hundreds of mourners for Long come in from all over the state and camp on the Capitol grounds for the several days before the Long funeral—a singular response to a man whom, through the Northern press, we knew only as a dangerous threat to American political well-being. Several days later, another shock: Dr. William A. Read, then head of the English department, dropped in at our flat to tell us that he wasn't sure that the university would open on schedule the next week. Longer mourning period was my first thought. But no; Dr. Read evidently feared that Senator Long's death would totally disrupt all the institutional processes of the state. This was a frightening possibility for a new instructor, heavily in debt, skilled only in ordinary classroom procedures, and at the bottom of the totem pole in what would continue to seem, for some time, a quite alien world. And what kind of world was it in which one man's death might bring a whole state to a standstill? Happily, Dr. Read's fears were not borne out by fact. Though still shaken, we began teaching on schedule.

In one of my wife's classes in freshman English there turned up a young man named Russell Long, then sixteen, the son of the senator who had just been assassinated; the next year he would appear in a section of mine in a sophomore course. If we felt any trepidations about having the son of a political dictator in class, they were groundless. Russell was an earnest, solid B-plus student, well behaved, unspoiled, stubborn in his positions, and having total faith in his father as a savior-figure. After all the shocks of that hot September, Russell's style as student provided some reassurance about Louisiana life, at least in the university. Russell was already set on a political career, and he trained for it by running rather flamboyant campaigns for student office. He once used a plane to drop leaflets to the electorate, and I believe small presents for those who could grab; I vaguely recall, also, handouts of ice-cream cones to the electorate. A few years later, as a married graduate student, Russell lived for a while in a house near ours, and we had occasional yard-work chats. He seemed on the one hand the responsible young householder, and on the other the politician-in-training, marked equally by a sense of hereditary mission and a sense of how the world goes.

ii

Term opening revealed an aspect of heavy-duty faculty life that perhaps went out when the Depression gave way to the War. All faculty members were supposed to work at registration, sitting in long rows behind tables in front of which students lined up for instructions and advice. This was in a gymnasium or some such large space. We newcomers to the game were given hasty instructions about requirements, sectioning, and so on, and then turned loose to impart information and wisdom to the students who were stuck with us. I never could learn about catalogs, I was a flop at registration, and in time I began to cheat by being mysteriously missing on opening day. Did Brooks and Warren also serve, if only by sitting and waiting? My sense of it is that LSU was not then making, for people of special attainment, any of the concessions which are now familiar the country over.

Like the city and the university, the English department was small: it did not have the magnitude that we ordinarily presuppose as a basis for large enterprise. Unless my memory is even worse than I take it to be, there were just nine people in the professorial ranks—Dr. Read, the head (*head* was not yet a four-letter word), and professors Bradsher, Uhler, Bryan, Joan Miller, Brooks, Warren, Olive, and Downey; there was also a considerable subprofessorial staff concerned largely with freshman English. It was a boost to our sorry financial situation when my wife was given a spot in this cadre; as I remember it, she was called an associate. Her schedule was fifteen hours—five 3-hour courses— and I do not believe·that it changed during her ten years of teaching. Her 1935 salary was $1,100, and it went up little, if at all, in ten years. Another member of this staff was Estelle Lower, later Mrs. T. Harry Williams.

As an instructor I had the same fifteen-hour teaching schedule. In my first year I taught two sophomore classes and three freshman classes. The former averaged 75 students, the latter 30; so my student total was about 240 per term. The ninety weekly themes I read myself. For the sophomore classes I had a student assistant, whose task was to grade the true-false, multiple-choice, and fill-in examinations on which we largely relied (as we likewise did in the freshman English finals).

After a year I was promoted to assistant professor, and my teaching schedule went down from fifteen hours to twelve. This seemed a relatively easy load, at least in the sense that it was what I had mostly had since I began full-time teaching in 1928. Toward the end of my time at LSU I believe I got down to nine hours for a term or two; perhaps Tom Kirby, by then the department head, was able to say that for the other three hours I had been assigned to do research. My impression is that Brooks and Warren never got below nine hours, even during the seven heavy-work-load years of the *Southern Review*.

My incoming salary, when I had my degree and six years of teaching experience, was $1,800. With my promotion to assistant professor I got a tremendous raise—to $2,400. It was my first salary over $2,000, which I had received in the pre-Depression year of 1928 to 1929, when I was still only A. B., but which I had been below ever since. That $600 raise was my largest at LSU. After that my salary rose slowly. Between 1936 and 1948, when I left, it had gone up from $2,400 to $4,700— an average of not quite $200 a year. Obviously summer-school teaching was desirable, indeed close to indispensable, and I stuck to it for about ten years. A standard teaching schedule was fifteen hours, that is, three 5-hour courses. In the summer of 1936 the salary for that load, at my rank, was $350. It must have gone up after that, but the figures escape me.

To cite these figures is in no way to complain or to introduce the well-worn how-tough-it-was-in-my-day motif. The figures may have some general antiquarian interest that is not out of place in a historical survey. But the principal function of the figures is to help give a concrete impression of LSU at that time. They clearly show that LSU was in most ways a parochial Depression place—penny-pinching, narrow-gauge, getting by, in no aspect of its style suggesting the capability of imaginative outlays for venturesome projects. It was, so to speak, not a place in which the *Southern Review* was a probable event; it might not be overstating the case to speak of the *Review* as an impossible event.

On the personnel front, too, there was little to suggest plan, program, or vision. Procedures seemed casual and hit-or-miss. Today, Brooks and Warren would be brought in, after the usual "national search," and expected to do big things. Then, they just happened to be here and, as far as LSU was concerned, were, I suspect, no more than a couple of guys that Dean Charles Pipkin happened to know, or know of, as fellow southern boys who like him had had Rhodes scholarships. I got my job at LSU simply on the personal say-so of A. J. Bryan, who had been in the department for some years, and whom I knew as a fellow graduate student at Harvard. An old boy vouched for some friend who then showed up as a new boy. I have no sense of there having been much, if any, institutional search and screening. Perhaps because of the Depression, perhaps because it was a different world, we who came did little screening of the university—certainly nothing of the tireless scrutiny that became rather too familiar when later on I was conducting an appointments process elsewhere. What research grants do you have? How good is your research library? How is your university press? Does it look to the English department for manuscripts? No, on both sides things were quite informal. I received no blueprints of what was expected of me; I heard nothing about standards for tenure and promotion. At this stage of the game the usual emotional cycle is Ph.D. exhilaration, post-Ph.D. depression, and then pretenure anxiety. Though I had enough anxieties to be quite conventional, I can't remember tenure tension. I do not remember whether I ever formally received tenure. One more or less assumed that a job was a lifetime affair, even if students did not entirely love one. There were, as far as I know, no teaching evaluations. The term *publish or perish* was not yet invented, and I don't think anything was ever officially said or implied about publication as a professional activity. Still, the subject was somewhat and somehow in the air. A friend of mine in another department, adopting a *faux naïf* stance, jested ironically: "What's this about writing? What do they want me to write? If they tell me what they want me to write, I'll do it."

iii

When I say that writing in no way seemed to be officially expected of faculty, but that the idea of writing was much in the air, I of course describe an aspect of that doubleness which, at the outset, I set forth as an identifying characteristic of the LSU of fifty years ago. That 1935 situation was remarkable and even now seems fascinatingly unexpected: on the one hand, the Depression, messy politics (they would get even messier in the late 1930s), a dictatorship, violent death, mass mourning, the fear of general collapse; on the other, the presence of gifted persons, a fusion of minds and personalities in an influential intellectual and literary flowering, all this evident in such phenomena as the founding of the Louisiana State University Press, the big literary conference in the spring of 1935, and the founding of the *Southern Review*. So far I have been mainly describing the aspects of that world which would lead one to expect institutional ordinariness rather than the extraordinary developments that took place. I want now to sum up or expand somewhat the contrasts or contradictions which created the "doubleness," and then to go on to a fuller look at the excellences which have become memorable.

Like the university itself, the immediate outside world would hardly have seemed conducive to a major literary enterprise or a think-tank world. Yet it is clear that a small southern city, not very centrally located, and not yet endowed with many comforts that we take for granted, did not impede a new creative outburst in the university. A certain spirit, however generated, triumphed over terrain, location, and discomfort.

In sum, LSU not only was an undistinguished institution in an un-distinguished city, but it had many of the stigmata of the Depression university. On the other hand, the Huey Long way of doing things, which included both securing new tax revenues and indulging a sin-gular passion for LSU, supplied the university with funds that enabled it to expand, at least in parts, when numerous comparable universities were retrenching. Brooks and Warren joined the English staff just be-fore 1935; three new appointees came in 1935, and two more in 1936. Within five years seven newcomers were added to the professorial ranks, which rose to a total of eighteen by 1947 (with at least the same number in other ranks). And given the general salary range in the 1930s, the outlays for the *Southern Review,* as well as for the School of Music, which was taking on a comparable distinction, were rela-tively enormous.

The creation of the *Southern Review* implied an interest in writing, even though scholarship and writing were neither enjoined nor un-officially recommended. But even in the absence of institutional pres-sures, they were getting done. Dr. Read had been writing prolifically about place names (I still remember his delight when he hit upon an etymology for the well-known Louisiana surname *Cazedessus*). Warren had already published a biography and was publishing poems and essays; Brooks was writing essays. Likewise people in other de-partments were writing. In some way the university had acquired members who wrote spontaneously, autonomously. Individual talent modified local tradition; we had personal examples rather than insti-tutional imperatives and codified stepladders.

It is this aspect of doubleness which brings into the open the ques-tion that lies behind all the contrasts and inconsistencies that charac-terized the LSU of the 1930s: how explain the doubleness? More spe-cifically, how did that LSU manage to bring in, in effect welcome, and perhaps even stimulate a number of fertile, creative minds that perma-nently changed the air? That problem leads more to speculation than to explanation. We may have to settle for that concept of chance which we usually phrase as the presence of the right people at the right place at the right time. But that tells us little. I want to make a guess which, while it still leaves the matter rather abstract, unanchored to precise historical facts, at least improves on the idea that all was chance. My guess is that what happened at LSU—specifically the remarkable influx of talent—had its ultimate roots in the imaginativeness evident in the very complex makeup of the man who ruled Louisiana for a time. It was an imaginativeness which could grasp ends beyond profit and power. Huey had it, and I suspect it influenced his appointment of some underlings who had the same quality, notably President James Monroe Smith. Smith was a very imaginative man, even in the stock-market venture that led to his downfall and imprisonment (Huey's statehouse followers seemed unable to imagine the consequences of conspicuous looting). And aside from that more or less direct channel, the impulse to imaginative leaps could conceivably have been carried more or less unconsciously by lesser university people than Smith who had some influence on the way things went.

Questions of source aside, the influx of some quite gifted people led to a certain internal doubleness in the thirties: the one between the productive or creative individuals who moved toward a more ecumenical intellectual or professional life, and the comfortable academic citizens who were pretty much content with life in the parish. Initially this was not much more than a contrast in style, with perhaps some reciprocal feelings of annoyance or irritation between what we might call new boys and old boys. (In no way, having been a new boy then, do I want this to be a diatribe against the old boys of the day. Throughout academe, new boys tend to bring with them a sense of the excellence of the ways of doing things at the places they come from, and a desire to transplant these ways to the place they have come to. Hence they tend not to have a very high opinion of the resident old boys. Having now lived long enough to have grown from several new-boy-hoods into old-boy-hood, and to have seen different versions of both classes, I am no longer sure that our new-boy criticalness of old boys was as entirely objective as it seemed then.) In time the doubleness of attitude took more solid form in overt action. Some of the more restless faculty tried to have some influence on institutional direction—procedures, standards, appointments, and so on. Nineteen of us got out a rather modest manifesto suggesting some alterations, by no means revolutionary, in LSU; the basic idea, I suppose, was the one put into words by Tom Cowan of the Law School, that LSU should be "more like a university." We probably achieved some stylistic abrasiveness, but I doubt that we stated more than academic truisms. Still, what a furore! In reply, 176 faculty members issued a countermanifesto asserting that LSU was absolutely first-rate just as it was. This was unusual school spirit by faculty members. The doubleness had an amusing side: one faculty member signed both manifestos. Comic doubleness within the individual soul. Still another version of that doubleness: some of the 176 said that they signed the second manifesto because they had been given no opportunity to sign the first one. Ah, the thwarted joiner instinct!

The make-it-new versus keep-it-the-same division did not involve two other kinds of doubleness, one of which we might historically expect, and the other of which was alleged at the time. If it was in some sense new boy versus old boy, it was not scholar-critic versus nonscholar. The 176 included some good established scholars, mostly, if my memory is correct, on the science and engineering sides. Again, certain defenders of the status quo complained about some alleged nogoods for whom the going term was *Yankee troublemakers*. But the division was, happily, in no way northerners versus southerners. The nineteen were about as evenly divided as a prime number could be between northerners and southerners, and the 176 had a healthy infusion of good old Yankee boys. The system of doubleness was not quite the simple affair that a doubleness can sometimes be.

Finally, there was one other doubleness, though rather more elusive than those I've noted. This one faintly reflected breezes blowing from the State Capitol. Some campus characters always seemed to have vague statehouse ties; some could quietly but audibly hint at a Long connection. Thus one could feel, in spots, a faint derivative air of quid-pro-quo-ism. (Minor example: one department secretary managed to let some staff members feel that professional goodies could be arranged if, and so on.) On the other hand, there were campus characters who hated Long and all his works and methods and successors. But these contrasting styles never shaped up into a clear-cut good guys versus bad guys split. Things were more complicated than that. After all, the statehouse characters, whatever they were up to on their own political and economic front, were committed to the Long tradition of magnifying the university. So they might gain tolerance, if not total forgiveness. At any rate, one expectable alignment seems not to have occurred: namely, that the "make it more like a university" group would also become a political-purity action demanding total divorce between campus and Capitol. We tended rather to utilize any slender political resources that might be tapped, or tactics that might be invoked. Rigid partisanship was doubtless made difficult by an ironic doubleness in the state as well as in the university. One aspect of this situation was nicely put by Robert Harris, then head of the Department of Government, after the 1939 scandals had made an official reform movement politically feasible. Harris said, "We have to vote for stupid reformers or bright crooks." Of course, some of the latter turned out not to be terribly bright.

To sum up: at its seventy-fifth birthday LSU was in a transitional period marked by many contrasts in aims, attitudes, and indeed sensibility. But the conflicting elements on different axes never came together enough to create an all-out polarization of objectives and styles. In retrospect one sees energizing differences rather than a potentially disastrous irreconcilability.

iv

The central doubleness, of course, was that of local tradition and individual talent. Not only was LSU expanding during a depression, but it was making some outstanding appointments. You might call it luck, or surmise the unusual availability of gifted people in a depression. On the other hand, when these people came here, the place did not discourage them or reject them. That's the big point. There was some sort of institutional vitality that could live with difference, even superiority. I have suggested a subterranean imaginativeness under the surface of ordinary humdrum existence, an undefined readiness for institutional adventuring, an intangible susceptibility to "conversion." But on the whole we can describe better than we can interpret.

There was a palpable doubleness in the Department of English into which I came in 1935. The department had long been in the hands of establishment figures of whom now it is fitting only to say *requiescant in pace*. Still, in the 1930s the appointive process was showing an almost mysterious imagination and feeling for quality. The opening wedge of a new order was of course the arrival in the early 1930s of Cleanth Brooks and Robert Penn Warren, who in relatively few years would be well on the way to national fame. Other new arrivals would achieve different kinds of distinction. In my first biennium at LSU the newcomers in English included Thomas A. Kirby, a rising mediaevalist who would soon become department chairman for a fantastically long tenure; Nathaniel Caffee, who later was provost of the university; Arlin Turner, who went on to Duke and served as editor of *American Literature;* Bosley Woolf, later a major figure at Merriam-Webster and the editor-in-chief of their eighth Collegiate edition. Harris Downey and a little later John Wildman revealed talents in both poetry and fiction, and Wildman did a good book on Trollope. George Marion O'Donnell, the promising young poet from Tennessee, was on the staff for a while; a troubled man, he died young. William Van O'Connor was there for a year or two, and was doing his book on tragedy— unusual in that it was a pre-Ph.D. affair; after military service he would become a very productive critic, teaching in various universities and finally assuming the chairmanship at California-Davis.

Other departments also made outstanding appointments, and these contributed to a widely felt vitality in the College of Arts and Sciences. In the next essay I shall recall various individuals whose presence contributed to the new academic spirit. Here I concentrate on the Department of Government, which had wide variety in its staff, and which exhibited another, and very significant, version of the doubleness that I have been attributing to the LSU of the 1930s and 1940s and have made an underlying theme of this account. (The department was not yet the "Department of Political Science." Robert Harris, department chairman for a while, declared that the field was not a "science." He quoted a Vanderbilt professor who, a practicing poet as well as a professional historian, declared at some public occasion, "I speak with authority, not because I *am called* a social scientist, but because I *am* a poet.") Two members of the department I knew only slightly: Charles Pipkin, dean of the Graduate School and nominal editor of the *Southern Review;* and Willmoore Kendall, the bright but perverse fomentor of scenes and schemes, later at Yale, and finally at the University of Dallas, where a program in literature and science was named after him.

I am glad to claim longtime friendships, some of them close, with other members of the department. Alex Daspit, an LSU alumnus and Rhodes scholar, was a delightful ironist, whose loss we felt when he went off to the State Department for what was to be a lifetime career (one August, years later, we stayed in the Daspits' apartment in Paris). Alden Powell, a genial midwesterner, had a natural ease with all kinds of people; he gained the confidence of established figures on the campus and hence became valuable as a mediator in some of the skirmishing between the old order and the younger insurgents. With an amiable reasonableness he could define different objectives and attitudes in un-quarrelsome neutral terms. Robert Harris, one of the distinguished Vanderbilt alumni on the faculty, was a wonderfully witty observer of academic and political matters; he was an artist both in the needling of folly and the deadpan teasing of complacency. It was he who said of a member of another department, "Yes, of course he is bilingual. He is illiterate in two languages." It was he who said to a dean evidently yearning for a presidency that everyone knew could not possibly come his way, "Please resist any attempt to get you away from us; we need you here" (as a butt, of course). Later Harris had a long period as dean at the University of Virginia, surely much better equipped than most administrators for verbal jousting with faculty complainants.

Three other political scientists came to LSU in the latter part of the period which is my subject, and by pleasant accidents of geography I was able to see a good deal of them in our post-LSU years. In point of time the last arrival of the three was Harold Stoke, who, with a degree in political science, came to LSU as president at the beginning of my last year. Giving up a successful presidency at the University of New Hampshire, and later becoming president of Queens College in New York City, Stoke was the first nonsouthern president of LSU in modern times. When LSU appointed him, it manifested an academic ven-turousness which is one aspect of the doubleness which is my main theme here. If Stoke did not wholly gratify all the constituencies that inevitably besiege a president, nevertheless his style and spirit won many longtime admirers, and indeed some observers believed that in the long run he might have triumphed over the difficulties that arose during his administration (1947–1951). To some extent the situation may be symbolized by a judgment made to Stoke by Earl Long, whose worldly intelligence Stoke much respected: "Of course you're right, Doc, but you can't make it stick here." Long's remark may have had to do (if, when Stoke reported this to me, he defined the context, I have forgotten it) with the admission of the first black student to LSU—a large issue of which I heard Stoke give a very objective, and yet also very moving, account in a paper read to a town-gown discussion group in Seattle many years later. Talking about this issue to me, Stoke paid a very great compliment to the student body of LSU: "If it had depended on the students alone, there would have been no difficulty in integrating LSU." This was three or four years before the Supreme Court decision.

My other two friends in political science I come to last because they best reveal another aspect of LSU doubleness. These two men have hardly anything in common except an odd coincidence in their life spans: born within a few months of each other at the turn of the century, they died on the same day in January, 1985. The *American Spectator* mentioned their deaths in the same sentence and asserted that their departure "lowered the I.Q." of the nation. The men I refer to were Charles Hyneman, who chaired the department at LSU from 1937 to 1942, and Eric Voegelin, who came to LSU in 1942 and stayed until the late 1950s, when he left to direct a Bavarian state research institute in Munich. Two more contrasting people could hardly have been found in one department: the student of pragmatic politics in America, and the political theorist, and indeed formal philosopher, of international repute. In their unlikenesses they illustrate the extraordinary range and flexibility of appreciation that LSU had acquired a half century ago.

Hyneman was an easy, articulate, and forceful speaker; he was effective in the public pressing of issues in faculty and AAUP meetings; in debates on policy, he was really the only competent public speaker among us who felt that we wanted to "make it more like a university." In his own field, I suppose Hyneman took theory more or less for granted; his abiding interest was in practical politics, in the public machinery of the American system, in the history and style of American institutions—a large field in which he would later do a great deal of writing. He liked to bring the academic view of things to the ears of working politicians, and discuss issues with them. He told me once of a very satisfactory session with Governor-Elect Sam Jones: they sat with their feet on the table and talked the same language. While Hyneman was at LSU he formed what would be a lifelong friendship with Hubert Humphrey, who had arrived in the influx of exceptional graduate students in English and in political science (Humphrey's future colleague in the U.S. Senate, Russell Long, was in the Law School at the time). Hyneman and Humphrey planned to collaborate on several books; but these projects were victims of Humphrey's primary devotion of energy to campaigning for, and holding, public office. During the war Hyneman worked in the War Department (part of the time with Harold Stoke, who would become LSU's president two years after the war). Later he became chair at Northwestern and finally Distinguished Professor at Indiana University. He was at one time president of the American Political Science Association.

In its welcome to Eric Voegelin LSU showed its extraordinary capacity for cherishing a totally different breed of professional scholar—the profound theorist for whom the truths of political life were inextricably interwoven with the history of ideas, with philosophy, with theology, and indeed with the practices of traditional aesthetic modes. He had little of Hyneman's interest in the immediate political scene, which for the most part he found obvious or amusing or at best a useful illustration of theory. But he surpassed many observers in his knowing precisely what given political actions meant. From the start he understood nazism completely, and he was always a heroically outspoken antagonist of the Nazis. (He was not Jewish; his heritage was Lutheran, and it always influenced him.) When the Nazis entered Vienna, he had to flee, leaving all possessions behind, and playing a risky hide-and-seek game such as one finds in melodramas of political intrigue. With his enormous intellectual and imaginative gifts, with his formidably extraordinary learning (he read a vast spread of documents and texts in Hebrew, Greek, Latin, German, English, and the major Romance languages, and he made some approaches to Oriental languages), and with his inclination to candor in observations on men and ideas, he scared off more than one major American university. He did not scare off LSU, he was made to feel at home, and in his fifteen years at LSU he not only won many student admirers but was an enormously productive scholar. The magnitude of his work will be overwhelmingly apparent in the multivolume edition of his writings now being prepared at the LSU Press.

Voegelin had another talent exceptional in the gifted group of LSU political scientists: he was a superb interpreter of literature. His study of James's *Turn of the Screw,* written first in a long letter to me eventually published in the *Southern Review,* is the profoundest of the many that have been called forth by that ambiguous novel. On the other hand, Voegelin and Hyneman, polar opposites as they were in professional life, were remarkable in having in common one interest that, as far as I know, neither spoke about. Eric was a gifted pianist with a mastery of many classical scores (he knew them by heart, I believe), and Charles had amassed, and used, a great collection of recordings of classical compositions.

To sum up: the traditional political philosopher, European in intellectual and personal style, combining graciousness with formality and punctiliousness; and the American pragmatist, a folksy, slangy, midwestern small-town boy, were both welcomed and made at home by a provincial state university, still strongly attached to its military tradition, and just emerging from obscurity at its seventy-fifth birthday. Its basic doubleness was to be its hereditary self and yet to be hospitable to these outsiders who would change that self; and its corresponding doubleness was to entertain such strikingly different immigrants. All this tells us something about its range, potential and actual. That range is otherwise reflected in the birth, fifty years ago, of the *Southern Review.* On the one hand, LSU was a medley of old boys, parochialism, and a more recent existence as institutional pet of a populist dictator; and on the other hand open to, and having a singular gift for, the kind of appointments that brought in a Brooks, a Warren, a Voegelin, and many other first-rate scholars and intellectuals. Those were not merely old times; they were extraordinary times.

I.2

LSU in the 1930s and 1940s: Diversity, Achievements, Personalities

(1980)

i

Samuel Hynes's *Auden Generation* (1977) takes off from the historical fact that in the 1930s to think was to think politically, and if
one was traveling anywhere, with or without fellows, the right turn to
make was to the left. By the time the more perceptive converts were
finding that the left was not right after all, the right was becoming sinister, so that by the forties there was no choice: one had to live with the
world's left in the hope that the center would remain a possibility. Historical pendulums of sensibility being what they are, it might have
been predicted that by the fifties the left would become generally sinister, if not that it would spawn excesses of exorcism by a right fallen
into gross manipulating hands.

To live in Baton Rouge, Louisiana, from 1935 on was to be pretty
much outside the pressures of the right thinking that turned utopian
seekers leftward. One kind of cultural critic might attribute this freedom from up-to-dateness to regional underdevelopment, to a back-
water failure to move up front, to a hand-me-down reactionary resistance to sure cures, innovation, the wave of the future, and so on, or to
a death-wish hostile to life (headline variety, of course). Other such
clichés will come to mind. But I can think of no faculty member at
Louisiana State University in that period who would wish to have been
more in the van of political fashion, more under constraint to get in
line with the Good. Unless one is lucky and has extra genes for skepticism, it takes too much energy to resist political haute couture or
haute cuisine. Thirty years later a colleague said to me: "You know
what saved you and me a lot of headaches in the Depression? We

weren't joiners." Just this might be said of most of the talented junior people who made LSU a better-than-average place to be. By a non-joiner I mean a person who doesn't join what everyone is joining at a given time—not a person without adherences and loyalties. Among colleagues with whom I felt most at home there was never a dominant movement of any kind. Instead there was an unusually wide range of sympathies or affiliations. There were many conventional "liberals," of course, and there were "conservatives" of different hues; part of my own education was hearing judicious people speak of liberals as persons whose depth, dogmas, and reality-sense did not always match their good intentions. There was a wide spectrum of ideas as to what the South meant and where it should go: agrarianism, regionalism, modernization, industrialization, internationalism all attracted capable voices. There were men and women with religious convictions, and most secularists were not fanatical evangelizers. There were several Communists, whether party members or just emotional kinfolk I do not know. One of these was a Trotskyite, a talented creative man who, a saint by inclination, later chose to limit himself to handicraft work in common life. There was one admirer of Nazi Germany, who may have reconsidered by the 1940s; he was a longtime professor elsewhere, and never a *cause célèbre*. One professor of art was ahead of his times in pedagogical theory: he sought to enrich the educational experience by gamboling on the green with students or cutting snowball capers with them during our quinquennial inch of snow.

Some of my generalizations are incarnated in specific memories. 1) One colleague, already approaching distinction, held a visiting professorship in a good midwestern university; on returning he recounted the classroom difficulties with Marxist emigrants from New York who had already mastered the truth of all things. They were the first wave of an educational type that would materialize in several later forms—the Unteachables. 2) A faculty Communist who might not be understood in Moscow persuaded a colleague that a true leftist would give away precious possessions. Enthusiasm led the new convert, little endowed with worldly goods, to lay giving hands on his wife's hereditary silver. She caught on in time. 3) A dinner invitation to the Naziphile's house created some trepidation. Would the host propose a toast to the führer? As it turned out, the only actual strain was looking at the juxtaposed likenesses of Luther and Hitler in the bedroom where we left our wraps, and using one's eyes instead of one's mouth when the truly beautiful blonde hostess naïvely extolled life in the new Germany.

Instead of having to contend with a forceful party line that would generate submission or resistance and thus determine the basic color scheme of existence, we enjoyed a remarkably free air and lived with an unquarrelsome diversity of preferences. I fully appreciated this comfortable pluralism only after I had moved to a northern university and found, at least in those areas of it where my professional and personal lives were centered, a dominant "liberalism" which meant not so much an easy living with different options as a set of specific beliefs to which it was understood that all good men would adhere. (Once, when I was serving on a search committee for a major position in another department, a member of it said of one candidate: "Let's get him; he's a liberal." The same department felt quite ill treated by a visiting professor, a distinguished scholar, who did not confess until he arrived on the ground that he was, of all things, a Catholic.) This somewhat puritanical air of constraint enabled me to look back on the Deep South university as providing a more open and flexible world. The evidence was not only the range of basic perspectives held but the personal and professional congeniality among those who held them. The differences in no way interfered with a broadly shared belief that the university was capable of better things (we had doubtless a large portion of the youthful impatience with actuality that we have since observed in successive academic generations), a common feeling for the larger worlds of letters and art and thought that should influence the local scene, and an ability to cooperate in institutional activities meant to benefit the place. (Not that the cast lacked people who could go principled at odd moments. One humorless humanist was driven to censorious apothegm by a colleague's wearing a borrowed Harvard Ph.D. gown at commencement: "A man who fudges in small things will fudge in large.")

This hanging loose instead of going rigid paralleled a certain living with differences encouraged by the demographic makeup of Louisiana. Baton Rouge lies roughly between the Baptist north (often called "hardshell") and the Catholic south, between the hill country from which sprang the Long revolution and the delta country rich in the plantation houses of the ancien régime. Besides, there were the rural Catholicism of the Cajun (Acadian) regions, and the urban Catholicism of New Orleans: the puritanical and the worldly versions of the church. These divergent communities evolved a modus vivendi, and the university made some adjustments instead of proclaiming its own infallibility. In our day there was some sort of local Index, and at times it included titles on the reading lists of English courses. So we had alternative titles ready, and readings could always be found which seemed neither sinful to the readers nor shameful to the instructors (though the stronger in mind could get a bit exclamatory about it). The Index had more influence with rural than with urban students, who tended to smile at the alternate-readings people but of whom few would have been up to the observation made to me by an English major from New Orleans: "The safety of the Church does not depend on what I read." My impression is that departmental accommodatingness allowed more persuasive maneuvers than high-toned combat would have. "Oh, you can't read that? Too bad. I think you would have enjoyed it." But if there was a fair amount of urbanity in the air, I must not claim a cosmopolitanism beyond the overall university talents. I remember some students coming in bug-eyed over the heroics of an intellectual desperado in geology who kept pounding his lectern in a fury over the cosmological shortcomings of Genesis. We took him to be a recent fugitive from the upstate hardshells or the Cajun Catholics; either neoworldling was likely to get the shakes from the new-thought alcoholism of graduate school. The unchainer of mankind was not an LSU special, though; to this day virtually every faculty endures a local Prometheus, who brings fiery thought to local mankind as he boldly discloses falsities in elders, powers, and traditions and thus becomes a darling of the youngsters and the press.

After the death of Huey Long in 1935, the Long movement fell into the hands of henchmen not gifted enough to let private perquisite be decorously shaded by public profit, and by 1939 they were heading colorfully into various state and federal jails. Among them was the president of the university, who was using state funds in a grandiose stock-market venture that didn't quite come off. Such doings seemed— if my impressions after many decades are reliable—less like appalling vice and crime that demanded an all-out fight by everybody than like

some kind of Gilbert and Sullivan picturesque and picaresque ras-
cality. If the principals had all been as wittily jesting as they were cynical, they might have been Falstaffs. Their doings hardly stirred us into
a crusade; on the contrary the ironic probability is that the non-
puritanical air of state politics contributed indirectly to the sense of
freedom and ease on the campus. Be that as it may, the university
could enjoy an increasing academic stature traceable ultimately, if not
directly, to Huey's almost paternal concern and, as I have proposed in
essay I.1, to a less-noticed quality in him, an imaginativeness which
rose above the usual ends of dictatorship. Granted, he was charmed by
sideline spectaculars such as football and the band, but still it was in
his day that some strong general impetus to new life sprang up in LSU.
The results on our side of the campus were a first-rate music school, a
superior fine arts department, a flock of good appointments in various
departments, and at least four new journals (among the ones with
scholarly specialties I remember those in history, sociology, and political science), of which the outstanding one was the *Southern Review*.
Its life spanned the seven years from the death of Huey (1935) to the
final winding up of the post-Huey scandals in a shift of political power
in the state (1942). The *Review* grew famous; the English department
picked up luster from it and attracted some very good graduate students; and through it the university as a whole gained respect in quarters that had hardly known of it before. Indeed it won some honor
among a laity of whom such reading might not be expected. Once a
Baton Rouge printer showed me with pride his own seven bound volumes of the *Review*. His sense of it as a regional achievement of national repute was surely not unique.

ii

Whatever the trick-and-treat musical-comedy shenanigans at the north
edge of downtown Baton Rouge, where the State Capitol shot up forty
floors above the endless flatness, there was great professional activity
some miles to the south where the campus spread over many acres.
Some of us worked a little for internal changes, that is, for the introduction of academic and administrative patterns that we had known
elsewhere and thought salubrious. I don't know whether we had any
impact; perhaps some on the filling of headships and deanships, which

may have gone a little less readily to good old local boys of dependable innocuousness.

Cleanth Brooks and Robert Penn Warren were interested in these strivings, thus differing from literary people who have since become fixtures in universities and who rarely care about university well-being. Brooks and Warren did not use the combined demands of their own writing, their editing of the *Review*, and their teaching to justify an indifference to institutional welfare. Brooks in particular was active on the university front, and many a caucus took place at his house. Our activities involved collaboration among instructors of different social and political views. This finding of common grounds, or of accommodation among diverse ones, appeared in such English department activities as planning curricula and setting up degree requirements. We new Ph.D.s, of course, drew on the practices of our own graduate schools, which now looked more nearly ideal than in predoctoral days, and these had to be reconciled. Yet in all of them the basic expectation was a wide knowledge of English literature as a historical sequence of events. Brooks and Warren, on the other hand, wanted to have candidates know critical methods and be able to apply them in specific judgments—quite a jump from the loose critical impressionism practiced by the older order of Ph.D.s and assumed to be reliable because the individual had such vast historical knowledge. I do not recall the details, but doubtless we worked out some conflation of disparate aims and methods. What I do remember is an absence of that furious and disruptive factionalism that theoretical differences can breed in English departments. Brooks and Warren combined conviction and urbanity; theirs was not the all-or-nothing stance of people newly come into Truth. Besides, Brooks had an especially beguiling way of buttonholing colleagues and explaining, gently and reassuringly, that their positions and his were really not far apart. Our faculty decisions (this was before the day when graduate students clamor via committees for degree requirements catering to their desires and what they take to be their needs) must have been at least workable, for we had a number of crops of very talented students.

Some graduate students in English went on to careers in scholarship and administration—such as Walton Patrick, longtime department chairman at Auburn; Melvin Watson, chairman at Chapman

College; A. H. Scouten, at Pennsylvania; Ernest Clifton, chairman at North Texas State; Patrick Quinn, chairman at Wellesley; and David Malone, chairman of comparative literature at Southern California. Two men who would earn critical status were enough in contrast to illustrate again an atmosphere congenial to people of unmatching beliefs. Richard Weaver, who was later to teach at Chicago, was "conservative": one of his books, *Ideas Have Consequences,* which he boldly asserted had a "decline of the West" tone, would excite indignation and reprobation in all liberal organs. Alan Swallow, son of a Wyoming banker, was leftish—a sort of philosophical Communist: he subscribed to radical publications but never made a big thing of it. I remember him as a first-rate student of the history of criticism, who read and placed all the documents with thorough detachment and without the condescension of the party faithful. (His leftism was perhaps a credal extension of a kindly nature. One client of his was a hard-up female graduate student who was a sort of public challenge with her neediness and her bland possession of intellectual riches from the *New Masses.* When my wife and I fed her, as everybody did, she looked around our box-house and said, smiling, something like "A charming suburban residence," meaning, of course, "Bourgeois thievery.") Swallow would later become poet and essayist and notable publisher with an unusual eye for unpublished talent. Yvor Winters was the most famous of the authors of whom Swallow was the only, or initial, publisher. In later years Swallow fell in love with foreign cars and became a famous fast driver. He told me that once he was rolling along from Denver to the coast at 115 mph and was stopped by a cop. The cop said: "I just wanted to tell you there's a lot of black ice ahead, and you better look sharp."

Still a different kind of graduate student was Robert Lowell, known as Cal, still a long way from his eminence as poet. His wife then was Jean Stafford, who worked at the *Southern Review* and was just on the threshold of her career as fiction writer. There was much interest in the chosen rigors of Cal Lowell's life when, the descendant of an old New England line, he was being guided to Rome by a campus chaplain generally felt not to represent the finest riches of Catholic thought; perhaps there was a bond in different strains of Puritan feeling. Another man of great talent was Lowell's classmate at Kenyon, Peter Taylor, who spent a year at LSU before going into the army; the *Southern Review*, which published several of his stories, did the main job of bringing him along in his career. Also appearing in the *Review*, probably with his first publications, was Pier Pasinetti, newly arrived in Baton Rouge from Italy and en route to an eventual Ph.D. at Yale and a career as novelist, Hollywood writer, and professor at UCLA. The younger poets on the scene included Archibald Henderson, son of the biographer of G. B. Shaw, survivor of many bombing runs over Germany, and later professor at the University of Houston; and Thomas McGrath, severe in conscience, who left Rome and turned left (in contrast with Patrick Quinn, who stayed Roman and ironic and was said to have engaged in great Thomist-Calvinist debates with a female graduate student, a Presbyterian who had a missionary turn of mind). Leonard Unger was an early critic of Eliot; he has long taught at the University of Minnesota, where he has helped edit a series of chapbooks on American writers. Albert Erskine and John Palmer, who came in as graduate students, soon revealed the especial qualifications—judgment, taste, the rare talent for dealing with writers, advising them, keeping them at work—that make outstanding editors and publishers. Erskine (he was married for a while to Katherine Anne Porter, who, it need hardly be said, was a very bright spot in the local scene) was the first business manager of the *Southern Review*, but also an editorial colleague in whose literary judgment Brooks and Warren had confidence; in time he went on to New Directions and eventually to Random House. John Palmer was first an editor at the LSU Press (which, working up a very good list, was a valuable arm of the new LSU); he succeeded Erskine as business manager of the *Review*, went into the navy, and some time after the war became editor of the *Sewanee Review* and then of the *Yale Review*, a post from which he retired after a long tenure.

I also remember some outstanding undergraduates who were visible in later life. John Edward Hardy, who collaborated with Brooks on one book, has been a productive critical writer and university teacher. Aubrey Williams went on to do a Ph.D. and teach at Yale, and to achieve a university professorship at Florida and distinction as a neo-classicist. Three students brilliant in English were to have notable careers in other fields. William Havard took a Ph.D. at the London

School of Economics, headed various departments, was for some years dean of arts and sciences at VPI, and finally became head of political science at Vanderbilt. He has been one of the effective expositors of the work of Eric Voegelin. George Hilton Jones, who would become a historian, was a genius in concision; I could never make up an exam that he couldn't handle flawlessly in two pages of script. Bernard Webb became a psychologist; he was to be chairman at Florida, and later graduate research professor. Webb used to cram fraternity brothers in a course of mine; after exams were over, he would come up to the desk, check through the bluebooks of his pupils, and often exclaim in disgust: "Look what the idiot put down! I knew you'd ask that question, and I told him what to say. What's the use?" Several journalism students who wandered into classes of mine were regularly heard of in their professional lives. Billie Laffler worked in various parts of the world for UPI, headed different bureaus in that organization, and finally became their literary correspondent. Wirt Williams, who took a Ph.D. in English and wrote a critical study of Hemingway, published half a dozen novels, of which at least one won a prize. Norton Girault, a cartoonist, wit, and aspiring writer, went into the navy when World War II broke out and had a long navy career, in later years commanding the ship that was picking up the first American post-sputnik shots in the Atlantic. After retirement he taught for many years in the dominantly black university in Norfolk and gradually edged into a late-life career as short-story writer and novelist. Mary Carolyn Bennett, a charming Mississippian, went to the *National Geographic,* survived the difficulties then faced by professional women, and advanced to a senior assistant editorship which she held for quite a few years.

I concluded the preceding essay with an account of some strong, and even striking, faculty appointments that in the 1930s signified a new era at LSU. I concentrated on faculty members of just two departments, English and Government, since they best represented the doubleness that I was identifying as a central LSU attribute. But there were excellent newcomers in various departments, and many of these people discovered an across-academic-boundaries congeniality that was doubtless easier when state universities like LSU had not yet developed the massive departments that can be self-enclosing. And this fellow-feeling within the university also surmounted some conspicuous differences in the secular faiths professed, as I noted at the outset of this essay, by various rather energetic faculty members.

There were, of course, some spectacular eminences whom one knew about rather than knew. I think of those brilliant arrivals from Metropolitan Opera, Louis Hasselmans and Pasquale Amato, both short and paunchy and equipped with canes and stiff straw hats like a vaudeville duo, to which, of course, they had no other resemblance. We felt close to Christian Jordan, the pianist, and Frank Collins, the pipe-organist. I remember some superior people in the Law School: Dean Paul Hebert, who we hoped would become university president; Jefferson Fordham, Mel Dakin, and the witty Wex Malone, who had an extraordinary knowledge of music and literature and who would become a national authority on torts. In fine arts there were Conrad Albrizio, a painter with a considerable regional reputation; the sculptor Armin Scheler, who came from Germany (and who, at the piano, could convert himself into a delightful sculptured parody of a violent, suffering keyboard star); the art historian Ralph Wickhiser; Duncan Ferguson, the creator of wonderful bronze cats (one of which we yearned to own but could not afford) and later a martyr to the Trotskyite faith; and Caroline Durieux, gentle ironist and satirical lithographer whose inventiveness and experimental spirit continued into late years. In languages there were Cecil Taylor (later provost of LSU) in French, and Karl Arndt and Robert Clark in German (Clark later taught at Texas and Berkeley). One remembers Allen Stanley and Robert Melampy in zoology, Lloyd Morris and Max Goodrich (later dean of the Graduate School) in physics, and in geology Richard and Dana Russell, Chalmer Roy, and Fred Kniffen. History included Lynn Case (later at Pennsylvania), Bell Wiley, the anglophile Walter Richardson, Wendell Stephenson (for a time dean of arts and sciences, and later at Tulane and Oregon), and of course the marvelously energetic T. Harry Williams, who won various honors for his studies in American history, spent a year at Cambridge as Harmsworth professor, and won the Pulitzer for his biography of Huey Long, which is the subject of my essay I.4. We all felt a considerable kinship with three very talented refugees from Hitler's Germany, men who had different degrees of gregariousness, but who conspicuously had the mark of quality that was becoming more frequent in the university: Rudolf Heberle, the sociologist from Kiel; George Jaffe, the physicist from Leipzig; and Eric Voegelin, the philosopher from Vienna. Heberle brought into sociology an intellectual dimension which changed wholly what humanists used then to call the science of manhole-cover-counting. Jaffe, an impressive man, was very reserved; Voegelin told me that Jaffe wrote mystical poetry, which is not exactly an everyday event in departments of physics. About Eric Voegelin's stature I wrote more fully in the preceding essay. Here I add only that his range and depth of thought undercut the prevailing intellectual clichés of both left and right.

I should probably remember other names, but I hope to have mentioned enough to identify clearly an academic generation in which there was great personal and professional vitality, and many beginnings of distinction.

iii

Another class of professionals who helped light up the area, not to mention the large and unbordered scene where ideas are the actors, were the contributors to the *Southern Review*. The casual 1990s recollector of the 1930s might suppose that the *Review* was the exercise-ground of a closed fraternity of southerners who pushed only agrarianism and the New Criticism. Regular southern contributors there were, a very fine stable of them: on the literary side, John Crowe Ransom, Allen Tate, Donald Davidson, John Donald Wade, John Peale Bishop, Andrew Lytle, Samuel Monk, Edd W. Parks, doing essays and reviews, often on nonliterary subjects; in social and political science, history, and philosophy, Herbert Agar, W. Y. Elliott, Frank Owsley, Robert K. Gooch, Lyle Lanier, James Feibleman, Virginius Dabney, Vann Woodward. Yet the *Review* was anything but the house organ of limited brands of sociopolitical and literary southernism; actually it pretty much held open house for all kinds of thinkers and writers from elsewhere in the states and from Europe. Contributors on the sociopolitical and philosophical side included a host of major figures: Rupert Vance, Manley O. Hudson, Lindsay Rogers, John T. Flynn, Crane Brinton, Pitirim Sorokin, Ernest K. Lindley, and Henry Bamford Parkes—representatives, it need hardly be said, of quite diverse points of view. Liddell Hart, the English military theorist, appeared at least once. But anyone with strong preconceptions about the tone and range of the journal might be surprised to find in its pages Norman Thomas, John Dewey, Max Lerner, Philip Rahv and William Barrett of *Partisan Review*, Max Eastman, and, quite frequently, Sidney Hook. If on the one hand the editors used the principle "Let's hear the best voices on all sides," on the other they were rarely content with a static juxtaposition of contrasting views: instead they strove for the dynamics of debate that would reveal weaknesses and strengths to the reader. They achieved some forceful confrontations; a debate on Trotsky naturally did not generate an air of knightly gentilesse.

On the literary front, which assumed dominance in the later years, there were contributions from such well-known English writers as F. M. Ford, Aldous Huxley, Herbert Read, Hilaire Belloc, W. H. Auden, and F. R. Leavis, and such Europeans as Paul Valéry and Mario Praz. T. S. Eliot appeared at least once, and Bonamy Dobrée, L. C. Knights, William Empson, Christopher Hollis, and Montgomery Belgion all several times. Among Americans the most frequent contributors were Kenneth Burke and Delmore Schwartz on the non-academic side, and R. P. Blackmur, Howard Baker, Morton Zabel, Arthur Mizener, F. O. Matthiessen, Mark Van Doren, Dixon Wecter, Cudworth Flint, and W. B. C. Watkins on the academic. Lionel Trilling and Jacques Barzun appeared at least once, as did Leo Spitzer, Theodore Spencer, John Gould Fletcher, Richmond Lattimore, Francis Fergusson, Harry Levin, C. L. Barber, Joseph Frank, Dudley Fitts, René Wellek, Austin Warren, Horace Gregory, and Wallace Fowlie. There are many stars here, and obviously many kinds of light: no one could organize them into a galaxy with a party-line orbit. The *Review* was clearly a liberal capitalistic enterprise: free and full competition in the marketplace of ideas. That meant taking risks, as is apparent in the range of ideas and values represented by the writers named. Besides these, Harry Slochower appeared once, James T. Farrell several times, and Herbert J. Muller repeatedly—drummers for still other kinds of intellectual merchandise. Once Muller was turned loose on the season's batch of critical volumes, and he lit into Blackmur, Brooks, and Ransom. Everyone was on his own, for no intellectual protective tariff was imposed. Nor did the editors try to flood the market with brands that would dominate it: instead they aspired to push buyers subtly toward the better of the available choices. Once they did intervene directly in an effort to depress a hot issue: they made an editorial attack on Howard Mumford Jones, who in opposing the New Criticism had betrayed some lamentable literary taste, for "selling literature down the river" and revealing "Ku Kluxery in one detail of his thought." "Selling literature down the river," *i.e.*, into a slavery under harsh doctrinal chains, was a kind of merchandising the free market was not bound to tolerate, even though in the idea-market of the day H. M. Jones must have looked like AT&T or General Motors.

Of these essayists and reviewers some were already well-established professional figures; others were fledglings if not bantlings, whose subsequent achievements make it difficult to realize that in the period from 1935 to 1942 they were virtual unknowns whose talents the editors were recognizing at an early stage. The mingling of the ancien and the nouveau is less marked in the writers of poetry and fiction published; among the almost fifty in each mode, newcomers are more frequent, and fewer of them became well known. In general the writers most frequently published were to be the major achievers—Katherine Anne Porter, Eudora Welty, Caroline Gordon, and Peter Taylor at the top, and then Mary McCarthy, Michael Seide, Thomas Thompson, and Pier Pasinetti. The editors' generosity to new talent clearly included an eye for potential. For spread there are two stories by Nelson Algren, as well as some verse by him. Of the poets published, the ones reasonably well established by then were Wallace Stevens, Mark Van Doren, Tate, Auden (singularly appearing in the same issue as another first-timer, Muriel Rukeyser). The poet most frequently published was Randall Jarrell, first introduced as a Vanderbilt student and then brought well along toward his eventual major status. John Berryman also had very early appearances in the *Southern Review*. Yvor Winters, R. P. Blackmur, and Josephine Miles were there, and in 1940 and 1941 Richard Eberhart and Rolfe Humphries were among a batch of "young poets" the editors wanted to bring in. The twenty-eighth and final issue included verse not only by Nelson Algren but also, with a symbolic suggestiveness doubtless not unnoticed at the editorial desk, by Emma Swan.

Though my omissions are at least as numerous as my inclusions, this section is, I know, bound to seem mainly a roster of names, rich in cataloguism and skimpy in criticism. But my business is less a judicial evaluation of the journal than a pictorial impression of it as a striking element in the life of LSU and of the larger community in which the university was not only a many-sided force but an object of devotion. The *Review* brought not only a larger, but a very large, world into the local scene; at the same time it took the local world out into the larger scene. The shapers of the ideas that shaped political and literary action were not merely untouchable exercisers of power or debaters on inaccessible platforms. They now came to display their wares in the local market; there they had to compete with one another and with regional voices; and this under the management of colleagues who were themselves persistently and independently influencing the way things were to go. Fashionable clichés about politics and society were all open to challenge; the going traditions in literature were surprisingly not sacred any more; and on a front closer to home, neither the sentimentalizers of the old honeysuckle South nor the get-with-it modernizers were going to get away with it. These were heady experiences. Yet they fell rarely, if at all, into a too easily gratifying "us" and "them" melodrama; anyone might find his own preferences and habits of mind tripped up at any time. One could often hear grumbling about the general directions or specific turns that the magazine was taking. Inevitable. But few could have failed to experience excitement over these notable, and widely noted, doings of the boys in the office next door. Behind that, in both university and its larger public, lay a new participation in both the current events of the mind and the nonhistorical issues agitated by the reflective in every age.

iv

If the *Southern Review* was, as I have so far treated it, a university-wide and indeed a regional phenomenon, still it was mainly edited in the Department of English, which beneficially felt a special Brooks-Warren impact. The traditional and the innovating mingled in other ways than the shaping of curricula. For one thing it meant a mixed crop of visitors and speakers (who were quite numerous even before air travel created a race of circuit riders). Our Hopkins colleagues brought in Kemp Malone and Raymond D. Havens, and G. L. Kittredge, a spirited trouper at seventy-six, came down from Harvard on a south-southwest safari (when we put him on the overnight train to

Houston, he was installed sitting up, dressed up, in or on the bed in his made-up roomette, and munching the apple which was his chosen and only postlecture refreshment). Brooks's Oxford tutor, David Nichol Smith, provided a breath of British air in the scholarly field. A flock of literary people came through—Ransom, Lytle, I. A. Richards. Marshall McLuhan dropped by on a family visit to Texas. Morton Zabel came for a lecture after we were in the war: we were doing the blackout thing with enthusiasm (we were allowed to think the big Standard Oil refinery in Baton Rouge was vulnerable to attacks from U-boats in the Gulf of Mexico), and Zabel spoke in a hall dark enough for a film showing, with the temperature matching the illumination. Zabel did a fine piece of literary theorizing, subtle and thorough; a virtuoso performance of about two hours gently complimented and sternly tested the audience.

The Brooks-Warren impact may have been most pervasive in informal and personal ways. The literary materials in their magazine were ignored by some and contested by others, but what the contributors said was in the air and could not be unfelt. Few teachers might move from literary-history-as-all to literary-structure-as-all, but it took a hardy soul to remain wholly closed to the concept of formal nontemporal characteristics as qualitative determinants of the work. Brooks, of course, could easily manage dialogue with the historical lads, since as author of a linguistic work and one of the editors of Percy's letters he was exhibiting established forms of scholarly reliability. So he could not be completely mad as he brought out essays that, tracing the revolutions in English poetry, undermined the romantics revered in, and exalted some sixteenth- and seventeenth-century poets undervalued in, the schools. It seems odd now, in the days of a different radicalism, that the upgrading of Wyatt and the metaphysicals, the new look at Shakespeare as something of a modern (including Ransom's denigration of the sonnets), and the deolympianizing of Wordsworth and Shelley should have stirred up so much of a professional kerfuffle. But still, whatever the contentious feelings occasionally aroused over specific issues, the new development was on the whole quiet and gradualist. It was persuasive revaluation rather than noisy revolution. There was no somber and self-righteous talk about undermining an unjust canon and securing canonical equity for the heretofore underprivileged.

There was simply a rather gentle pushing for the larger, though hardly exclusive, use of new insights.

Brooks was a bit of a corridor missionary: the gospel was "Read Empson," "Read Richards; he's no longer just a mechanical psychologist," "Read Eliot." Brooks was busy with Yeats's *Vision* but probably did not try to push it as a public park for literary exercises by everyone. (I recall an occasional invitation to try *I'll Take My Stand*, and the expending of some energy pro and con on the Agrarian front.) *The Waste Land*—later to be called by Eliot an "insignificant grouse" and "rhythmical grumbling"—became an index of one's literary progress. One faculty wife said that "Shantih shantih shantih" made the tears come. Graduate students, with ears ever receptive to new voices, could easily turn *The Waste Land* into a separator of human cream from human skimmed milk. Nathaniel Caffee, master of an easy geniality with students, once walked into an office where a half-dozen graduate students were in sober discourse. "What is the text?" said he. "*The Waste Land*," said they. Caffee said, "I do not understand it." One of them, later a well-known professor, said, "We do." Caffee chuckled as he reported it to me.

Understanding Poetry appeared in 1938. But it had a departmental preview in a mimeographed edition which was the text in a multiple-section basic course. (This may have happened for *Approach to Literature,* 1936.) For most of us it was a baptismal experience in the detailed objective analysis of poetic method and quality. Once we had just announced *ex cathedra* what was worthy; now we had to make a case for it, as well as come to terms with the asserted unworthiness of some poems heretofore assumed to be worthy. Doubtless our responses ranged from conversion to intransigence; others must have shared my own attitude, which was instinctive hospitality to the method, but difficulty with some of the new tools and with some judgments that were not congenial. We were, of course, in on an educational revolution, though we had no way of knowing this then. It is now gratifying to look back and say: "Great things were happening, and we were there." Perhaps it is just as well that what was to become quite an event in the history of academic humanism did not seem, to us who worked near the birthplace, much more than procedural innovations introduced by amiable and talented colleagues who did not look or sound like revolutionaries. Had we been able to say "We are at a historical crisis," the passions of collaboration and resistance might have been greater; the latter might have led to such declarations as "My sentence is for open war" rather than stopped at that unprogrammatic grousing with which the profession usually greets proposed alternatives. Besides, oppositionist zeal tended to be defused by a genuinely experimental air. Brooks and Warren had strong convictions, but my impression is that they were quite open to all kinds of responses, did listen to arguments, and were willing to make adjustments, certainly in approach, perhaps occasionally in conclusions reached. Unlike most revolutions this one did not exclude a sense of humor. Brooks told me that Warren had said that applying their method to Wordsworth was like "manicuring an elephant."

There was excitement, then, on the teaching front. There was also the excitement of internal efforts to alter the university, and, more peripherally, of the statewide political goings-on. The denouement was the "scandals" of 1939, when facts caught up with adventurers, and prosecuting attorneys had better headline and campaign materials than usual. It was also in 1939 that Brooks's first, and enormously influential, book appeared—*Modern Poetry and the Tradition*. And it was in 1939 that Warren's first novel appeared—*Night Rider*. Then in 1940 appeared Kirby and Caffee's *Studies for W. A. Read*, a festschrift (before festschrifts had become monthly events) for the distinguished linguist who had been department head since 1902 (a charming gentleman, as well as a scholar, of the old school: a Virginian, he had taken his Ph.D. at Heidelberg and had studied at Göttingen, Grenoble, and Oxford); it had local, national, and European contributors. I mention these three books together, with their dates, for two reasons. One is that neither external events in a spectacular style, nor a diverse schedule of activities by department members, interfered with the major professional activity that led to books. The other is that the three volumes represent all the kinds of activity that are expected of a department of literature—the critical, the creative, and the scholarly (and two of them not then expected). *Night Rider* must have been almost the first novel by a full-time professor of English, and in its extraordinary fusion of physical violence, moral sensitivity, and philosophic inquiry—these would be the characteristic Warren triad—it had a fullness infrequent in later floods of faculty fiction.

This touching of all bases open to scholars and writers reflected not only a widespread productive impulse but also a nurturing background in which there was much to modify the provincial. Long before international travel had become a cliché of American mobility, southerners had an affinity for things European. There was a small symbol of this in the presence of six Rhodes scholars on the faculty in my time (Brooks, Warren, Palmer in English; Pipkin, Daspit, Kendall in Government.) The LSU faculty were drawn from all sections of the country, and it is worth noting, I think, that the many nonsoutherners on the faculty never felt any real regional antagonism, though the community had an exceptionally strong southern sensibility, and, among intellectuals, the Agrarian movement tended to create a sense of exclusive southern identity. There was always good nature in the frequently revived old joke about people who for a lifetime thought that *damnyankee* was a single word.

The large Esso installation in Baton Rouge included the experimental laboratories; these were populated by scientists who often had intellectual and artistic interests. They contributed to a citizen-of-the-world flavoring, especially when the war meant evacuation of Americans from European fields. But in justice I must record one disappointment of my own, this one administered by a recent evacuee, a southwesterner I believe, from Ploesti. It would be some years before I would get to Romania myself, and I must have thought of it as some sort of Graustark or Ruritania. I pushed and pushed, my curiosity engendering a cross-examination of the recent arrival. Two answers still stay with me, surely a fair summation of the oilman's analysis of picturesque Balkan life: "The Romanians make good servants," and "Yes, it is an interesting place to be. Any time you get tired of your own outfit you can go down the street and talk to the Shell people."

V

Obviously these flashbacks to the period from 1935 to 1945 at LSU—and more peripherally in Baton Rouge and Louisiana—do not add up to an authoritative record. In this memoir at its best the reminiscential

may not reach the quintessential. One hopes less to pin down an ultimate history than to suggest—evoke, if one is fortunate—an atmosphere in which certain activities of the mind and imagination flourished. A gossipy pictorial retrospection need not be wholly chancy and
vague, and for concreteness I have taken some risks on the catalog-
and-annals side: roll calls of publications and of students, colleagues,
and journal contributors, owning or earning names in their fields.
Though they may seem a mechanical alternative to reflection and
analysis, such lists should in their definiteness give a clue to the tone
and style of the period. They improve, I hope, on hyperbolic abstractions of praise. Their computer-printout air implies the "Down, nostalgia" which one must keep uttering to the ingratiating petlike pasts
that bounce up through kindly filtering memory. The spur to memory
is reliable, however, when its source is not the ordinary but the extraordinary, not the common man but uncommon men. There were
enough of these to make a true history that can afford some pleasure.
In half a dozen ways there was a striking New Deal for the Old War
Skule (the popular name of LSU from early days).

When a literary and intellectual florescence of more than local visibility occurs in a seventy-five-year-old school with a dominant military
tradition, one inevitably starts prospecting for causes and influences.
But the ore of historical explanation is elusive, and all the dowsers
serving Clio may find their rods remaining stationary in the air. Obviously everything turns on the presence of some quite uncommon
men, and a student of that phenomenon may be able to do no more
than genuflect before the old divinity Fortuna. Luck there had to be. If
one aspires to go a step further, he can trace some slight veins of development. The first Rhodes scholar on the scene was Charles Pipkin, an
early faculty critic of local mores, soon made dean of the Graduate
School, and no doubt it is fair to make him a sort of academic pro-
genitor of the considerable line of Rhodes men who were large figures
in the period. But then he and his presence and his influence still need
explaining, as does the contemporary influx of first-rate people in
other departments which had independent appointive processes. Aside
from seeking the new spirit that brought talented people in, one has
also to look for the energizing spirit that led them to work produc-
tively instead of languishing in pleasant sloth or wearying in futile

combat. Congeniality among individuals helped, and perhaps it first made itself felt during the efforts at institutional improvement which I have already mentioned. Happily these efforts never expanded into an exhausting reformism. On the other hand, even in a day when university administrators still could cashier "uncooperative" faculty, I never heard of any untoward pressures from above, much less any overt actions that could make the AAUP charge into the fray. Potential polarizations did not really mature, notably the kind generated by ideological pressures—a lucky absence of dictators above, or uptight utopians around, discoverers of a final good and willing enforcers of it. To put these matters affirmatively, one can recognize, in retrospect, a kind of laissez faire which, while it may have disadvantages for the ill-organized and self-indulgent, is admirable for those with talent and direction. The underlying puzzle, of course, is that laissez faire, and with it a literary and intellectual flowering of a distinctly highbrow sort, should accompany a populist revolution at the heart of Huey Long's rise to power. One rummages around in the historical armoire for psychological and cultural materials which could beget a seeming paradox. The urban worldliness of New Orleans (since then a refurbisher of its has-beens into one of the country's great tourist traps), a brake on the tendency of revolutionary energy to roar into narrow channels and gain destructive force? The ironic and imaginative sides of Huey, too gamesome ever to become a Robespierre? An ambitious expansiveness through which he inadvertently set up kinds of achievement hardly embraced in the formal programs?

May there have been, more generally, a subterranean kinship between the freedom conducive to art and thought, and a statewide sociopolitical easygoingness with its obvious built-in risks of messes, rackets, and worse? One playful speculation of the time suggested analogies with the Italian Renaissance, when the masters of commercial and political banditry were also the patrons of a great art. But if Baton Rouge could not quite be taken for Florence (as Arno, the Mississippi is a bit grandiose), the scene was still marked by a coexistence of apparently contradictory elements. Such unlikely juxtapositions, in their resistance to logical clarity, are always a little troublesome to observers from other sections, who expect the distant to have a unitary identity. When Warren's *All the King's Men* appeared in 1946, many readers knew that any good man and true who glanced at Huey in any way—never mind how fictional art employs raw materials—was obliged to scarify him; since Warren's mode was in no way polemic (it was tragic, which is much less easy on both writer and readers), the knowing critics in other parts of the country decided that Warren was committing an apologia for a monster, and indeed for all people who lived in Louisiana and had failed in their civic duty—a duty as defined at a safe distance in time and place, the duty of becoming tyrannicides. I doubt that any other novel of our day has been the object of so much self-righteous misreading. I shall present some of the misreaders in a later essay (III.14).

In 1942 the war was nominally responsible for the death of the *Southern Review*, and it was indeed responsible for the departure of various faculty people, some into lifetime careers elsewhere. Professional activity made other professors widely visible, offers kept coming in, and various good people left. A few observers felt that some sort of bubble had burst. Hardly. If the state's old mingled tonalities, picturesque and tantalizing, were more muted than before, still it was not that a stolid ordinariness had superseded imaginative venturesomeness. The Longs survived Huey's henchmen and returned, never a dull company. Some excellent faculty members stayed on at LSU, and its subsequent history has shown that the university has never flagged in the taste for quality that became conspicuous in the 1930s. The *Southern Review* spiritually survived a budgetary execution; then its life-after-death was followed by a formal resurrection and a new life that still flourishes.

In looking back at the LSU of the 1930s and 1940s, we keep talking about Huey Long, a singular man who in some way was behind all the new developments, and about the *Southern Review*, which was a striking symbol of the new vitality in the university. My comments have been mainly those of an amateur observer depending upon impressions and memory. I want to solidify the account by reporting, in the next two essays, on books by professional scholars who have taken a longer look at the concrete evidence on which history and biography depend. The books are Thomas W. Cutrer's *Parnassus on the Mississippi* and T. Harry Williams' *Huey Long*.

I.3

Cutrer on the *Southern Review*

(1985)

In *Parnassus on the Mississippi* (1984) Thomas W. Cutrer has made a very interesting book out of a brief period—and out of what at the time seemed less than a main event—in the life of a Louisiana State University that, concluding its generally unnoticed first seventy-five years, was drawing a burst of national headlines as one stage for the fantastic melodrama of political revolution and corruption that had run for a decade and dominated the state. Cutrer's story, in brief, is this: a Huey Long henchman, President James M. Smith of LSU, authorized a young dean and two junior faculty members (aged 30 and 29) to start a literary journal, and he funded it amply; it achieved an extraordinary *succès d'estime*, nationally and even abroad; everybody who was anybody wrote for it; the editors spotted and published many a youngster who wasn't anybody yet but was to become somebody; bright young people came from both coasts and intermediate points to study under the editors; the war came, budgets were cramped, the *Southern Review* was dumped by a new president, and R. P. Warren went to Minnesota (1943) and Cleanth Brooks to Yale (1947).

The *Southern Review* is the centerpiece in a panoramic story, as the subtitle of Cutrer's *Parnassus on the Mississippi* (a metaphor both gaudy and inexact) reveals: *The "Southern Review" and the Baton Rouge Literary Community, 1935–1942.* Cutrer's approach makes a lively public book out of materials probably too specialized for general consumption—the short happy life of a highbrow quarterly. Cutrer does not treat the *Review* as a philosophical voice or phenomenon, nor does he become simply an annalist tracing subscriptions, budgets, contributors, etc., year by year. Instead he finds in the history of the *Review* a nexus of themes that, as he traces them individually, give the tale depth, spread, and variety.

Several initial chapters tell the pre-Long history of LSU; the impact of Long on a university that by money and enthusiasm he pushed toward distinction even as he harmed it by trying to control the student press; the arrival of many new young faculty members, such as Brooks and Warren, who would achieve notable careers at LSU and elsewhere; LSU's pre–*Southern Review* investment in an intellectual quarterly—namely the brief uneasy collaboration with Southern Methodist University in maintaining the *Southwest Review,* endangered by the Depression; President Smith's authorization of a new magazine at LSU in February, 1935, the intense labors needed to get out the first issue in July, the death of Huey in September, and the widespread fears that the *Southern Review* might suffer Sudden Infant Death. Chapter 4 records many writers' responses to the *Review,* its high rate and slow pace of payment to contributors, the editors' policies, practices, and work loads (for instance, reading ninety short stories for every one published), their insistence on being catholic rather than local-colorist or cause-bitten, the disappointment of some Agrarians and other southerners that the quarterly had not become the house organ for which they had hoped, and finally the publishing history, and some of the personal history during those years, of two contributors who were to become famous, Eudora Welty and Katherine Anne Porter (Porter lived in Baton Rouge for several years). In chapter 5 Cutrer looks at Brooks and Warren in terms of their ties with, their complex attitudes to, and their disagreements or even splits with some other southern writers, primarily the Agrarians. Chapter 6 traces Warren's career in the LSU period—his first two collections of poems, his short stories and essays, his first novel, his textbook work, the early stages of *At Heaven's Gate,* and his struggles with a play that later turned into *All the King's Men.* Chapter 7 deals with Brooks and Warren as teachers, as authors of influential textbooks that transformed the teaching of literature, and as magnets for many gifted students who would achieve literary or professional distinction. Chapter 8 concerns the scandals of 1939, the resignations or jailings or both of many Long henchmen (including President Smith of LSU); Brooks's role in the battles over university reform, the department headship, and the university presidency; the outbreak of the war and the end of the *Review*, despite protests both local and national. The epilogue sketches the subsequent careers of key *Southern Review* figures and mentions the revival of the *Review* in 1964.

Cutrer uses many secondary sources (he provides a good bibliography), and he also draws heavily on unpublished material from interviews and archives: hence he tells much that could not be generally known at the time. I don't mean dirty linen, of which none appears, but such significant matters as the complex negotiations that preceded both the birth and the death of the *Review*, and above all the communications between editors and contributors, southern intellectuals, and members of the Vanderbilt group, some of whom could be testingly irritable at times. But Brooks and Warren maintained an easy, well-disciplined, gentlemanly manner not always evident in the literary business, especially when Marxists were banging away at the erring with customary rude self-righteousness. Great talent, relentless hard work, and exceptional courtesy—these combined to form a special editorial style.

Cutrer notes, but does not harp on, such matters: he is not doing a campaign biography. His manner is factual, his prose sensible, straightforward, and utilitarian, though some lapses in style and accuracy are bothersome. Cutrer's especial gift is, as I have said, to grasp all the ramifications—personal, literary, institutional, educational—of what might have been a much more circumscribed narrative. The one that most spurs our reflective energies is the Huey Long connection, since it most engagingly needles conventional expectations. Populist bosses don't subsidize elite quarterlies. If it is unlikely that Huey ever knew about the *Review*, barely born when he died, nevertheless it came to life in the Louisiana which he had remade and almost wholly controlled; it was directly commissioned by a Long underling not likely to make moves that would irk the top dog. Yet its independence was guaranteed from the start, and there was never any infringement of that sine qua non, even by Long epigones who were quite unsubtle people. Having improbably survived an order of life that we might suppose would be throttling, the *Review* died, apparently of budgetary complications, under reform administrations in state and university. All that is somehow not as we suspect it should be. The key lies, as I have already suggested, in imagination—in Huey's primarily, and then in the lack of it in other quarters where it may be desirable or relevant. A dictator can hardly do without some of it, but the more of it he has, the less likely it is to be circumscribed by the simpler rules of political haymaking. Huey's imagination clearly gave him visions of excellence in LSU, an excellence beyond band and football fame; hence, in the university, an atmosphere of freedom, aspiration, and adventure (despite Huey's crude interference at some points)—precisely the atmosphere in which a critical journal could be conceived. Huey's successors lacked imagination both of limits to pilfering and of public ends to be kept in mind: hence ensued gross misconduct, scandals, and reform. Reform means severe accounting and auditing; accounting, indispensable as it is, is hardly a friend or servitor of the imaginative life, which is much too freewheeling for budget-watchers. Perhaps there is a kind of dialectic progression: the charismatic leader is a man of imagination who, though being boss is primary, can envision achievements beyond power and profit; his followers cannot have imagination, which might well inspire rival adventuring; freed from the control of the leader, they fall into excess and vulgarity; hence reform; hence accounting as a weapon against fiscal misdeeds; hence a regimen of bookkeeping naturally suspicious of cash outlays for book writing and such imaginative goings-on. The great imaginations, political and literary, leave the stage as anti-imaginative auditors catch up with unimaginative looters.

The model has some usefulness, though it oversimplifies the actual historical process in Louisiana: it does not take into account the war and its impact on a public sense of necessities, new budgetary constraints, some misunderstandings, and the sheer weariness of Brooks after many crises in the university. Cutrer dispassionately traces all these. He enables the reader to see how a social and political revolution in a then-backward state, and under a leader who evoked love and fear, reverence and detestation in equal proportions, singularly contributed to a widespread revolution in literary education. Yet the literary activity was wholly independent from the start, and Cutrer traces in detail its inner workings and its outer influences.

From whatever point of view we look at LSU, we sooner or later find ourselves having to take some account of Huey Long, in whose time the university began to leave its old essentially provincial self behind. We are ready for a full look at that complex, ambitious politician.

I.4

Williams on Long

(1970)

i

T. Harry Williams' *Huey Long* (1969) is perhaps first of all, and most of all, a remarkable work of composition. In part, of course, I allude to the creation of a unified narrative out of almost overwhelmingly plentiful primary and secondary sources; the sheer quantity of evidence—journalistic, eyewitness, documentary, archival—on many scores of episodes, most of them complicated and elusive, might have intimidated a less bold historian, making him ponder for a lifetime instead of yielding to his control in the dozen or so years in which Williams put together this 900-page study. I mean, however, to stress not only the intellectual task of assimilation and synthesis, but the literary achievement of coherent presentation—that is, the "composition." It would be understandable if in so massive a production one had a sense of stops and starts, of ragged edges, of overlapping, of discontinuities and self-conscious piecings together. There is almost none of this. Instead there is a fluent forward-moving tale, in which the joints are either concealed or appear as graceful articulations. Williams has had to deal with four components of the total narrative—the overall chronological account, the often prolonged episodes (*e.g.*, Huey and the university) that share in the general chronology but have a certain intermittent life of their own, the thematic currents that are not amenable to chronological discipline (*e.g.*, Huey as social thinker, as legal strategist, as would-be president), and the essential background situations (the nature of Louisiana politics, the Louisiana constitution, educational habits, etc.) that have to be understood if one is to be clear about foreground events. Williams fuses these admirably; transitions are hardly noticeable; the elucidation of background matters seems to float in almost casually when needed, not to be forced in by an arbitrary traffic controller.[1]

It is not likely, when the organization is as effective as Williams', that even a critical reader will think of much that might be ordered differently. There is one point, however, at which the placement of material reveals the intention to make one kind of book rather than another. Chapter 26, "Power in Himself," might well have been the final section of the book; it is the longest directly analytical section, and its subject is fundamental—the role of power in Huey's thought and personality. As the curtain chapter, it would have focused attention on the psychological and moral problem more interesting than even a life that resembles a succession of theatrical spectacles. It would have invited us to pay Huey a final tribute of meditation, not only on a certain greatness which did "influence the course of history" (ix), but on the profound human representativeness, in capacity for both good and evil, of the especially gifted man. But "Power in Himself" is followed by an-

---

1. Williams' tendency to render machinery inconspicuous appears in the formal documentation. He numbers footnotes from 1 to 9, thus evading the large figures that scream scholarship. With few exceptions, he puts a footnote only at the end of a paragraph and includes in it all the sources used in the paragraph. The one difficulty in this otherwise laudable procedure is that when there are multiple sources for one paragraph (there can be as many as 25), it is not easy to apportion the textual material among the indicated sources, though the latter are doubtless listed in the order used. The present reviewer must leave to specialists the task of evaluating Williams' use of "oral history," which here means a systematic, though by no means exclusive, reliance on recorded interviews with 295 informants. In such source material there is an exciting liveliness, that of gossip or of intense reportage by knowing participants; on the whole the orally provided material seems more spontaneous than calculating. Often, of course, testimony is expectably incomplete or conflicting, and Williams has to do some skipping around on the floating ice-cakes of conjecture; probably his most frequent adverb is *probably*. Finally, this experiencing of oral history makes one speculate about its psycho-cultural role: Does oral history drain off the energies and substance of mythmaking into controlled, nearly verifiable portraiture? Huey's life has all the makings of myth, but here, in a sense, the myth is reduced to, and by, history. If we gain scientifically, we may lose aesthetically and culturally through the noncreation of a figure potentially most useful in the ordering of experience. On the other hand, it is possible that telling one's tale to a trained listener may be less cathartic than stimulating; the informant may be turned on by the recording experience and go around echoing and expanding his impressions to whoever will listen. If this is the way things work, we can foresee a mythic Huey and a historic Huey both emerging, competing, each striving to correct the other.

other hundred pages on the colorful, tense, and sometimes ominous events of the last seven or eight months of Huey's life—a well-paced tale that becomes increasingly stark as it leads up to and recounts the shooting of Huey on a Sunday night in September, 1935, and his death "some thirty hours" later. There Williams stops abruptly; the final impact is that of shocking cessation, of a blow and a void. Biography here borrows an artistic method, that of a mimetic form: the tale of a life imitates the life. In art as in life, of course, the sensational tends to sneak in its kissing cousin, the sentimental, and there is just a touch of this in the final pages when Williams fictionally re-creates the "visions" seen by the dying Huey—visions of all the needy and unlucky and oppressed who "looked at him and trusted him" (876). By *sentimental* I mean, not that the vision is false in itself, but that it is simply not complex enough to correspond to the very complex character that the book has created. The vision would have been ampler had it contained, side by side with the humble and the powerless on their knees begging for help, the humiliated and the overpowered on their knees begging for mercy (but still ready to try a quick butt in the gut). It is not that Williams is unaware of the latter, but that his instinctive posture is one of defensiveness against a simplistic and undiscriminating anti-Hueyism, which on its side of the fence has also not grasped the complexity of the subject.

ii

If the effect is sentimental, the motive behind it is understandable. I have had some experience of listening to facile condemnations of Huey by people whose evidence was little more than headlines, but who could leap over great abysses of difference to equate Huey with the purely negative and untalented Joe McCarthy. I am here thinking of the kind of northerner who localized original sin in the South and simply viewed Huey as another manifestation of that regional delinquency from which we nonsoutherners were fortunately spared. This has always been a little bit trying to us who had lived in Louisiana for a dozen years and had ample firsthand knowledge of a state in which human nature remained constant even as latitude declined, and in which no one denied Huey's great achievements, achievements amply documented in Williams' book. Our lessons in the complexity, both in the Louisiana style and in this unusual man, who seemed equally to evoke reverence and revulsion, love and hate, began for my wife and me in our first week in Louisiana—the last week in the forty-two years chronicled in Williams' biography.

I have already described (in I.1) the finale of our first week in Baton Rouge: our being present in the Capitol; seeing Senator Long, newly arrived from Washington, direct the activities of the lower house; and hearing, just below us, the firecracker-like sounds which we would shortly learn were the shots that killed Dr. Weiss and fatally wounded Huey. I have mentioned, in passing, two events that brought home to us the meaning of Huey's death (a day and a half after the shooting)— the fear of a senior professor that the university might not open at the scheduled time, and, more broadly significant, the statewide mourning for the dead senator—mourning which needs more than a mention. From all over the state mourners came to Baton Rouge and crowded the city up through the day of the funeral. Hundreds camped on the Capitol grounds just across the street from our apartment. They seemed to be mostly backwoods, bayou, and hill folk, spare, somber, strange, Yoknapatawpha emptied out at our doorstep, devastated and per-haps—who knew?—savage and even revengeful. It was not one of those ghastly organized "spontaneous" demonstrations that we saw so often in the late 1960s; it was the real thing. What it taught us was that Huey was a far more complex figure than the press often made him. No mere demagogue, no mere dictator, such as Huey had seemed to be and as in part he was, could have evoked this outpouring of grief and indeed of worship. (It was a little too easy to join in the rationalist chuckles when paid ads in the papers gave joint thanks, for blessings received, to a Catholic saint and to Huey Long.)

We learned more about Huey in the next five years as we watched his legatees, just as he had prophesied, heading toward and eventually landing in jail. They crowded too grossly around the public trough. Maybe dictatorial leaders simply do not attract first-rate henchmen. What we watched, from 1935 on, was a singular mixture of disturbing political melodrama, hazardous for the losers, and a sort of hardboiled low comedy. When a political leader, accused of graft, replied publicly to the state, "What if we did steal millions? Look what you got out of it," the script might have been written by Joe Orton.

Finally, we learned about Huey through our experience of the university, about whose doubleness I have already written. On the one hand it managed a certain abstention from high seriousness: a kind of analogue of a political style in the state, and a condition deplored by some of us newcomers (as is the wont of new Ph.D.'s, ever alert to the shortcomings of campuses at which they arrive). But we also knew what went along with it: a great feeling of freedom, particularly of expression. We sensed vigor, imaginativeness, gusto, and, along with the ever-present political sense in some quarters, a great feeling for quality in various departments of the university. All this had to reflect a Long spirit, one that continued in the Long afterglow. If Long liked to lead the band and head the football parade, the Long and post-Long administrations provided funds for growth, and even distinction, on academic, cultural, and artistic fronts. Distinguished refugees from Europe in no way felt lost there. Eric Voegelin, true, did not come until 1942, but without the impact of Long on the university, no one on campus would ever have heard of Voegelin in the first place. Indeed, better-established universities were repeatedly said to have been afraid of him. Interestingly enough, T. Harry Williams arrived at LSU about the same time as Voegelin. Their different intellectual styles once led to an illuminating clash at the meeting of a discussion group. Voegelin said something to the effect that, if this was indeed the "century of the common man," as it was often called, things were in a bad way. Williams bridled, since he tended to be rather an admirer of the "common man." Their difference became clear when someone asked the disputants whom they meant by the "common man." Williams said, "Lincoln." Voegelin said, "Hitler." He meant by "common man," he said, anyone who had not felt influences—religious, cultural, educational, whatever—that would raise him above the beasts of the field. He thought Lincoln not a common man at all.

Perhaps this exchange sheds a little light on the biographer of Huey Long. It concludes the brief sketch of events that reveal the sources of my own attitudes. Though I was post-Long at LSU, the time was dominated by the immediate past, and we constantly pondered that past. We kept trying to define and evaluate the man who evoked powerful responses of opposite kinds, who had often used methods and a style that were repugnant and even ominous, and yet who against great

odds effected vast changes which, by standards then and now, were all
to the good, and who indeed, in his sense of the economic foundations
of human well-being, was ahead of his times. The chief bias of which I
am aware in myself is a strong dislike of simplistic explanations of a
very complex man, be they idolatrous or, as more often in my own
experience, contemptuous and condemnatory. In this central feeling, I
believe, Williams and I come pretty close together, though some of our
emphases may differ.

iii

To Williams' eye Long is an antiprivilege, anti–ancien régime political
and economic reformer with solid, broadly based humanitarian programs that, though they were to win wide popular acceptance, had to
be forced through by any available means because of the intransigent
resistance by the old sociopolitical order (the plantation class and the
New Orleans machine) and its commercial-industrial allies (sugar,
lumber, and especially oil). Though in time Williams pretty much
settles on "antis" to designate the opposition, he very frequently uses
conservatives as a synonym for *opponents* and rather relishes their
discomfitures; with him, too, *aristocrat* and *gentleman* and *social elite*
usually connote a kind of anti-Long original sin. This usage, which
comes out of the populist sensibility in Williams, is a little tedious,
since it begs a big question—the nature of the anti-Longism that could
grow into actual murder plots. A feeling so intense would seem to involve more than conservative or class feeling, however much these
were involved, or simply the distress of defeat or of diminished powers,
or even the fear of change that can sometimes make men frantic. In
immediate post-Long days, according to my very amateur sense of
things, the anti-Longism seemed to come from people who would ordinarily be called "liberal," people, that is, who thought well of the
programs and welcomed rather than deplored change. Trying, in later
years, to find a word for the anti-Long emotion I ran into, I would call
it a disinterested sense of danger. If this was also true in pre-1935 days
when opposition groups flourished all over a state that had by now
fully experienced the benefit of the Long programs, then we have the
profound problem of the benefactor who excites fear as much as rever-

ence. Williams does not directly address himself to the problem, which still presents a large field for meditation.

If Huey took what methods he had to, he used them skillfully. The phrase "good principle and good politics" (168) reveals Williams' sense of the joining of desirable ends and successful means. Huey had "chosen . . . the way of the artist in the use of power—the way of the great politician" (410). He was the "typically pragmatic American politician, one who liked to appear more terrible, and more powerful, than he actually was" (332). Often he could pull off a "brilliant coup" (398). Even near the end he could be "pragmatic . . . negotiate . . . offer concessions and accept compromises—all very unlike a dictator" (854). What Williams admires is Huey's good sense of what works at a given time and, in a given context, his "ruthless skill" (290) in doing what is needed, his "shrewd calculation, smart politics" (309). Sometimes it seems as if his only errors were pragmatic; his drinking was politically troublesome, or a foray into LSU was "one of the worst mistakes of his career" (773). (Williams can also admire political sagacity in others [300] or laugh at the lack of it [363]. In the opposition he can discern "pious enemies" [665], "a petulant effort at revenge" [424], "demagoguery" [447], a "vicious press campaign" [660] or an "excessive devotion to principle" [299].) I do not mean that, in presenting Huey as a "mass leader" (rather than a demagogue) who was also a "power artist," Williams is uncritical of anything but tactics. It is true that at times, perhaps unjustifiably, the reader anticipates some kind of evaluative note and then finds it brief or implicit or apparently missing—Huey's making accusations without evidence (148), dictatorial conduct of a hearing (169), apparently undercutting a benefactor (193), treating the Klan issue as a matter of expediency (208ff.), and so on.[2] But whatever the moral problem of various actions and kinds of

2. His loss of interest in the Public Service Commission (225), making unjust charges against another politician (230ff., 238), the relationship with Maestri (254), political payoffs (406), and political "deducts" from state employees' salaries (465; "de ducks is flyin'" was the word in the later 1930s), the Senate methods that a colleague called "unscrupulous" (620ff., 681), the use of military intimidation in the state (called "improper," 660), the resistance to reforms which would reduce his patronage (661), a document snatch (804), the firing of teachers on political grounds (855).

activity, one keeps hoping for a theoretical critique of pragmatism, or at least a pragmatic critique of Huey the pragmatist: one has a growing impression that the methods used, win battle after battle though they did, aroused so much resentment and hostility that it was becoming increasingly difficult to win the large wars that Huey was always projecting.

Obviously Williams does not shy away from adverse judgments. These come a little more easily, I feel, in external matters of style or in peripheral issues—of Huey's early bad taste in clothes, his poor speaking style, tactical blunders (257, 298), use of nepotism (314), a racist speech (328), his "reckless disdain for sound financial procedures" in handling certain funds (377), his methods of putting pressure on legislators (391), his musical ignorance (434), eating and drinking too much (436), tactlessness in victory (527), "crude clowning" that would not work at the national level (576), "specious reasoning . . . to becloud the issue" (607). But Williams can be quite sharp in censure. In practicing "savage retribution" Huey once revealed the "sinister" view that "anything he created or supported was his personal possession" (515); in another case his reason "may have been sinister, but it was probably quite simple" (617); again, his "reason . . . was not exactly sinister, [but] it was not very much to his credit" (638). He "interfered frequently and often improperly" in the operation of the state colleges (524). He vetoed appropriation bills in "a ruthless display of power, and with utter disregard for the public interest" (529). Of a package of laws which, as United States senator, he sent to the Louisiana legislature: "They were power laws, blunt, blatant, and unashamed" (726). "His activities were within the law but highly improper" (824). The Win or Lose Oil Company, whose profits Huey shared, "had done nothing illegal" but "the morality of its operations was open to grave question" (827).

One could quote many other such passages, and one should remember Williams' statement that Senator Russell Long "has strong objections to some of my generalizations" (viii). Hence it may seem rather picky to register the impression that the adverse judgments are often brief interpolations, unavoidable but not to be lingered over. But I do not mean to be censorious; rather I notice moral and aesthetic problems that his subject imposes upon Williams. One always writes in a certain context; every context has its own imbalance; and every writer must want to contribute, insofar as he can, to righting this. One context for the biographer of Huey is that Huey's vices have been far better known, and much more talked about, than his virtues; hence the biographer may well feel something of an obligation not to dwell on the known, but to bring into adequate focus the less well known— a step toward the Olympian judgment that can only be made long after. Another context is the Louisiana political style: it is always possible to say, as Williams often does, that the opposition would have practiced, or did practice, the same or equivalent vices. Here, of course, one runs into another nice theoretical problem: is the extraordinary man somehow obligated, by his extraordinariness, to find something better than an intensified carrot-and-stick way of doing business? The aesthetic problem is of a different kind: the situations in which the ambiguous or the apparently questionable might elicit judgment are frequent enough so that the critical observer, intent on fidelity to role, might well seem to be only a nagger. One can't appraise every act explicitly; often the story itself has to serve as its own moral commentator.

iv

The "story itself" is the center of Williams' biographic art; he is at his most spontaneous as a narrator; in fact, in scores of episodes he is genuinely zestful. In part he is a vivid teller of tall tales, and in Louisiana doings he finds much raw material for this mode. He says, in effect: let's enjoy the story, the comedy, the drama. He uses fictional techniques—advance buildup of scene and situations, flashbacks, vivid imaging of physical appearances, suspense through unrevealed facts or outcome, intertwining plots, foreshadowing to create tension, climax, "continued in our next" (figuratively, that is). The impeachment of Huey is treated as a colorful drama with "moments of rare and unforgettable comedy" (371); one phase of it was a "stellar attraction" (385). Huey's Senate appearances tend to become spectaculars; farce (the word is often used) is always around the corner from melodrama ("most hilarious moments" [609]). Williams often adds ironic wisecracks ("as proof of his devotion to rural interests [Gene Talmadge] wore red suspenders" [814]) or arranges a summation for ironic effect, as when he checks over Huey's possible choices for the next governorship: "Leche was from New Orleans, which was almost as bad as being a Catholic. . . . Noe was too closely allied with the oil business. Ellender was too short" (856). Williams is the energetic, often-gay raconteur or impresario. He has a direct, flexible, vigorous, sometimes-breezy style that avoids academic vices and embraces journalistic excellences—plainness, pace, variety, informality, unpretentiousness, and an occasional pinch of the slapdash and folksy. He can be colloquial and slangy: "eateries" (30), "making noises like a candidate" (191), "smart dopesters" (229), "rundown" for account (259n), "report laid over" (371), "gag" (773). Referring to Dudley LeBlanc, an inept politician, as Dud rather labors the joke. But "government by goatee" (187) is a witty phrase for the old order that plays baronial villain to Huey's white knight.

Instinctively Williams is less drawn to moralizing the fable than to dispensing delight, whether it derive from the sheer shenanigans of politics, from a persistent theatrical quality in Louisiana public life, from the strange cause-and-effect relationships, sometimes farcically mechanical (a story on p. 715 might be modelled on Snake's line in *The School for Scandal*, "You paid me extremely liberally for the lie in question, but unfortunately I have been offered double to speak the truth"), often singularly devious or elusively sinuous. This mingling of the serious business of history, which is never trivialized, with the spirited conduct of show biz—a new version of Horace's *prodesse et delectare*—reveals, in Williams, a temperamental affinity with (that is, an understanding of, an imaginative openness to) a remarkable two-toned quality in Louisiana politics. What was a life-and-death struggle was in some ways also a game; the quest for victory had a histrionic quality; a sense of goal was balanced with a sense of audience; the aggressor's snarl might suddenly metamorphose into the comedian's jest; one might ignore all scruple and danger to destroy the enemy, and next day amiably use the rule "If you can't lick 'em, jine 'em." The ambiguity recorded by the book, even in the last year or two when Huey's moves against opposition became more fiercely destructive, was very much in the air in the later 1930s. One wasn't quite sure whether one was in a severely troubled modern state or in a fascinating Graustark; whether one was in *Macbeth* and was obligated to fight real tyrants, or was in *Oklahoma*, its troubles originating only in a host of poor Judds garnished more by dirty fingernails than by foul psyches; or in a *Hamlet* imperfectly turned into a musical comedy with a happy ending. When the post-Huey quasi Hueys had run their course and the "scandals" broke out in 1939 and 1940, one might have seen nemesis inevitably taking over, but it was also like watching a theatrical denouement in which a set of brazen, lively rascals were, by dramatic convention, getting their comeuppance. One is constantly reminded of Gogol's *Inspector General*, where serious matters are implicitly at stake, but where the satiric thrust virtually disappears amid the buffoonery and the ironic structuring of incident. One petty grafter in the play is rebuked: "You take bribes too big for your rank"; compare Huey, who knew that "some of his men were taking in more money than they should" (820) and who could also violate "his own rule that politicians should be moderate in taking extra money" (827). Then there is the politician (an M.D.) who testified, concerning jobholders stuck with the "deduct" system, that indeed they were not coerced; on the contrary, he said, they "had to pay that ten percent voluntarily" (612).

Irony was everywhere, in the system and in the observers of it; the melodrama of highly intense combat is repeatedly drained away into gargantuan hilarity. Part of the irony is that much that might hurt seems not to hurt: this is the mode of farce. But amid all the farcical events, all the translation of moral burdens into a nonmoral key whose very incongruity is laughable, some people did get hurt, enough to pile up stores of vengeful feelings on both sides; or the hurt might be that of the young idealist who could kill, and knowingly accept death, because of moral outrage. And back we come, hardly believing it, from musical comedy to utterly serious drama: the ultimate in the ambiguity of this political theater. Whatever its traditions, however, they were immensely complicated by the fantastic diversity of the leading man, and on this one can ponder as long as one will. Williams calls Huey's *My First Days in the White House* "a mixture of nonsense and wisdom, of frivolity and gravity" (845) and at another time alludes to "a curious duality in him" (803). True enough, but we need the still stronger phrase of a reporter whom Williams quotes: "this man who seemed to be so simple but really was incredibly complex" (759). In dealing with that complexity we are perhaps driven to describing its manifestations rather than discovering its roots. Williams says that Huey's *Every Man a King* reveals little about his "inner nature" (647). This is partly applicable to Williams' own book, where the perspective is more panoramic than analytic: Williams sees the excellence of the program, the skill of the pragmatic politics, and the fascinatingness of the spectacle. An important part of the fascinatingness was the multiplicity of the hero, in whom, in addition to all his virtues, Williams can at times detect "spite," "meanness," untruthfulness, a tendency toward "persecutions that were primarily expressions of his personal animosities" (159), "deep personal hatred" of Standard Oil (173), unforgivingness (407). But alongside vindictiveness there are various actions of political magnanimity; alongside a passion for political and economic reform there is a buffoonishness that might be a weapon or a handicap; alongside great courage and daring there are expediency and triviality; alongside a puritanism that appeared in an extraordinary talent for hard work, for organization, for getting things done, for doing homework and knowing what he needed to know, there was the tendency to eat and drink too much, to get into rows of a farcical sort, to misbehave brattishly; alongside great agility, ingenuity, and innovating imaginativeness in crises there was a passion for, and a relentless skill in, self-promotion that anticipated every device, insinuating and vulgar, that public relations firms would later market at high prices; the seeker of justice for the underdog was all but obsessed by a histrionic need that demanded center stage in every act; the most calculating of operators is at times driven by irrational motives, some of which border on the clinical; the political virtuoso, acting with real guts or bravado or political trickery, could be a wit, jester, ironist, even cheap entertainer; the antipoverty crusader an insouciant nose-thumber. Rarely can one find such a mingling of the brilliant and the boorish, of principle and play, of the clownish with that ultimate indefinable gift of the man who would lead—the charismatic.

Williams lays out all this variety fully. To discover a principle of coherence by which many unlikes are integrated in a definable unity, we may need the perspective of a great deal more time—plus a freedom not really available for a generation (at least for significant aspects of private life that may have defining value). For the time being we can be grateful for Williams' abstention from easy psychological simplifications, the kind that so often harass literary interpretations. In the end, I think, Williams' book offers something like a literary experience: in the best sense, he presents a realistic fiction—that is, all the actions, all the behavior, all the relationships and battles that externalize the personality and the character of the hero. Our interest tends to shift from historic inquiry—what events actually took place?—to the human problem and the moral experience: what manner of man is this? In moving from one question to the other we illustrate Aristotle's notion that poetry is more universal than history.

V

In observing Huey, one instinctively looks for the universal types that are the foundations of literary modes. Repeatedly Huey's attitudes, calculations, and strategies as "power artist" remind one of the Machiavellian leader (Williams himself makes the comparison several times), whose ethical imperative is the maintenance of stable order through power grounded in a knowledge of man's fears and lusts—the utopia of a total realist. There is no doubt that Huey was continually brilliant in sensing the kinds of human need and desire and responsiveness to which the "mass leader" might effectively appeal by being feared, admired, unpredictable, inscrutable, ruthless, faithless on occasion. To read Huey by the Machiavellian light, however, is to face a real dilemma. One can either say that the Machiavellian sense of human reality—as essentially will-less, appetitive, mechanical in responsiveness to stimuli—is inadequate in the long run (it does not adequately allow for rebellion against humiliation), or say that Huey did not adequately apply sound rules of maintaining the power needed by both ruler and ruled (by being unable to control the corruption not tolerable in a Machiavellian view of political order). But Machiavellianism can at most be a clue to Huey on the operational side; in other ways it is not an effective measure. Nor can one seriously think of Huey as a "machiavel," that inadequate literary offspring of Machiavellianism who during the Renaissance was a favorite stage villain. Yet many, it is clear, wanted to, or did, think of him thus—as a purely evil plotter whose machinations were to aggrandize himself and ruin others. Oddly enough, Huey at times reminds one of one of the most striking of all machiavels, Shakespeare's Richard III—in a slight tinge of what was an abiding passion in Richard, the need to humiliate victims; in a somewhat sardonic sense of the human scene around him; in a tactical simulation of piety (588); and in letting himself be persuaded to do that which he had already resolved upon (120).

A certain gamesomeness in Huey—especially early in his career, but later, too—suggests the picaresque hero: the incredibly skillful salesman who lives by his wits, is partly a con man, charms people, is a virtuoso in putting things over on others, who either deserve it or don't feel injured. Once Huey boasted that he "could sell anything on earth to anybody" (47), and he could make it good, literally or metaphorically. "Gall was one of his specialties" (51). Williams often alludes to his "impudence," his "effrontery," his remaining "unabashed" where other people might have been abashed; he had plenty of bluff, boldness, and audacity, and at the same time skill, ingeniousness, trickiness, a turn for the quick irresistible ploy. There was in Huey at least a part of the genial rogue with charisma—the man to become a faith healer and, beyond that, a minor secular divinity. It is a type we can love as long as we have faith in its ultimate impotence; the true picaro is a hit-and-run operator destined for the jug. If along with his jesting peccadilloes appears a permanent quest of power, not over an individual only but over the community, the strange union in itself is frightening. (Huey had an almost hypnotic effect upon people; hence we must remember the reaction against the hypnotist in Mann's "Mario and the Magician.") Put it another way: Huey had a flair for low comedy, for slapstick episode—a symbol of innocuousness; join this with ruthlessness, and the hardly imaginable combination naturally becomes sinister and terrifying. Slapstick and the big stick, farce and force are antithetical; combine them, and the grotesque merger is ominous. Perhaps unlimited diversity itself is frightening; a man who goes off in all directions is centrifugal, hinting the latent chaos in all of us, and thus implicitly extending a threat of a very subtle kind.

But we have also to remember Huey's espousing of programs that are his objective hold on historical fame. As crusader for causes he is another type, the hero of melodrama who does battle against enemies in the world. We have already seen Huey construed as melodramatic villain; to see him as hero is to note again the ambiguity that elicited opposite responses. He had in him a little of the revenger, the melodramatic figure who was both just and unjust, and who always came to a violent end. He liked the role of a heroic David against evil Goliaths, especially Standard Oil, and there is no doubt that to many he was literally that. In melodrama the chief figure may be defeated because he is actually evil or because he is the victim of evil men; or he may triumph. These are the simplest alternatives, and clearly they are too simple for the Huey story. There are two more-complex outcomes, however, that are possible in the melodramatic situation. One is compromise; some get more than others, but no one loses entirely. It is the outcome of forbearance and half loaves, the virtues espoused in Molière's *Misanthrope;* it is really the solution of high comedy, which is what eventuates when the intensest emotions possible in melodrama do not finally undercut a sensible worldliness. It is the outcome ideally suitable to the Louisiana story, where the soundest note is one of a pragmatic politics in which, as Williams shows, Huey at his best had great skill. But too much passion entered the story on both sides; too many antagonists were willing to risk the world rather than practice the worldliness of finding a modus vivendi. What happened, then, we can think of as complex or ironic melodrama: the protagonist wins the battle, but at a terrible cost, here finally that of widespread bitterness and of his own life.

Even this may not be complex enough, for it implies a unity in the protagonist; the cost seems to be only assessed against him by others. But suppose the cost is one that he brought upon himself? Then we have the tragic mode (which is what Robert Penn Warren saw and used in *All the King's Men*). Indeed, one keeps hoping throughout that the story will finally assume the tragic form that is latent in the historical materials. Granted, the Louisiana milieu was not conducive to tragedy; it had that form of worldliness which could accept corruption as inevitable in political life and even admire it "when it is executed with style and, above all, with a jest" (185). This is the mode of the most sophisticated comedy, a comedy where the danger is cynicism, the polar extreme of tragedy. And yet Huey's very diversity is the raw material of tragedy, which turns on the inner divisions that are the ultimate fact of human reality. Williams is drawn to this view ("a great politician may be a figure of tragedy" [x]) but seems to hesitate between attributing the catastrophe to the "relentless opposition" and finding its genesis in certain qualities in Huey. Williams amply reveals these qualities, but he does not formally concede to them primacy in determination of the outcome. He can call Governor John Parker "a prime example of the tragedy of the progressive reformer limited by his own vision" (136) but never quite say of Huey, at least overtly, "a tragedy of the social idealist destroyed by his own lust for power"— one possible formulation of the drama.

Oddly enough, the circumstantial fabric contains many strands of traditional tragedy. The Longs feuded with other families, and their own internal feuding, sometimes actually treacherous, is not unlike the internecine bitterness of royal lines in Greek myth. Of the circumstantial ironies in the Long story, none is so striking as that final one when Huey was shot: the doctor who took charge, a Long appointee to several medical posts, was not up to saving a life that might have been saved. Huey was an eminent public figure and in many ways a representative one. He had the "feverish and almost abnormal energy" and "encompassing curiosity" (26) that often appear in tragic heroes. It is not difficult to think of him as the "good man" with the "flaw." These traditional terms imply an inner division, a conflict of motives, such as Williams attests to a score of times. Huey "had his ideals, but he also loved politics for its own sake" (108); "an instinctive sympathy for the poor and a sure sense of what would be a vote-getting issue" (112); his "motives" were "a mixture of self-interest and idealism" (155); he could veer between "ruthlessness" and "reasonable compromise" (482); he practiced patronage but disliked it because of "the idealism that lingered in him" (755). But in time all the divisions in him are subsumed under, or merged in, one fundamental division—that between the rescuer or even savior of society and, to employ a comprehensive enough term, the egomaniac. The latter side appears in many ways, from vanity of authorship to feeling that "anything he created or supported was his personal possession" (515) to "consciousness of mission" and conviction that he was a "man of destiny" (106). But for the mission he needed power, and the whole question turns finally on the degree to which power, in the manner of an indispensable drug, becomes addictive, or to which a means becomes an end. Williams discusses this at length in his excellent chapter 26, in which, if I read him aright, he neither justifies Huey's rationalizations of power seeking nor quite identifies an obsession with power as the tragic feature of the story. But he shows the obsession operating not only in direct grabs of power but in various kinds of arrogance—scorn for rivals and followers (107), the need to humiliate (758). On one occasion Williams describes Huey as "exhilarated by the exercise of power" and hence overconfident and misjudging "completely the depth of the reaction he had aroused" (348). The episode has thematic value: sense of power diminishes sense of actuality. Whom the gods would destroy, they first make mad. The metaphor might even have a tangential literal applicability: at various places Huey is described as manic or depressed or paranoid. But the clinical, if it is that, is only illustrative, not central.

Yet we seem to have, not the oft-told tale that power corrupts, but something profounder—an antecedent disposition, of a phenomenal sort, to demand the primacy that is the ultimate symbolization of power. Huey, in the words of many observers, "couldn't be second to anybody" (7). The final grand dramatization of this is his taking on of FDR, being cast out by powers too great for him, setting up a lower base for revengeful efforts to gain power over FDR's New Deal children, and planning to seduce them with bigger apples. Obviously I'm stretching the analogy a little, but it is not really a *tour de force;* it has enough verisimilitude to suggest the tantalizing mythic potential in the Huey story. And if it does nothing else, it reveals the magnitude, in Huey, of that hubris which in some form or other has always marked the tragic hero.

The last seal of the tragic hero is self-knowledge. Williams says that Huey was a "remarkably introspective politician" who reflected on his own use of power (748); on one occasion he blamed himself for the corruption in his organization. Still, he seems not to have looked at himself in the more profound way called for by the moral contradictions that I have been sketching in the last several pages. Rather like the protagonists in some Ibsen quasi tragedies, Huey is cut off from the full reach of reflection by sudden death. Williams' final arrangement of materials, indeed, suggests rather the pathos of incompleteness than the tragedy of an errant will.

On the one hand Huey's story can call to mind the greatest myth of the demonic hatred of second place. Along with it we see heroic achievement, roguery, and low comedy. We have not yet a key for

whatever center may be assumed to lie behind these centrifugal out-
pourings of personality. We are bound to keep looking for it: Huey's
challenge to the imagination is a great one. He died young, but he
makes a strong impact on the psychic centers from which flow the arts
of historical and literary interpretation. *Hugellus, brevis vita, arte
longus.*

My comments on Williams' portrait of Huey Long conclude a series of
four essays which have focused primarily on the university as it was in
the 1930s and 1940s. It is of course not possible to separate the university from the individuals who constitute it, and hence I have already
had much to say about professors and others who were significant in
the institutional life of half a century ago. I turn now to sketches of
several of these colleagues as individuals, not entirely bypassing what
they did in the university, but recalling them primarily as members of
the profession generally, as friends, and as human beings. The move
from place to persons is a natural one in the grammar of the volume.

II

PERSON: Some LSU Individuals

II. 5

RPW at LSU: Reminiscences

(1980)

When I began to put these notes together, I was struck by a geographical irony. Here was I, a native Pennsylvanian, writing literally on an island shore in Puget Sound, about a Kentuckian whose colleague I was forty years ago in Louisiana and who has long lived in Connecticut. What we had shared, for a few years, was a Deep South which we had both left in the 1940s, and which no longer is what it was then. Yet that past still asserts its vitality for me in our now-distant present.

My glancing back, in a Kentucky scene, to that old Louisiana reality reminds me, if only faintly, of Red Warren's going back to Todd County to see again the Jefferson Davis monument, begun long before, finished much later, and then in 1979 a key point in a Davis commemoration. It should be amply clear that I am not a Warren—that most of us here are not Warrens—and that he is not a Jefferson Davis. Granted that, rough parallels between the backward looks, or the absence of them, will come to mind. I can start with no childhood images to be partly unlearned and partly confirmed later on, though I might seek a parallel by claiming that my first images of Red, forty-five years ago, were products of my professional childhood. But my early images came, of course, not through a grandfather, but directly from the subject; they were tentative rather than decisive; they were to be added to

This talk was delivered on the morning of October 29, 1980, in the Department of Special Collections, King Library North, at the University of Kentucky's Robert Penn Warren 75th Birthday Symposium.

65

rather than revised or justified. And the native Kentuckian who is the center of our rites is happily not at the stage at which stone monuments are the required idiom. Or better still, he has been building his own monument, not quite so localized as the Davis one, a little longer in construction, and visible in all scenes and at all distances. So in our present pageantry we can see both man and monument. In 1979, Red Warren, glancing back over a century and a half, could meditate a little on the passage of things and even, in the totally dry-eyed way that marks his style, on the *lacrimae rerum*. One might be tempted to borrow that mode here, even with less than half a century to think about, and to record the sense of something gone besides the years. But that sounds like standard septuagenarian mournfulness, which I do not feel. As to what slides away, then, better to borrow the silence that held between the Warren brothers as they looked at markers of time past.

So on to bare annals. When I arrived at LSU in September, 1935, Red seemed like some kind of old-timer there. He was well along at thirty, and I was a mere twenty-nine. To me, a new instructor with a new Ph.D. and old debts, an old-timer was almost anybody up ahead; there they all looked secure and entrenched. Red was an old-timer of a year or two, and what is more, an assistant professor. From where I stood and waited, it seemed an exalted status. At that time one was not spotted in advance as a period man or a type man (say a medievalist or semiotician); one was just signed on to teach freshman English and the peripheral goodies in literature, if any, that might drop into one's lap when and if the fates were kind (that is to say, unkind to someone ahead of one in the pedagogical chow line). So I had only extreme juniority, an everyman's generalized teaching role, and no record of any kind to make me an identifiable individual. Established assistant professors seemed a different breed to whom one spoke only if spoken to. Besides, this was the Deep South, and my first sight of it; all was foreign, and anything one said might be a goof. Too, this redheaded assistant professor was a strange duck who had the most extraordinary accent, not the Louisiana speech I was learning to hear, and with no trace of the Oxonian which sometimes sweetens the tongue of old Rhodes boys. For such reasons it was quite a while—perhaps a year—before I began to get acquainted with Red at all.

As seasons of mists and mellow fruitfulness go, that autumn of 1935 was an unusual one, with an ironic ripeness at the core, and even fumes of poppies of a sort. Huey Long was shot on the Sunday after Labor Day and died two days later. These somewhat Shakespearian events took place during my wife's and my first nine days in Baton Rouge, and, as I have already described, we were in the visitors' gallery of the lower chamber in the State Capitol when the shots snapped out just below us. We could hardly know that, in being on hand at the spectacular cut-off of a spectacular career, we were standers-by of an ending that was also a beginning. This rounding out of a life made it visible as a whole, the raw material available for transmutation, a decade later, into the different life of one of the great American novels, as I can say with assurance, of our day. Was Red Warren's imagination already beginning to play tentative games with that life, brief but now complete, and to see it extending into a mythic existence beyond time and place? I wish I could report that I had spoken with Red about such matters, but I cannot. There are always large vacant spots in one's past luckiness. Still, just being a bystander when shots bloodied the statehouse floor seems a little like having been a passerby where the Daulia road meets the Delphi-Thebes road—they still point the alleged spot out to tourists—when an arrogant old man ordered a young chap off the road and got hacked down. Out of such brief episodes come, in time, works you don't forget. One knows this, alas, only through hindsight and not at the hot moment.

Did Huey's death raise any qualms in the editors of the *Southern Review,* which was just aborning? The editors might well have wondered whether the budget for the *Review,* a paradoxical product of the very complex Long era, would survive in a new post-Long regime. If the question had occurred to me at the time, I would not have been up to asking it, and I never thought to bring it up later. A casual retrospective observer might see, in the coincidence of Huey's death and the *Review*'s birth, a simplistic symbolism: ring out the old, ring in the new; down politics and up culture. The truth, happily, deserts such obviousness for irony: the *Review* did not meet its death until seven years later, and then during a reform administration in the state.

Well, Huey died, and a few weeks later the second issue of the *Re-*

view came out. Assistant Professor Warren, as I have said, seemed an entrenched old-timer. He had been at LSU long enough to have engaged in the preplanning—they did a year's work in six months—needed before the first *Review* could come out. On the literary side it seemed, I guess, a rather strange beast to the majority of us who had been brought up, in college and graduate school, in the old historical tradition. Some of us wouldn't buy it at all—I use *buy* in the figurative sense, since purchasing anything but necessities was a slender practice in those Depression days—and some of us were teased into its orbit despite ourselves. To some it was a freak, to others invisible, to others a godsend. In general the usual distrust of the new and the usual envy of growing success were in time more than matched by a sense of the class of the *Review* and hence by local pride in it. Surely no one foresaw, however, that in a brief septennium the *Review* would become memorable, would take such almost unknowns as Eudora Welty at least through the vestibule of the house of memory, would give some glory to its university, would help qualify its editors for major posts in distant states, and incidentally would send forth its first two business managers into notable editorial careers elsewhere. Again, as with Huey's death, how comforting is hindsight.

After I became acquainted with Red Warren and Cleanth Brooks, I got the impression, more from chance remarks of theirs than from outright assertions, that they saw pretty much eye to eye on contributions, or could argue vigorously but peaceably; that their tastes sometimes differed sharply from that of Charles Pipkin, the political scientist who was nominal headman at the start; that some editorial agreement was necessary for acceptance of a contribution, but that two tepid yes-votes were not enough. One strong yes was essential. But still, these are impressions that may be sustained, modified, or demolished by the principals who can speak from knowledge instead of impressions.

Time-consuming as the *Review* must have been, it was only a fraction of Red's life. I do not know, as I have said, whether his imagination was already beginning to work out from the Huey Long story. His imagination had to be at work, if not in 1935 at least pretty soon after that, on the Kentucky tobacco wars, for *Night Rider* would appear in 1939. *Night Rider* began his long series of treatments of middle-South subjects, especially those of Kentucky and Tennessee; if Nashville was not quite his Dublin, still the analogy is suggestive. Memory of where one is not is the catalyst; after all, the Louisiana story came into its transformed fictional life only after Red had moved to Minnesota. Unless my memory, with customary fidelity, is deceiving me, Red's decade in Louisiana did not generate fictional themes beyond the large one of *All the King's Men*.

Back to the late 1930s, when *Night Rider* was in gestation. These were incredibly productive years, even in the context of a long life never exactly torpid. For Red was working on both stories and poems (his second volume of poems appeared in 1935, that wonderfully full year), coediting the *Review*, collaborating with Brooks on two textbooks, *Approach to Literature* and the more famous *Understanding Poetry*, both of which appeared in the later 1930s. And then of course there was *Understanding Fiction*, and along with it the second novel, *At Heaven's Gate*, both in 1943. All this is in the public record, though the casual reader of the record might not envisage the great gushing forth of intellectual and imaginative energy. But like most of its kind, that public record is incomplete. It does not reveal, though it may imply, that Red was teaching full-time (the full-time probably included some nominal allowance for editorial work). It does not reveal that the teaching was more than providing the casual classroom semipresence which some scholars and writers think is enough. It does not reveal that he was busy in department life, first in helping shape up a new Ph.D. program (not to mention working on examination committees for M.A. and Ph.D. applicants), and then in that busyness of correspondence, caucus, and corridor which broke out when the department faced a change of chairman and was shaken by the urgent campaigning of one candidate who to many of us seemed a walking anthology of administrative disabilities. Nor does the record reveal that Red was one of a relatively small faculty group who, when the post-Long scandals broke out in 1939 to festoon the state like the decor of a colossal musical comedy, tried to make hay by pushing for some small betterments of the university. All these doings not on the record prove a large conscience in university affairs—the kind of conscience often choked off at birth by scholars, and rarely even a gleam in the eye of writers, who are rarely seduced into institutional citizenship. Put together the doings on the record and the unrecorded doings, and they give a picture of Warren work fantastic in its variety and quantity. It was an early model of the diverse creativity—which extended of course to social criticism—of that rare being, the full-scale man of letters.

If only I could claim that, as a colleague of Red from his thirtieth to his thirty-eighth year, I foresaw the future achievement. But I can assert only that I did spot him as an unusually able figure in the English department and university. At the same time the man of talent and the nonstop worker was a very attractive human being. Let us not, however, shrink him into a standardized charm-school midget, smiling his way into all unjudging hearts around. He had a deadpan, almost stern, mood, a sort of flat withdrawal or uncommunicativeness which could make one wonder, "What have I done?" Then there was another style that seemed to go naturally with the lined face and hardbitten look which were there early—a skeptically ironic twist of expression and of speech that could effortlessly deflate any foolish ideas, or for that matter popular ideas, that might be floating around without getting many questions. It neither reflected a suspicious nature nor fell into easy sarcasm; it was rather a natural inquiringness of one not easily convinced or converted—a sort of Kentuckian Missourianism. His critical questioningness seemed to issue from near the corner of the mouth, without drifting into what a college teacher of mine called "sidemouth philosophy." Perhaps in his close look at things there was also a touch of that strong wariness of sentiment which helps toughen up the fiction. Then finally there was the joyous and laughing Red, whose full face crinkling into merriment meant a fine display of teeth and that long little suck or hiss of breath, an inbound or outbound sibilance, that somehow doubled the sweep of delight. I thought of this aspect of Red while reading Eudora Welty's comment, in a recent interview, on a visit from Red: they just "sat around," and he, leaving, said, "I have never laughed so hard—not a serious word all evening."

And that brings us to the gregarious or social Red. *Social* is probably the better word, since *gregarious* connotes a habitual search for company, as if solitude were a kind of flu, whereas I'm talking about the basic hard worker, who has to be solitary, and then the variations on that base. Whatever his working schedule inevitably was, Red was a better-than-average social being, as a guest ready for whatever fun

and games would break out, and as a host easy, amiable, and generous. He was a mean gunner in a battle of charades; it was easier to be
on his side, and not to have to face his look of the unmoved mover,
pitying, condescending, amused and a little amazed at the obtuseness
of the interpreters. I remember him as a host at occasional big parties,
the guests a wide spread of gown and some town, making each guest
feel sought after, and seeing that the supplies of food and drink were
located and utilized by the guests. I don't mean, of course, that Red
really came up to Colonel Sanders, though within the last few days he
seems almost to have made it here in Kentucky.

In those spring years one could eat and drink with more abandon,
and with little hint of the watchfulness that would later overtake us.
I still have a clear picture of one Warren guest, an instructor in English,
standing there with his back against the wall, and a little cross-eyed by
now, like a happy late-nighter in a cartoon, and then suddenly starting
to slide gently down the wall, his feet moving slowly forward and outward until, never losing contact with the wall, he was seated solidly on
the floor, his legs making a big V, and his face coming apart in a
slightly puzzled gaze. The Warren party air, though not intent upon
such a fall, was comfortable with it; first aid and a comic sense were
both there in suitable measure. At such a time all the king's men could
reassemble the wall-fall guy.

Red was not only a ready party-man, and an apt host, but a great
entertainer. In him I saw and heard, for the first time, the southern
storyteller, who is what he is, I guess, because he does not live by the
punch line alone but has equal zest in the spread of detail along the
way, the filling-out of scene and action that have their own life, and are
not to be hurried over as mere props for the finale. Not that the finale
is trivial, but that it completes a structure instead of being merely the
pop for which alone the popgun exists. I heard him do the great tale of
the mountain folks' big family bed, the sleeping place for pappy and
mammy and their large brood, the brood all equipped with coonskin
caps which they kept losing at moments of crisis during the long night.
Perhaps the best of Red's tales—which by the way he credited to
Andrew Lytle—was the one of the city-slicker salesman who came to a
southern hamlet, snatched the local belle from the arms of her less
crafty village swain, and then threw a big wedding dinner. It reached a

climax in prose epithalamia by the male leads. We listeners rejoice in a wonderful archetypal contrast in rhetorical styles as winner and loser work with a common image of bridal loveliness. I stole the tale and for years presented it, without demand but with by-line, once winning a large acclaim with it at a dude ranch near Kerrville, Texas. But my version was no Warren work of art; Red invested it with a fullness of body and ornament that an alien amateur narrator could never come up with.

It is surely clear by now that the rising academic man, the on-coming literary man, and the instinctive social man was a very likable human being—not a personality boy, never a gusher, rarely without some reserve, having a sharp edge when needed, capable of impatience, but never self-assertive, and always unostentatious, decent and courteous. He was a rare denial of the four-letter definition of literary people which, a decade or two earlier, T. S. Eliot had vented at a luncheon with Conrad Aiken, and he was a negative answer to Osip Mandelstam's inquiry, "Might there not be some inverse ratio between the moral and dynamic development of the soul?" When I first came across Thomas Mann's wrestling with the problem of bohemian and bourgeois, I felt that Red had solved it by combining the virtues of both, or, if you will, of writer and citizen, or better, artist and gentleman. From Red I learned so early in life to associate good art and good manners that over the years, when my academic job involved me in regular contact with poets and fictionists, and of course professors, I found myself impatient with those who took tantrums for talent, or boorishness for genius. When Red came to Seattle to do the Roethke memorial reading a few years ago, he was one of our best visitors, famous now, but a wonderful trouper, tired from travel and performance, but amiable and even jolly with scores of introducees. Early and late, he has been essentially modest—not unconfident, not muddied with mock humility, but open to the rest of the world, as good a listener as he was a talker, talking about things out there and not in here, ready to belong rather than dominate, and dominating, when he did, only by others' sense of quality in the man. There was no side, no knowing insidership, no need to go by current standards, no affectation of high-toned with-it-ness. He once told me that he couldn't read Thomas Mann. Maybe that changed later; I don't know. Anyway, it enabled me to take the risk of saying I couldn't read *Finnegans Wake*, that polymorphously perverse anagram, fitter for dissertations than for delight. He once claimed to be tone deaf and thus to shun all musical events. I heard him say this at a time when an artist friend of ours was showing especial delicacy of ear by insisting that even symphony was too noisy, and that only a quartet was fit for civilized listening. Well, Red's alleged absence of musical ear made me less cringing when, in a community of opera buffs, I finally realized that I simply did not like opera. Red would listen patiently to criticisms of points in the text-books. He sent me the typescript of a novel—*At Heaven's Gate,* and perhaps later *World Enough and Time,* though incredibly I am unsure of this—and asked for comments. This was genuine modesty, as was his handling of my doubtless square responses. He would say, "Yes, I'll have to do something about that," or, more often, "No, I think I'll have to stick with that; you see . . ."—as usually I hadn't seen. A reader of my present memoir wondered whether Red's work might have been influenced by the comments of such manuscript-readers as myself. I doubt it very strongly. Perhaps an occasional point made by a reader led to some local modifications, but spurring local modifica-tions is not quite exerting influence. Anyway, most of Red's career has been in the years since I was in close touch with him, so I am an incom-petent witness on this point.

Perhaps his ultimate modesty is the willingness and ability to write the lucid and unaffected prose that has always dominated his critical work—a prose often imaged and allusive, yes, but with no touch of the Byzantinely opaque mode that now and then rampages in academe, unhousebroken. He took the risk implicit in an Oscar Wilde charac-ter's observation: "Nowadays to be intelligible is to be found out." And then there is that comment in a recent interview: "I am trying to be a good poet"—this by a senior writer a little later to be called, in *Newsweek,* "America's Dean of Letters."

But I must stick to my role as recording non-angel of an earlier phase in the three ages of American man—minority, middle age, and Medicare. (I do not include "maturity," which may happen in minority but may not happen in middle age.) Most of my memories are miscel-laneous, but three of them naturally fall together to show Red in com-bat. I take them in anticlimactic order. The scene of the first is a con-ference on southern affairs hosted at LSU. The only aspect of this event that I remember is Red's rising in the middle of the audience and re-buking the conference. The conference was on the wrong track, it had no idea of the true South, and no decent picture of its future. Though this occurred during general discussion, Red was reading his remarks from the back of what looked like a large manila envelope—a great comfort to us who can extemporize only from a prepared text. Well, this injection of an alien view seemed very brave to me; alas, I cannot recall what followed. In the second episode, the main character was a student caught in, or at least charged with, some kind of theft. Authori-ties were about to throw the book at him, and he was a likely target, for he was not a very lovable lad—perhaps a 1968 type born too soon. But he was evidently a good student, and that is probably what brought Red into a sturdy defense that was not altogether easy. A scholarly youth should not be treated with a severity unlikely if the culprit were a football player. Anyway, it took some conviction and guts to be on the boy's side. But with my unusual faculty for forgetting the next chapter, I cannot report who won. The scene of the third episode is again a bar, not of justice this time, but of a convention hotel. A num-ber of us were sitting around a table, the boy brought the drinks, and Red exclaimed quickly, "But they forgot to put the whiskey in mine." I didn't know whether that was a literal statement of an accidental omission, or a metaphor for a slick barman's cheating half-jigger. Whatever it was, Red spoke firmly to the Ganymede of the place. Though I said that I would use anticlimactic order, I am now hedging, for this was the only one of the three episodes of bold dissidence that could invite the attentions of a bouncer. But there was no bouncing; bourbon was brought; and whether the bill grew, I don't know.

A medley of images is scattered about in the frail storage room of memory. If only they were ordered in an assiduous diary; if only one had had the wits to be a Boswell when there was much Boswellizing to be done. But my images are random and chancy, relics tumbling from a messy attic room when one opens the door in search of old gold. The real gold is one's memory of an association, which isn't kept in the at-tic. But the attic has the purse trimmings, those signs that the real thing is there. One trimming: the time when Red was first teaching a course in Shakespeare. For some reason this involved the splitting of a class assigned to senior professor John Earle Uhler. Maybe it was just that the class suffered from overpopulation, since Dr. Uhler was quite a drawing card on the classroom stage. Be that as it may, Dr. Read, the department head—in those days having a head was not considered a piece of gratuitous tyranny—told Dr. Uhler to divide his class equally and send one half to Mr. Warren, who would be waiting in another room in Allen Hall (the arts and sciences building named after Governor O. K. Allen). Dr. Uhler went back to Dr. Read and reported that alas he could not split the class because no one would leave. Though Dr. Read was aged and fragile, his Virginian eyes sparkled, he grasped his cane, he snapped, "Well, if you can't split the class, I can," and he limped off to do battle. Thus began Warren's career in teaching Shakespeare, a subject in which he has never known a shortage of students.

A junior colleague told me once that Red had wanted to swim—a bit of a problem in Louisiana, where the thick brown waters are generous hosts to moccasins and alligators. The young man provided the swim spot at a country place, either a pool of sorts or a river eddy relatively safe from unseen currents and water wild beasts. He reported to me, "Red put plugs in both ears, waded in, and swam madly in a little circle for five minutes, and that was it." Not much hot-tub indulgence there. I do not know if this whirlpool style was altered in later years and other climes. I move on from warm water to ice tea. In Deep-South summer most of us got addicted to Coke or ice tea; I swilled both, but especially ice tea, and the habit clung even in the off-season. It seemed a bit of a secret vice, like sherry in the office-desk drawer. I confessed it to Red, the kind of man who would understand weaknesses. He said, "Live on ice tea? I work on it—and all year round. I couldn't write without a pitcher of ice tea." Saved again; one no longer had to justify guzzling ice tea in winter. In the hot and humid months I would drink about a quart and a pint at the evening meal, an intake made simpler when my wife found some ice-tea glasses that actually held a pint. I told Red once, "At supper we have only two things—ice tea and salad." "Good God," said Red, "if I came to the table and found only salad to eat, I'd just sit down and cry." I don't know whether forty subsequent years have either reduced the tears or removed all such occasions for them. I move on to a third liquid, and it happens also to be my third drawing on it—whiskey. This time Red is narrator. He was good not only as tale-teller but as reporter on persons, places, and things. The person in this story was Tom Wolfe—the Eugene Gant one, that is. The place, I think, was a writer's conference somewhere in Colorado. The time—an after-work-hours party. Wolfe arrived in a capacious jacket—or maybe topcoat, but jacket makes a better story— with large sidepockets, each one stuffed with a fifth. He was costumed with the ammunition for a bull-shooting that was to last most of the night. Wolfe was evidently a Gargantua in monologue. Red, as I have said, was a good listener, and this time his listening system must have got an extraordinary workout. No complaints, though; only lively details of the roaring boy on stage.

From fluids to dry goods. As dresser, Red could be equally colorful and constant, occasionally shiny but more generally old shoe, never one to turn out an old faithful. Any other Louisiana relics who are here today will probably remember as well as I do an old reliable jacket, a jacket that went on and on. It was of a reddish-brickish- orange-ish hue, with touches of the two geranium shades, and maybe a dash of horse chestnut. At first it riveted the eye in those precolor days of haberdashery, and then it stuck with one like a mistress dwindling into a wife. One noted it invariably, but inattentively, as one does a spectacle, like hijacking, that has become daily news. Maybe it was an indestructible tweed of Oxford provenience. It gained a special bou- quet from Red's habit—I report this secondhand—of sticking a not- yet-dead pipe into a pocket and thus setting up a double smoke. John Palmer once said that the beast had seen its best days and, like the horse in *Animal Farm*, was ready for the knacker. Only a good friend could be so inhumane.

From dry goods to dry statements. The subject was the Civil War. Red said of a southern general (I'm too uncertain of his identity to mention the name that comes to mind), "Lee should have had him shot." It was my first experience of so uncompromising a judgment of a member of a class that somehow seemed exempt from stern censure, though in this matter, times are much changed. And for me, in my pa- rochial naïveté, it was also very early evidence that southern loyalty did not mean unqualified admiration of everyone in southern ranks. I insert a more trivial moment, this one after Red had moved to Min- nesota. It was a meeting early in the fall, maybe in Chicago. As we were breaking up, Red said, "Well, nothing to do now but go back to

Minneapolis and wait for the first blizzard." It was his only comment on that city that I remember. Another dry statement later on, in a probably less trivial moment: "Some of my friends want me to become a Catholic, but I haven't the vocation." What his vocation was had long become clear. As for the products of that vocation, I have written about one or two of them. One of my happiest assignments was reviewing the reviews of *All the King's Men*, for rarely did one find so many big guns, commingled with various small side arms, cannonading such downright nonsense. I found that nonsense appetizing in two ways. One, it relieved any fears one might have that criticism was getting too rational. Second, it was the kind of nonsense that positively made one salivate epithets; abuse came flowing out like automatic writing. These victims were fun, however little fun their victim might have got out of that extraordinary flux of astigmatic holier-than-thou judgments. (My account of *All the King's Men* appears in III.14 of this volume.)

Once I planned to write something about a poem of Red's—"The Ballad of Billie Potts." When I first read the "Ballad," probably some time after it came out, I recognized the plot as very much like that of two plays, George Lillo's *Fatal Curiosity* (1731) and Camus' *Le Malentendu* (1944). Obviously the story that Red had picked up from an elderly relative in Kentucky was one branch of a mythic family that had migrated widely. This kind of parallel or relationship interests me, and I mentally outlined an article on the literary history of unwitting filicide; I think I was going to call it "Laius Acts First." I mentioned the plan to Cleanth Brooks, who said, "Go ahead. Red will be glad to play dead." Somehow this chance phrase made the historian of filicide seem like an unwitting homicide, and I let almost three decades pass before outlining the worldwide travels of the Billie Potts myth. Meanwhile, others had got into the act. My sketch of the myth, and of its other sketchers, is now embalmed in a long footnote on page 346 of a book I published in 1973 (*The Iceman, the Arsonist, and the Troubled Agent*).

It seemed like filicide and homicide when a misunderstanding—this is my guess—resulted in Red's departure to Minnesota in 1943. Maybe departmental suicide would be the better term. We felt the loss in many ways. Doubtless Cleanth would leave next. Fortunately he stayed another four years. My own departure, a few months after

Cleanth's, is a small footnote to this memoir. The University of Washington was looking for a chairman of English. One of the people they asked for nominations was a man who had been a visiting professor there—Joseph Warren Beach. Beach, of course, was at Minnesota. Maybe he couldn't think of anyone; maybe he just wanted more names. Anyway, he met Red Warren in the hall one day and casually asked him if he could think of anyone. How many names Red gave him I don't know, but one of them was mine—a gutsy gamble by him, and then by Washington. And so off to Puget Sound, about as far away as possible from New Haven.

A final word on the subject from which I have slid off into parentheses—Red's vocation. Two products of it, in some ways alike but both different enough from the expectable elements of a literary career to prove an extraordinary creative range, are beautifully spaced just about fifty years apart. One might call them the alpha and omega of the writer's life, except that the omega time is not yet. The study of John Brown in 1929 is surely the alpha, but the study of Jefferson Davis in 1980 is hardly a terminus. How nicely these studies balance out— the history of the northerner who hoped to start a revolution but died before the war he helped precipitate, and the history of the southerner who, unfitted though he was for the task, had to "manage what was, in one sense, a revolution," and a war; and to survive it, with little happiness, for a quarter of a century. And how nicely, too, the characters balance out—the fanatic and the logician. Ironically enough, the logician survives better in memory; the fanatic, who knows no law but his own will, exhausts his imaginative impact in his own time. Red's work on Brown might be called "The Unmaking of a Martyr." In a quite other way Red reversed his first subject: the Browns came from Connecticut, and John got to the South via the Midwest. I wish I had read the Warren *John Brown* when it first appeared—just a year after Stephen Vincent Benet's *John Brown's Body*. It just might have added something to my presentation of the Benet work, which in the early thirties was required reading in our freshman course at the University of Maine.

It may seem a combination of excessive pernicketiness and sheer banality to say that the *John Brown* is not as good as the *Jefferson Davis*. Yet even in the earlier work there is much of the echt Warren—

the dominantly direct narrative style, with nothing purple or pretentious; the concretely imaged scenes and looks of people and things; the occasional magnificent description, such as that of Brown's prosecutor; the dry observations; the ironic perceptions; the snatches of wit, with now and then, cliché though the combination is, the wisdom that one wants to feel is beyond the writer's years. (And speaking of years, I was delighted to see Red calling Brown, then in his fifties, an "old man.") There is always the penetrating moral sense that never announces itself with a fanfaronade, and the grasp of the convoluted self-deceiver in Brown which restrains what might be pure polemic. Good as this first work is, we miss a steady control of style and form: the writing is not always graceful, the focus slips, the historical narrative is not always clear, the structural lines are at times more bulgy than crisp.

It is by the control of form that the Davis piece achieves excellence and I believe distinction. It is not merely that it comes fifty years after *John Brown;* that is too simple. Its virtue—any work's virtue—is not an automatic product of half a century, a fiftieth-anniversary gift of the gods. Time does not guarantee grace. Red might have peaked at twenty-four, as many do. In the Davis narrative there is rather an achieved quality, the spontaneous imagination nurtured by experiences, yes, but, more than that, governed by disciplined striving. Well, these words may be a more than usually futile effort to describe quality. In brief, Davis, a very complex man, is portrayed by an equally complex art. Warren multiplies perspectives or context or framework; there are more points of view than in *Wuthering Heights,* but they all belong to one narrator. They are all on leash. There is the frame of the young boy listening to a grandfather who is seen in his local context. There is the frame of the second Jeff Davis, the sad hometown ne'er-do-well. There is the frame of Guthrie and its ways of creating the narrator's "uninstructed southernism." There is the frame of the monument story, which began when the narrator was ten or eleven and went on for many years. There is the meditative frame: what are monuments for? There is the frame of World War I. Take away these frames, of which the reader is periodically reminded, and the direct portrait of Davis is a different thing, perhaps a lesser thing. And then within the portrait itself there are other framings, improbable as my imagery may sound: the sketches of Lincoln, of Lee; the ironic linkages with Simon

Buckner, Zachary Taylor, John Brown, Gerrit Smith, and others; the national context, the minglings of attitude in both South and North; the frame of the twentieth-century line of vision, of political principles and wartime practice, of conflicting theories of war; and finally back to the first personal frame of the narrator, now merged with the new frame of the modern celebrations which only thinly echo the celebrated; and then the new personal frame, that of the family graves. I sink into catalog, I fear; I do not try to show how these diverse perspectives work; I omit much that is important; I only assert the unity. Well, if I am lucky, this sketch of what I take to be the *unum e pluribus* may suggest something of the combined substance and elegance of the Davis study.

But I must return, for a closer, to my assigned subject, which is not so much the work as the man, and indeed the man in that distant no-man's-land, or everyman's growing land, between minority and middle age. In my recollections of the man I fear I have been mostly knee-deep in trivia. But when the trivia concern a big man, they lose, I hope, something of their triviality. And I hope that, however peripherally, they may help evoke the image of a young man who at the time seemed a little more than the common man celebrated in modern myth. In retrospect we can see clearly what we did not all spot at the time—the creative energy that would still be surging long beyond threescore and ten. He was, and is, the gentleman who has an uncommon sense of the ungentleness of the human tribe. Know what he may, he still remains among the artists that, in Elizabeth Bowen's words, "were intended to be an ornament to society." But not through not seeing through it when it needed seeing through. And not only society, since it is for all of us that he can ask, in that summer-afternoon hypnotic state that brings certain truths to the surface, "Was this / The life that all those years I lived, and did not know?" So one remembers John Stuart Mill's claiming for himself a "large tolerance for one-eyed men, provided their one eye is a penetrating one: if they saw more, they would probably not see so keenly." Red saw, and sees, not only keenly, but more.

II.6

Cleanth Brooks: Selected Snapshots, Mostly from an Old Album

(1976)

It is a truism that Cleanth Brooks has greatly influenced the criticism and teaching of literature since 1935. He helped provide a vocabulary, and behind it a set of attitudes, that seemed to change the nature of literature. The beholder gained a new eye, and with it he saw in poetry what, though of course it had always been there, had not been readily or steadily beheld. *Beholder,* however, is slightly misleading, for inevitably there were beholders and beholders: many stubborn adherents of the old vision, many enthusiastic readers by the new light, and another breed who I think best reflected the Brooks and Warren cast of mind, the bifocalists who were aware of literature both in its dependencies (the stamping ground of the old history) and in its independencies (where the New Criticism was breaking new ground). Whatever the varieties of literary experience, the overall change was so great that the "revolution in literary studies" is a historical cliché. In its most important aspects, that revolution is likely to be permanent; unless we are very unlucky we will not lose our knowledge that literature exists in its own right, not as a subheading of social history, and that its structures define its essence. At the same time, the revolution had the "popular success" that begets its own penalties. Some enthusiastic converts seized new terminologies and brandished them so relentlessly that useful instruments seemed hackneyed. For years it was as if some seductive ad had proclaimed, "Symbols can be fun" or "Make every day your symbol day." (As late as 1971 a British play, Simon Gray's *Butley,* could base a farcical scene on an undergraduate paper solemnly dishing up image-and-symbol, paradox-and-levels, birth-and-death, night-of-the-soul criticism.) Then after some years a new generation, never having known the New Criticism as a struggling newcomer, saw it only as an established orthodoxy needing remedial rebellion. One persistent form of remedy has been political abuse; at times Brooks and associates have been called fascists, and recently I have heard them called racists (this by a black critic). But ordinarily reapportionism elects a more staid politics of headshaking over wrongheadedness, lengthy listing of shortcomings, announcing the decline of the oppressive doctrines, or alluding to their demise at some past time: "We have done with all that." To charge Brooks with error has become one way of symbolizing one's professional reliability, independence, and deserts.

I sketch this well-known history only for context. Since it is a history of some magnitude, it reveals how much more Brooks has been than even a well-known academic figure. To associate with him was inevitably to feel the energy of his mind, its habitual probing in many directions, its trying out of hypotheses, earnestly of course but many times playfully too, the rigor of thought infused with an imaginativeness that would often add gamesomeness to an enterprise serious enough at heart. I found in him a largeness of spirit that appeared not only in the deployment of knowledge and ideas, as hardly needs saying, but also—and this kind of thing does need saying—in generosity to the ways, the styles of others and in habitual authentic courtesy (I would say "courtliness" if that would not connote, in days of diminished self-discipline, an archaic heaviness) in relations with others. I have not slipped unawares into an anticlimax here: manners do image the man, the man is my subject, and graciousness is the everyday version of magnanimity. Magnanimity, or its cousin urbanity, does not always mark the intellectual, who alas may be given to the unawareness of others, the self-righteousness, and even the arrogance that betray malnutrition of spirit.

Though I say that the man is my subject, it is principally the man that I knew at Louisiana State University in the 1930s and 1940s. "Portrait of the critic as a young man" would imply both too much and too little: a portrait is more than the sum of a few snapshots (which I think is the right image for these informal notes), and "young man" wrongly suggests that all belongs to the past. Neither virtues nor crotchets disappear with time, and in Cleanth Brooks a greater-than-usual stability of being may be assumed.

Since I have already expressed my professional indebtedness to Brooks (and of course to Robert Penn Warren), I will stick to another kind of history here. When a flock of us new Ph.D.'s from the North came to an expanding LSU in the thirties, the liveliest members of the department were the Vanderbilt-*cum*-Oxford young men who were beginning to have some impact on literary and social criticism. Since newcomers such as myself knew nothing about the South or southerners and were not prepared for the innovating thought of some southerners, and since the southern critics were not convinced that an influx of nonsoutherners with the long-entrenched Germanic graduate training was the deus ex machina for higher education in the South, the situation was more than usually favorable for antagonisms and feuding, which are a central way of life in more than one English department. But as I remember it there was little more than initial cautiousness or tentative suspicion, the preliminary feeling out of others to see what human realities lay beneath styles that to either side may have seemed alien or even a little threatening. What developed was at least a thorough working amicability among men of different ways or beliefs, whether personal relations were more or less intimate. I introduce this agreeable history to make clear that it was not an accident and to give Cleanth Brooks credit for an important part in it. I have already said that he was a generous and courteous man; he could win confidence even when he did not win converts, and liking if not allegiance; he did not carry commitment into contentiousness or private judgment into the expectable next step of semivisible antipathy. What he had was not so much "tolerance" or *laissez vivre* as friendliness or social sense or disposition to keep doors open: a spontaneous getting on with people without modifying his dislike of that liberal spirit which in fear of being dogmatic tends to make no judgments at all. When we got better acquainted I knew that he made many judgments, always probing for the moral center and therefore often severe and doubtless sometimes as biased as other people's. But the constant need to be clearheaded was quite compatible with an easiness of intercourse that could survive almost anything short of indecency or failure of obligation. I am glad to be unable to say that Cleanth did not suffer fools gladly, for this banal pseudocompliment nearly always means that a man is rude to those who do not share his prepossessions. Cleanth gave fools the benefit of the doubt: they might be re-prepossessed. But he did have an extraordinarily vivid expression of dismay and pain—a plaintive, mildly accusatory falling and dimming of face—even when nonfools did not get the point.

There was a lot of getting along with diversity among a number of faculty members who in 1939 joined in a move that had unexpected repercussions. "Liberals" and "conservatives," anti-Francoists as well as sympathizers with the New Germany and with Trotskyism and perhaps the New Russia generally, we had in common mainly a feeling that LSU was capable of improvement, and we got out a statement on this subject, naming a few things that could be done. To our astonishment, its appearance filled the air with the noise of denial and denunciation. Nineteen of us had signed the statement, which, as I have already reported (I.1), led to a counterstatement ("Everything is splendid here"), signed by 176 faculty members. I reintroduce the affair of "the 19" (a term of opprobrium which lasted for quite a while) here because Cleanth was very active in the movement that led to the manifesto. We often held meetings at his house. He had a high degree of institutional concern and, if I may risk an almost defunct word, loyalty; unlike many members of the profession, he did not use the pressure of other concerns (teaching, editing, an extensive program of criticism and scholarship) to justify indifference to the university. And I can clearly remember his taking the lead in looking at one way in which opponents tried to discredit "the 19." It was an old southern ploy, historically understandable but not quite expectable in a university: calling them *damn yankees*. One night Cleanth said, to a group of us who were at his house, "Let's check this out." We simply had not thought about origins before, and we began counting on fingers; the truth was that the 19 were almost evenly divided between northerners and southerners. What is more, we checked as many of the 176 as we could remember and found them to be likewise a mingling of northerners and southerners. There were two lessons in this affair. One, this use of *damn yankee* was an amusing example of a low-grade literary method that Cleanth had been inveighing against for some time—the easy use of stock terms to get a quick-trick stock response. Two, all of us were finding bonds, not in regions, but in qualities that have nothing to do with regions. Perhaps I seem a bit wide-eyed in naming this as a lesson and in valuing it, but I hope I am doing more than revealing my own naïveté. Even today we manage to feel strong regional barriers, but that feeling surely was more thoroughgoing in the 1930s. More than that, Cleanth and like-minded men were sometimes stigmatized as "professional southerners," and their ways of defining and defending southern interests were not always acceptable to other southerners, not to mention northerners, who doubtless did not always find it easy to reconsider long-held assumptions. Hence the professed regionalists might easily have antagonized many and become withdrawn, indrawn, holier-than-thou, combative, and therefore unable to find common ground with anybody else. The point is that that is precisely what they never did in any way become, and to say that is to provide some evidence for what I have been saying about Cleanth. He contributed not to divisiveness, but to esprit de corps and even before that to assembling the corps itself.

His institutional concern led Cleanth to invest a great deal of time in seeking desirable appointments when the department chairmanship and the university presidency became vacant—time for caucusing, trying to persuade colleagues, trying to reach the powers that were, and so on. Since most people want to put allies into chairmanships, it is worth reporting that Cleanth's candidate shared with him, I am sure, not one literary or social or political idea; Cleanth was simply supporting an honorable man. The university presidency became vacant when the incumbent, a genius of a sort, a big thinker before thinking big had been thought of, an imaginative man who like other men of imagination felt the letter of the law to be irksome, found history and the market refusing to cooperate as a financial dream had told him they would—and decamped. We were immensely busy about the succession, saved from hopelessness by ignorance of our own impotence. One Sunday Cleanth and several others in our thirties (volunteers? commissioned representatives? and if so, of whom?) drove several hundred miles to call upon the president of the board of supervisors at his home, hoping to urge our candidate upon him and to register dismay over the rumored front-runner, an army officer (who was soon to get the job). On such occasions Cleanth adopted what seemed to me a very ingratiating approach: a sort of naïvely earnest throwing of us appellants on the mercy of a court admittedly dedicated to all worthy ends. Cleanth did not have to be a serpent to be a little less the dove that he was content to appear, trusting to the goodness in men who have crumbs to toss to hungry mouths.

The sixtyish-or-so president (lumber? oil? sugar? I don't recall) was courteous and friendly, professed gratitude for our concern, and said he had the best interests of the university at heart. Then with Cleanth and me he took a tack that was devastating in effect, though I am unsure whether he just fell into it, made honest use of a good thing, or took a deadpan demonic revenge for our bothering him. Having found that we professed literature, he took on the air of a kindly benefactor: "Gentlemen, I know that you will be interested, etc." Then he revealed to us a manuscript or privately printed pamphlet, the poetry of his wife, and introduced us to the maker herself. He was like a plantation owner letting an oil prospector in on a hidden gusher in the back forty. I am not sure whether we were to assay the crude on the spot or send in a laboratory report by mail. On the scene I limped in clichés while Cleanth managed benign words, in which the chilly critical spirit was somewhat muffled in the folds of courtesy and in which he gave only the mildest of gentlemanly turns to the screw that might have capped that well of English a little defiled by gentle reading and unfettered memory.

I have especially wanted to picture Cleanth as at once the very responsible man and the very genial man. I will only allude in passing to a strong filial piety of several kinds and to a quasi-paternal devotedness that exacted much in time and energy; Cleanth took on large responsibility for a younger relative and probably surpassed most fathers in giving literal day-to-day assistance with studies and other problems. Various family calls upon him were, I suspect, unusually demanding, but they never elicited any sign of his being burdened or harassed. Patience is the link between this side of his personality and the social and academic sides, in which openness, concessiveness, and forbearance prevented casual touchiness and unintentional sharpness and mitigated the criticalness which no first-rate mind is without. It was a matter of common report that, if a student's recitation were even faintly capable of being interpreted to the student's credit, Cleanth un-

failingly came up with that interpretation. He tried to pull the student
in rather than put him down. (I borrow the latter phrase from students
whom, when I was department chairman, I often heard use it to complain of instructors rather less gifted than Brooks.) He would make as
much of a concession as he could even to self-confident prejudice and
perverse attitudes, somehow gain a foothold in the student's terrain,
and try to lead him from there to better ground. He was quick to find
the tactics suitable to the occasion. He could be very persuasive and
certainly was winning even when not wholly persuasive. I can imagine
him in class, in an effort to guide the student, using the mild invitation
that we often heard in personal talk, "Now looka here." Behind the
urbane manner was the basic social act of giving the student (or for
that matter the colleague) confidence that Cleanth had confidence in
him. He did have that confidence or its surrogate, a practical accept-
ingness, to a marked degree; this could even make him a little vulnerable to an occasional academic calculator or self-deceiver who managed to seem more of a true believer, or a true thinker with worthy
beliefs, than he was. Having accepted, Cleanth would be slow to re-
value—a steadfastness once or twice enjoyed by people who might
have felt an earlier chill in associates quicker to judge. To those of us
who tended to start with a protective suspicion and to yield trust only
when it seemed earned, it was rather a lesson to see a style in which
trust came first and suspicion was reluctantly granted even when it
seemed earned. Cleanth would guard against possible harshness in the
public or formal evaluation even though in the confidential assessment
among friends he did not button up his acute sense of reality. There
used to circulate a charming story that Cleanth once said of a student,
"He is no good. He doesn't know anything. He can't write a sentence.
In fact, he is illiterate. I just had to give him a B."

It is only a small leap from one kind of family piety to another,
from kindness to colleagues and students to kindness to animals. For
some years the Brookses had a little dog, a Boston bull I think, to
which they were much devoted. The story was (as these pages may
suggest, stories tended to accumulate about Brooks—the makings of
a saga) that Cleanth had participated in a caesarean section by which
the dog was brought into the world, and I think the beast was named
Caesar. The true kindness of his foster home seemed to have little

impact on this dog, in whose case benevolence was evidently, in our more recent cliché, counterproductive. Perhaps a birth trauma had rendered him constitutionally uncooperative. In "training" he managed only to distinguish between floor and paper (an achievement that would have counted for more in a nonwriting and nonreading household), and he was paranoidally aggressive, able, with his ears back, teeth out, and voice piercing, to cause trepidation among timider guests. Once when some caucusing group was meeting at Cleanth's house, Charles Hyneman, who was not at all timid but probably got weary of sitting protectively on legs and feet, barked at the host, "Cleanth, if you don't do something about that dog, I will never come here again." Charles had the gift of combining candor with geniality, he and Cleanth remained good friends, and he continued to visit. David Nichol Smith, Cleanth's tutor at Oxford, once visited Baton Rouge and in similar circumstances expressed himself differently. Caesar did not so much chew on Nichol Smith as run all over him, yapping and snarling. Once when the Brookses were both busy in the kitchen (Cleanth did not establish himself as an intellectual by conspicuous incompetence on the food-and-drink front; he was always a most helpful husband), Caesar ran up Nichol Smith's long legs, which, stretched out, formed a sort of ramp from floor to chair, and began a noisy demonstration on the distinguished guest's middle. With a very quick but just perceptible turning of his head toward the kitchen as if to be wholly sure that he was not seen and heard, Nichol Smith made a vehement, sweeping brush-off, hissing fiercely at Caesar, "Get down, you cur!" My wife and I may have cheered.

Cleanth was a frequent host not only to colleagues, as I have been saying, but to visitors from elsewhere. At his house we met not only Nichol Smith but John Ransom, Cleanth's old Vanderbilt teacher; Katherine Anne Porter, for many years an intimate friend of the Brookses; Andrew Lytle, novelist and for a long time editor of the *Sewanee Review;* I. A. Richards; Marshall McLuhan. Cleanth was always indefatigable in chat and jesting, in good-tempered argument, in elaborating delightful fantasies for the discomfiture of the erring, in drawing Red Warren and Lytle into the storytelling of which they were both great masters, and occasionally in organizing charades. It is not easy to forget one episode in which the team that I was on failed mis-

erably to interpret a charade, even after demanding alternative enact-
ments and sweating it out for an hour or more. Our opponents' mon-
strous images, obscure and immorally ambiguous, were devised, as I
recall it, by Mrs. Brooks, Lytle, and Warren. With glee they finally revealed the words presented, *The World's Body*—the title, of course, of
Ransom's book of not long before. It was a little comforting that the
defeated team was headed by Cleanth and John Crowe Ransom himself.

From Cleanth as host we can move in two directions: to an analo-
gous activity that tells us more about the Brooks mind and to reminiscences that lightly sketch the personality. The hospitality that Cleanth
practiced at home appeared in another way in his work as editor of the
Southern Review, work which may not be remembered now. (Obviously one cannot separate the role of one editor from that of another,
but one may assume that each editor helped create the policy evident
in editorial practice.) Here *hospitality* is applicable in two ways—as
an openness to contributions by writers who held beliefs not shared by
the editors but who developed their positions with acuteness and
depth, and as a welcoming of many new writers who had to be judged
on their typescripts alone. The latter offers the opportunity of getting
new writers off to a start, as with Eudora Welty, and also involves the
risk of giving space to one-story or one-essay people. The *Review* had
some of these one-timers too; the only point is that the editors were
willing to take the risk instead of playing it safe with writers already
arrived or on the way. On the other hand they could subject the latter,
who might be acquaintances or even allies, to the same independent
critical scrutiny that they gave to known and established writers studied in class.

On the side of reminiscence I have to record what happened some
time after I. A. Richards had been a houseguest of the Brookses.
Richards wrote to ask about a pair of shoes he thought he had left
behind, and the Brookses looked everywhere, but fruitlessly. Then suddenly Mrs. Brooks said, "Cleanth, what do you have on your feet?"
Cleanth, I believe, resisted the imputation, but his wife insisted that the
shoes he had on were too long and narrow to be his. Cleanth's reply,
according to legend, was "But you know my shoes don't fit me." In a
similar episode—missing articles, surprising reappearance, and reasoning by the wearer—the property that changed hands was some

gloves I had left in the office occupied by Cleanth and me. This was during the war when most of us were teaching an ASTP English course that included some logic lessons prescribed by the government syllabus. The clothes episodes led someone fresh from struggles with logic (I think it was the late Esmond Marilla) to say, "Cleanth, you watch your enthymemes. Your implied major is, 'All clothes which do not fit me are mine.'" Well, the foggy man has had his run in anecdote and fable, and every campus has its specialist in absentmindedness. But the Brooks story, aside from its lesser role as an amusing footnote to biography, serves mainly to illustrate the paradox advanced by someone a year or two ago: that absentmindedness is the other face of presentmindedness, a firm focusing of attention on essential matters, whatever others become blurred in the process. This applies exactly to Cleanth, who may have had more hazy moments than most people about extrinsic matters, but who never failed in lucid attention to the intrinsic ones.

The lucid attention is of course richly established in his manifold writings, which are not my subject. But I want to make one observation: that lucidity is not the by-product of unwavering adherence to a party line, for which consistency of thought is sometimes mistaken. Loyalty to causes, for instance, has not made Cleanth any less clear-eyed about either the devotees or the raw materials of causes. In *The Hidden God,* speaking to a Christian audience, he chides Christians who have taken up T. S. Eliot because they have heard of him as a "good churchman." He could chide southerners who found the "southern cause," however defined, a good thing. His objectivity should be taken for granted, of course, but I make the statement precisely because many people who do not know or digest the record have thought of Cleanth as an unwavering apologist for all things southern or once southern. I am sure that he more than once felt pushed into the apologist's position by stereotyped attacks upon the South—ones that continue even after northerners have unveiled some aptness in vices once thought to be southern specialties. In public combat one does not always have much choice. But lest the figure of public combat seem all of the man, it is worth noting that, in contexts where the object was understanding and personal confidence rendered misunderstanding unlikely, no nonsoutherner could be more incisive than Brooks in detached evaluations not only of the present South but of the past South too. His persistent sense of ambivalence even in areas of devotion appears in some words he uses to define the "special heritage of the South" (the subject of chapter 14 in his *William Faulkner: The Yoknapatawpha Country*): "the past experienced not only as a precious heritage but as a crippling burden." In looking at traditions that he valued, he was no less hesitant in cutting through any accumulated flimflam than he was in seeing through contemporary intellectual fashions. One of these fashions, now doubtless forgotten, had a great run in its own day: the fashion, set off I think by some words in *Partisan Review,* of screaming "failure of nerve" to demolish anyone not irrationally devoted to the current metropolitan rationalisms. Cleanth's shrewd comment was, "They've given themselves away. That's all they're going on—nerve."

The lucidity of mind is reflected in a lucidity of style that has always stood out in a day when professorial critics often achieve a gruesome murkiness of vocabulary and syntax, whether by lack of discipline, by a sentimentally self-indulgent trust that whatever tumbles or writhes out is invaluable in its initial form, or by a cynical sense that impenetrability tends to pick up some market value because many people don't like to say that they can't understand the impenetrable and hence quote it more than they would otherwise. How much conscious disciplining of style Cleanth found desirable I do not know; my impression is that his easy naturalness and unpretentiousness were almost congenital. On special occasions he could strive for, or perhaps fall into, a very muted irony, sometimes a little too sotto voce for complete effectiveness if one did not have a special key. His written style is really a spoken style with a barely perceptible heightening through ordinance and embellishment. His conversational style was perhaps a shade less colloquial than informal faculty discourse tends to be, but easy, plain, essentially decorous, and expectably much freer with punch lines than his platform style; it was quite varied, ranging from literary wit to pungent or racy earthiness, the former neither self-conscious nor buttonholing, the latter keeping its force through a restraint and appropriateness prodigally discarded in our present adolescent phase of the free-speech epoch. This style reflected a thorough familiarity with nature in all her aspects, and Cleanth delighted to observe her workings in individuals who seemed to inhabit a more exalted plane (as in the high-toned sculptress whose male nudes were hyperbolically male). There was much contagiousness in the merriment with which he laid bare somebody's pettifoggery or self-deception or logical or Freudian slips (he rather enjoyed playing games with this last mode of thought, of which he has made only sparing formal use). There was always an impish glint in his eye in jest and banter; he was the gleeful rather than the deadpan phrasemaker or epigrammatist.

His deftness in words and tenacity in issues naturally made him a leader in academic matters in which he took part. He led best in smaller group meetings, in sessions to identify ends and plan means; he had a mildness, courteousness, and inclination to subtlety that were not the best equipment for open combat. When planning became, as it could, a sort of exercise for freeing emotions, Cleanth could gaily extemporize fanciful schemes for capturing the citadel, booby-trapping the ungodly, etc.; he delighted in ingenious war games which by deception and unexpectedness would have to confound even the wary. I suspected that in some little corner of consciousness he harbored the notion that, if some of us were only a little less unimaginative and stolid, we could execute some blueprint of his to storm the heights and make the bad guys cry uncle. One trifling example, though only by analogy. Junior faculty members of our department would occasionally get into a game of touch football with our opposite numbers in other departments. It was about all we could do to get the ball from the center to a back, and then get it handed off to a runner for a sweep or passed to some receiver (I have a clear picture of myself throwing horrible passes on one such occasion). But Cleanth would devise, and urge upon us, complex reverses and hidden-ball plays, and his characteristically good-natured face would stretch into sad lines of disappointment in us when in our self-doubt we clung to less taxing offensive designs. Not for nothing had he come from the Vanderbilt that invented what was then called razzle-dazzle football. Besides, he was an instinctive quarterback, and in university affairs he loved the metaphor of the quarterback sending the fullback crashing through the enemy line (single-wing power plays had their lure too). The only trouble was that in the academic game our side tended to be weak at fullback.

Not a large man physically, Cleanth had not a trace of the Napoleonic. In him, behind the mildness of manner, one felt the solid strength. Along with the confidence springing from talent there was much modesty about given performances. Of a completed lecture script he could say, "It ought to be better, but it's too late now." He could jest about a lecture as a makeshift redo of a prior lecture, though the modesty was probably excessive. Along with the firm maintenance of position there was a sweet reasonableness about opposition, a disarming effort to find the common ground rather than a well-armed rush to the battleground. Along with great patience with young learners about or in literature (students and writers), there was considerable impatience with old boys to whom literature hardly existed as literature. Along with a basic charitableness that I have mentioned more than once, there was a vigorous challenging of what I might call the clichés in the atmosphere, the positions apparently accepted by everybody but examined by nobody, the faculty club fashions and unconscious assumptions. Was the *New Yorker* really a wise and sophisticated journal? Was the New York *Times* really an exemplar of omniscience and dispassionate right reasoning? Why did faculty rationalism miss so much of reality? Was standard liberalism an instrument of truth or a device for shirking hard decisions? A freedom from dogmatism or a ragbag of counterdogmas? Such inquiries, offered gently but repeatedly, made it difficult to beg questions or to suppose that there were no questions to be asked.

Other images, recollections, tales. The story that Cleanth delayed the start of his honeymoon to fill his suitcase with books; the story that he was racing through dozens of detective stories to find the central key or pattern that would enable him to turn out a master sleuth tale to ease the bite of the thirties Depression. He did have the makings of a figure of myth. His having enough energy left, after everything else, to learn bookbinding as a hobby and to become rather proficient at it. His becoming interested in the construction of an outdoor fireplace, following through with the project, and, on the day of topping out, asking his wife whether she happened to have at hand any "raw dough" with which to test the new construction. His blueprinting, at least in words, inventions of various kinds: there was a series based on the football ethic, as he rightly read it, that anything goes which is not specifically prohibited. The most memorable of these, for me, was a defensive uniform covered with external suction cups that would make it impossible for any ball carrier to break a tackle unless he tore out the arms of the tackler. His and my making a long automobile trip to do lectures at another university in a dry state, taking along a carload of spirits needed by thinking men there, and, after what seemed to be the perils of rum-running over the border, being taken slightly aback when the consignees felt some of the goods to be too costly (one price that raised eyebrows, as I recall it, was $2.10 for a fifth of bourbon). Cleanth's regularly riding a bike during the war, perilous as it was for a nearsighted man, and several times, once to avoid hitting a dog, pitching into the street and coming up bloody—but ungrounded. The total absence of anything like self-pity even when there were heavy strains of institutional uncertainty, special family responsibilities, and the Depression generally. Cleanth going to the University of Chicago for a year and giving us a taste of department life without the intellectual vitality and the general zest which he contributed. Then, finally, the offer from Yale. On a very beautiful moonlit spring night in 1947 the Brookses and we were driving back to Baton Rouge from what had been an especially pleasant party at a country home in Mississippi. Trying as one does at such times to strengthen the irrational barriers against departure—the apparently rational ones are always the most fragile—and knowing that anything rhetorical would not do, I came up with something no more eloquent than "You would miss all this very much." These flat words may have contained some truth, but any nostalgia that he did feel was clearly no brake upon an impressive career at Yale.

After we both left LSU for opposite coasts it was a decade and a half until I again saw Cleanth with some regularity. This was from 1964 to 1965, when my sabbatical spent in London coincided with his first year as cultural attaché at the American embassy there. His basic virtues were unchanged. He maintained equanimity under difficulties (bad prior information about rentals, persistent housing difficulties, several robberies, the strenuous demands of a new kind of life). For me, as for many, Cleanth's work pace would have been exhausting: his keeping in touch with academic and literary figures both English and American, setting up lectures at the embassy, keeping up with embassy life generally, being a host in a variety of situations, taking part in literary symposia and other such gatherings in Britain and on the Continent, lecturing often at universities and schools—all in two years. Of many occasions at which he was an official American representative I saw him at two—the memorial service for T. S. Eliot at Westminster Abbey and the ceremony at which the Society of Authors made an award to the laureate John Masefield (at eighty-seven an impressively sturdy figure)—enough to glimpse his unobtrusiveness but alertness and readiness to play his part. I do not think any man could have performed a great variety of tasks more willingly or with more consistent dignity and graciousness. We were fortunate to have a rare kind of public servant abroad—one who could meet the intellectual and artistic communities with the infrequent combination of high intelligence and an unstraining and unfeigned amiability. Behind the scenes Cleanth had less inclination for the merry or impish *jeux d'esprit*, the playful fantasies that imaged the pretensions and inconsistencies and vulnerabilities of the world around. Doubtless there is less incentive for jesting invention when one perceives more sharply the precariousness of such order as we have. But he still exercised the large talent for asking hard questions about prevailing attitudes and fashionable assumptions, both British and American, about truth, belief, policy. The physically nearsighted man had, if anything, sharpened his eye for the dubious clichés of thought that flourish because many remain blind.

But these reminiscences of the London year are only a brief postscript to recollections of earlier years. Though the years are long gone, these pages are not an elegy, which would be a bit early. Nor are they a eulogy, which would be too easy. I have considered them rather a collection of snapshots which might, in sum, give an impression of a more varied personality than could be known through the critical writings. Even if that personality had seriously altered with time or disappeared, it would still have the interest that naturally attaches to an individual active at a crossroads both in a very colorful institution and in a larger academic and literary scene. In general, the scholar-critic is no less likely than the poet or novelist to be interesting as a person. Of course, the writer may have the easy appeal of a talent for creating spectacles or of a hyperactive id or libido, and the professor that of eccentricity or the faculty for histrionic self-display on many topical stages. Even an essayist may make his pages a projection of an emotive and turbulent self, a quivering body of sympathy, antipathy, and prophecy. Cleanth, on the contrary, has always been an unusually well-disciplined and self-contained man, no heart on sleeve either on printed page or in social intercourse. The easy friendliness and the generous ways that I have several times mentioned accompany a fundamental reserve that I suspect is not often penetrated even by regular associates. Hence the exhibitor of old snapshots cannot suppose that he is presenting more than a few surfaces. He can only hope that there are enough of these to give a general impression of the man that will seem valid to those who know him and at least a little revealing to those who have known the writer less than the writings. In showing snapshots one knowingly risks the trivial, and, as a hedge against the solemnity which one's sense of quality may betray one into, one admits some touches of the innocently amusing and some glimpses of occasional foibles that do not diminish essential largeness. If one is lucky, he contributes to the pleasure which we ordinarily take in the personality of the gifted man as it appears on the less public side and in remoter doings and which survives even the absence of the discreditable.

I started with a brief sketch of the historical context in which we see this gifted man, and I will finish with another short note on it. Not so long ago a talented younger man said to me, "Your generation revolted against the old history, found out about literary structure, and discovered the major tools for understanding structure. What is left for my generation to do?" I thought of Cleanth Brooks at this time, and now I remember the rhetorical question because the need for self-creation which it implies is one of the reasons for thrusts against critical methods which Brooks helped establish long ago. It is a much less distressing reason than a self-conscious and all-but-pathological mobility in our day: the delusion that all change makes for improvement and hence the worship of chronic innovation in the very academy that ought to know better. I am not complaining about the gradual perennial revisionism that is the substance of literary history or the restatements that come with changes in perspective or with terminological wear and tear. Neither of these, I suspect, would seriously endanger the indispensable insight on which Brooksian criticism relies—that the work is independent, a thing-in-itself, obviously not without significant external relations, but in the end to be understood and judged by internal relations (the kinds of elements related and the ways in which they are related). That is what in my initial statement I predicted would not be lost. But it would be wrong not to see that it is indeed threatened by various academic fashions, such as, among others, the fashion of interdisciplinary studies. Whatever advantages these may have in social and scientific fields, they tend when including literature to lose sight of the literary and to treat literature as only one of a mass of undifferentiated printed objects that go along with other sorts of objects to prop up whatever kinds of synthesis the researcher is concerned with. The trouble with the every-man-his-own-Toynbee program is that truly significant syntheses can be made only by very exceptional minds and by them only after long, hard thinking and heroic assimilation of facts. It is depressing to see graduate students who at best have a skimmed-milk knowledge of literature thin it out still further in order to secure a still more watery knowledge of other fields under the illusion that this pale mix of assorted superficialities will be intellectually enriching. This process can have only trivial results, but what is worse is that it will trivialize any one literature by cutting it off from its proper relationships with other literatures, by destroying the boundaries between literature and nonliterature, and by failing wholly to secure the in-depth, inside knowledge by which the stature and value of literature are known.

This brief note of disappointment in trendy literary studies is not, I hope, an excrescence in what is mainly a personal memoir. The memoir comes into being because the subject of it has done notable things; the personality interests by belonging to a person whose works naturally excite interest. Retrospective as it is by definition, the memoir is still prospective in tone; it implies the durability, the future of the man's work. I only make that overt when I point to new fashions through which, contagious as we find the flux, we could drift away from solid ground slowly won. I would like to see and hear Cleanth Brooks, in a congenial group, pinking such fashions—the shrewd, heart-of-the-matter analysis coming through either in sober, trenchant argument or in mild-mannered but cutting jests, the serious point outlined directly with firm and sober mien or translated into a merry game with its own light fantastic steps, the nimble imagination wittily pricking modish masks and brightening the fencer's face with delight in the rational and figurative cut and thrust.

II.7

Mrs. Cleanth Brooks: A Memoir

(1988)

My wife's and my acquaintance with Cleanth Brooks and Mrs. Brooks began in 1935 when we Heilmans arrived at Louisiana State University. The Brookses had preceded us into the department and into matrimony by several years, so to us newly wed newcomers they seemed like old hands in the department and like old married folk. We did not quickly work into what, long afterwards, we would think of as a lifelong friendship—a good illustration of my private rule that quick intimacies do not last and that slowly developing friendships do. Aside from a certain native reserve in both couples, there may have been a touch of hesitancy reflecting our northern and southern origins. It takes some time to learn, through experience, that people do not base personal relationships on geographical identity—that accents, speech habits, and perhaps some aspects of social style do not define the centers of personality and character which permit enduring congeniality. It took quite a while, in those days when ceremony had a little more sway, and instant first-name intimacy was hardly known, for us to call them Cleanth and Tinkum, as I shall do from now on in these reminiscences. When I first heard "Tinkum," I thought it was a family name used as a given name. But, as I learned, it was rather a childhood nickname which survived, as it was to do for another fifty years, because Tinkum preferred it to her given name, Edith. We did not use *Edith* even in playfulness.

This memoir was read at the University of Southwestern Louisiana on March 27, 1988, in connection with Cleanth Brooks's delivery of the eighth annual Flora Levy Lecture in the Humanities.

98

At LSU we were colleagues for twelve years. In that period we found enough congeniality to create a feeling of old friendship that persisted later even during long separations, they on the east coast and we on the west. Now and then they were generous hosts to us in their eighteenth-century house on a rural hilltop some distance outside New Haven. Tinkum was an easy and informal hostess, even with a large party; if she felt any tension, it did not show. Almost two decades after leaving LSU—we left within a few months of each other—we were together in London: my sabbatical year coincided with the first of Cleanth's two years as cultural attaché at the American Embassy. It seemed remarkably easy to pick up a relationship, in a sort of old-hometown-folks way, after a long separation. We saw a great deal of Tinkum because Cleanth had often to be away on embassy assignments. In the subsequent two decades we saw a great deal of Tinkum through letters. She became more and more the family correspondent, and her letters always made good reading.

I do not mean to claim more intimacy than we had. Rather, in recording a long-enduring sense of easy friendship, I identify such grounds as I have for my comments on Tinkum—comments made because such an account seemed fitting to the University of Southwestern Louisiana people in charge of the present occasion.

Though I think of Tinkum as a greater devotee of private life than many people I know, I can still imagine her as a figure in business or public life. Her mother was active in both cultural and political affairs in New Orleans and indeed in the state. So Tinkum had the genes for activity outside the household. In fact, during the 1940–1945 war she was active in the Blanchard family business. She told very lively stories about what she called the "Sunshine Bus," which transported workers to the workplace, and which was one of her responsibilities. If I were writing a full account of her life then, I would entitle it "The Boss as Humorist." There was much call for both humor and managerial perseverance when the Brookses moved to London in 1964 and, partly because of bad information and advice from the State Department, and partly because of an unusual series of misfortunes, ran into housing difficulties that went on and on. Since Cleanth was head over heels in new embassy duties, Tinkum had pretty much to take charge of things. After various moves, they found themselves at length in a new apartment house—"block of flats" to Londoners—in which for quite a time the only other renter was a wealthy, mysterious Middle Easterner. The situation seemed a natural for unexpected and perhaps alarming events. Several times, when Cleanth was away, we stayed with Tinkum in the Brooks apartment, unsure, of course, of our ability to deal with any strange Levantine operations we might run into. In all her accounts of grave housing problems, in which she showed both competence and courage, Tinkum spoke wryly rather than plaintively.

But over a long life her energies and talents went mainly into a private life that was a very successful career. She was devoted to nieces and nephews, and with Cleanth created a domestic atmosphere in which these younger people, sometimes with new-generation styles that could not be wholly congenial, always felt very much at home. She was a good hostess, casual and dry and witty rather than overflowing with a mechanically glowing graciousness. She had a vigilant eye for social needs, however. She could tell Cleanth and another guest, who had fallen into the male social vice, a long private duet of ideas in a corner, to break it up and try their tunes with other guests who needed partners in song. She was a remarkable assistant to Cleanth the writer—consultant, research assistant, and one who on herself the humblest tasks could lay. I mean not only the endless ordinary typing jobs over many years, but in time the quite special ones made necessary by Cleanth's visual problems. In some literal physical sense she was, if you will, Cleanth's seeing eye. I like to think of her, too, as providing a kind of second sight—a way of seeing things that was of course not alien but still was different and independent. I have in mind now both her insights—into situations and people—and her voicing them. Cleanth tended to be reserved and tactful and scrupulously intent on fairness; it took a considerable outrageousness of conduct in others to elicit from him the sharp open words naming mental and moral flaws. Perhaps in private life he felt something of the inevitable constraints of university and embassy life, but it was probably more a matter of native reticence. Tinkum was different. Not that she was tactless or inappropriately outspoken, but that she was much less reserved. She seemed to us very acute in seeing through things and people, in having a sharp sense of subsurface realities, in not being taken in, and yet happily without working at not being taken in. I trusted her sense of the underside of things, of the reliability of what was visible, for her judgments always seemed objective, in no way a dressing up of private hostilities, and hence of private needs and ends, as judicial pronouncements. She could be vastly amused by embassy solemnities and by the pieties of university life, the self-importance of public officialdom and of the professoriat. She had an acute eye for the modes of showiness and for the follies of trendiness, and she could nail fashions and fads to the wall. She could be matter-of-fact without being bound to the factual. Her common sense could become uncommon sense.

Her sharpness of observation came across in candor and tartness. She could be plain and direct, or wry, or ironic. Though she could be sardonic, she was never bitter. Obviously she and Cleanth shared fundamental feelings and ideas, shared the ideas that people live on. But she had, at least now and then, a somewhat different perspective. Hence they could disagree overtly, and occasionally did. But the big thing here was the openness and ease, the essential urbanity and civilizedness, of expressed differences and challenges. It was rather a lesson to those of us who tended to withhold disagreement lest it lead to disagreeableness. Cleanth could say, "Tinkum, you're not being fair," or "Tinkum, you're missing the point," and Tinkum could say, "Cleanth, don't be stuffy"—sharply, on both sides, yet without discomfiting cantankerousness, or awkward confrontation. It was simply a fundamentally amiable candor, a direct counter-criticalness, allowed by a basic compatibility of thought and feeling. Tinkum's gift was to manage an unusual range of talents: she was a fine typist, a helpmeet (I knowingly use an older term) in many ways, and a wholly independent equal in assessing the world, its ways and its people. The final measure of quality lay in Cleanth's unstinted valuing of her merit. No husband that I know has alluded more frequently than he to a wife's skill and insight as a kind of watchdog on the world, and to her keen expression of her watchdog insights.

To praise Tinkum's eye for pretenses and delinquencies should in no way portray her as an essential debunker. Her insights into true virtues were no less reliable. I sometimes think of her as an art critic in personalities: she had a sense of their true color. And if that true color was different from, or not wholly evident in, the surface shades and tints, she could discern it just as sharply if it was praiseworthy. She had a good eye for the less evident decencies, solidities, and talents. She could hold merits and insufficiencies in a nice balance, not only in people generally, but in friends. If she had few illusions about friends, she was nevertheless immensely tolerant and even protective. Yet she could speak out at times when the rest of us were reticent or hesitant. Once when we were talking about a writer we all knew and thought well of, it was she who could say, without any trace of commonplace disparagement, "Let's face it; so-and-so is just not a novelist."

She could always come out with it. When Cleanth had to deal with another sudden request for a lecture—he was always in enormous demand, in England as well as here—she could say, and she alone I am sure, "Well, back to the scissors and paste." She once told my wife that Cleanth always wanted her opinion of things he was writing or had just finished. She reported, "All I do is say, 'That's very good, dear,' and he feels better." My wife reported this to me gleefully, for she knew that I would recognize the words "That's very good, dear." What Tinkum did was express archetypally one of those roles of amiable wives whose husbands struggle with pencil and paper. On another occasion she jested, quite merrily, "What a pair we are to be abroad in the world: Cleanth blind, and I deaf." She once said, of a nouveau tycoon's wife, a woman a little given to intimations of especial refinement, "She's a phony—but a nice phony." Once she managed what I regard as an act of wit not in words, but in things. She had bought a garment which she then thought was inherently superior to its assigned function. So by personal magic wand she wholly altered its role: a nightgown became an evening dress. She punned in clothes.

She was very bright. She could be playful; she often jested; she was earnest in season; she was shrewd, and always sturdy in the face of difficulty. Perhaps the best summation of her qualities would be wisdom and fortitude, and I mean wisdom to include humor and wit. All these qualities showed in letters, in which, as I have said, she was gifted—businesslike in reporting, agile in concrete detail, fluent in style, ironic in observation, witty in accents. Her last letter to me (my wife had died a few months before) was written just three months before her own death. In it she reported the medical diagnosis that had been made, and she treated it as if it were a surprising, but not quite fitting, jest. Her central concern was for her husband, and that concern, too, was put humorously: "Poor Cleanth is going to have to get to work."

During her last month she was on oxygen, attached to the supply by plastic tubing of sufficient length to permit some movement around the room. Once she stretched the tubing as far as it would go. She commented, in a remarkable union of the wit and fortitude that we knew in her, "I have reached the end of my tether."

There could be no better ending to an attempted portrait of a remarkable woman.

II.8

The Past: Fact, Fancy, and Luck

(1973)

i

Not long ago I was surprising myself by performing a great act of Christian charity. I was writing a letter to Tom Kirby even though he owed me a letter for a year or probably two. But I didn't want to carry the charity so far that I would be suffering from spiritual pride. So I spent a good deal of the letter pointing out his errors to him; I made out a bibliography of all the letters he should have written but hadn't. Thus I helped save both souls. I kept him healthfully aware of his own defects, but by being censorious I kept my own charity from getting out of hand and becoming a vice.

Now that letter to Tom, believe it or not, crossed a letter from Professor [Lawrence] Sasek, of the committee arranging this party, which generously invited me to be here and to say something, as the letter put it, "appropriate." The first thought that crossed my mind was that I would come and read aloud the letter I had written to Tom, spreading before all, at his final moment of vulnerability, a record of astonishing nonfeasance. The title would be something like "The Non-Responsive Administrative Fraternity Brother, or, The Perils of Epistolary Infidelity." But then a little voice within—or more probably a not-so-little voice from across the dinner table—said that no, this was not an occasion on which such truth was called for. Besides, since then Tom has written me five of the longest letters I have ever received. Maybe I

An address delivered on December 8, 1973, at a dinner honoring Professor Thomas A. Kirby on the occasion of his retirement as head of the Department of English at LSU–Baton Rouge.

awakened his conscience. Or maybe he guessed what I would be up to and set out to defeat me in advance. With that easy start taken away, I had to return to the drawing board and see if I could discover a role that would be "appropriate." Was I to play a sort of Antony to Kirby's Caesar, a head-of-state not felled by men of principle but freed by the principle of gentle superannuation? Or a Winston Churchill lamenting the abdication of a warmhearted ruler who preferred another mistress to the throne? Or a kind of secular Saint Peter at the gate, welcoming a new saved soul into post-administrative, *i.e.,* a post-purgatorial, bliss? Or just one of the boys in the old backroom telling how it was in the backroom before the boys in the backroom sneaked or aged into the front office? Suddenly I realized that I was making Tom into a sort of meatloaf compacted of Julius Caesar, Edward VIII, an unnumbered but saved royal soul, and some sort of ex-politician who had become a statesman, and also that as a chef embodying Antony, Winston, Saint Peter, and an academic wardheeler, I might do something unfortunate to the stomachs of the dinner guests. It seemed well just to charge ahead and hope that the appropriate might drift in from somewhere.

One thing was clear: whatever my role, I would be most happy to be here and to be in on the triumphant completion of one of the longest academic reigns in history. Not only that, but to be in on the ending of the second of the two longest reigns in history in one department, stretching for three-quarters of a century. It's a little bit like having George III and Queen Victoria as back-to-back rulers—a sort of ultimate in stability in a world that often mistakes fickleness for progress, and the revolving door of routine change for a fixed entry into a promised land. To shift from royal simile to my favorite metaphor, I must, in a day of unlimited substitutions, say three cheers for the sixty-minute man.

Compare my present school. To get through just two-thirds of a century at Washington, it took, not two chairmen, but three, plus one acting. You can see that I look admiringly at LSU from the perspective of a much more changeable, impatient, impetuous world. It makes me pretty humble. The only way I can keep up my pride vis-à-vis Tom is to say, "My, you've been in a rut for a long time." Unfortunately we can all see that, for a man trudging in an endless rut, Tom shows no signs of dust or mud, doesn't limp, and seems to have no holes in his shoes.

ii

The rut began in 1940. It was five years earlier that the class of 1935 arrived on this scene—Tom, Nate Caffee, and I. That was 38 years ago. With the twenty-years-after approach in mind, I thought I might translate us into Dumas' three musketeers. Unfortunately musketry was not our strong point—except the verbal kind. The only shooting that ever went on at Kirbys was done by Josie, to the great discomfiture of the local moccasin population. Once Dr. Earl Bradsher took me out to teach me to use a revolver, and when I blazed away for the first time, he disappeared and was found hiding behind a bunker twenty yards away. He said, in a quavering voice, "Where did you learn that wrist motion?" With such problems in mind, it seems better just to settle for us as the three new Ph.D.'s, ready to inflict upon LSU the annual university penance of enduring new light fresh from out-of-town graduate schools.

My degree was from Harvard, and I was prepared to import Cambridge ways into LSU at any time. Soon I met Tom and Nate and found out that they had got their Ph.D.'s respectively from places called Hopkins and Virginia. I began to wonder what kind of standards they had at LSU because I had never heard of Hopkins and Virginia. Then I found out that Tom and Nate had never heard of Harvard. You will recognize our common state: philosophically it is called solipsism, and culturally, provincialism. In time we painfully broadened our horizons. It wasn't long after that that I learned more about Hopkins. This was at an MLA meeting, and I was with Tom and some Hopkins friends of his (very tolerant people). One of these, a female Ph.D. in English (a girlfriend of his immature years), said that she had at last discovered the identifying mark of Hopkins degree-holders. She said it was their integrity. This was the first time I had ever heard of integrity being passed out with the diplomas. Again, this made me feel pretty humble. Around Harvard I had never heard anything about integrity. After all, we were producing presidents and secretaries of state.

Well, in time the three non-musketeers merged their separate provincialisms in a new kind of local institutional loyalty. Now the institutional loyalty of new members always takes the form of pointing out what is wrong with the institution. By this you mean that it doesn't do things the way they did at the place you just came from. "Now at Harvard we"; "now at Hopkins we"; "now at Virginia we" (and as you know, the phrases should read "Now in the yard we," "now at the Hopkins we," and "now at the university we"). In our zeal for betterment we had perhaps some idea of getting help from Cleanth Brooks and Robert Penn Warren, who had arrived at LSU a year or two earlier. But the trouble was that they hadn't been to Hopkins and Harvard and Virginia and so did not have much familiarity with our kind of high standards. They had only been to Vanderbilt, which we had never heard of, and to Oxford, which was only a Tom Brown sort of place. On the whole, we had some problems in educating our senior colleagues in the department.

What obnoxious junior staff members we must have been! Of course, I don't want this brief note of ritual modesty to make me sound like a remorseful defendant in a Stalin treason-trial; so I will only add that our obnoxiousness of those days was of a more refined, more elegant, less obnoxious sort than the junior obnoxiousness we have known in latter decades. Now let me try to explain how this is so. Tom once said to me (in latter decades, that is), "When I was an assistant professor I used to walk along the corridors and pass the old-timers, and I would think, 'How did such untalented people ever get so far?' But now it's got so that when I walk along the corridors and pass the assistant professors I can *feel* them think, 'How did such an untalented man ever get so far?'" "Heavens, Tom," I replied in excited relief, "I've had exactly the same experience at Washington. But surely they are more obnoxious than we were." "How so?" he asked, hopefully. I said, "They try to conceal it but don't succeed. We didn't even try." "But," said he, "doesn't that make us more obnoxious?" "On the contrary," I explained. "We just looked prejudiced, and so no old-timer had to take us seriously. But these youngsters look like men of such strong convictions that they can't conceal their disdain, and you have to take men of strong convictions seriously. That's what makes them more obnoxious." Well, anyway, he hoped I was really making a case for our superior brand of vice.

Here I pause for a private note or two—purely family notes. In 1937 Ruth, my wife, was in Our Lady of the Lake Hospital for the rather precarious bringing of our son into the world. Tom and Josie made a

special trip to the hospital to tell us that they were going to be married.
It was a gracious gesture, a thoughtful attention at a difficult time—
the sort of considerateness that I know has been shown to many who
have followed us in the department. I turn now to a second gesture
that was connected with this same engagement. At a party someone
said, with elaborate grandioseness in quotation marks, "Tom is marrying a flower of the Old South." Nate Caffee, the gentle Virginian,
added, in his most urbane way, "You mean he's marrying an old flower
of the South." The bold wit, you see, turned on a pseudo-putdown;
Nate daringly used untruth as a metaphor for the truth of charm. Like
Verner modifying Grimm's Law, Nate modified Chesterfield's law,
which was that you praise a woman only for a merit that is not obvious to everyone; the Caffee variation is that you best praise a woman
by attributing to her a nonexistent demerit. As we look at Josie today
on her birthday, we can see that when she resolved to dwindle into a
wife, she obviously had to get parental permission before she could
secure a license.

iii

I go back to the days when Tom had got into his 35-year rut and was
beginning to learn about life in the front office. About offers to colleagues, for instance—alleged offers, unscrupulous offerers, colleagues
whose free souls require them to ignore the catalog descriptions of
their courses or refuse to turn in grade books, about finding a literate
instructor in wartime. I remember one we had whose desk disgorged
eighteen sets of unread themes; I seem to have been showing the right
attitude to the administration by assisting the boss in a pre-Watergate
break-in.

Meanwhile he had to deal with all of us who thought that raises
would be nice. I was one of his chief problem children, for every now
and then I would go in and try to improve myself. I remember when
my salary had been $2,800 for a while, and I was recklessly trying to
get it up to $3,100. Tom wondered whether I wasn't seeking too big a
jump. He said he didn't want me to get spoiled. I said I didn't want to
be spoiled either; I only wanted to be solvent. What, says he, in a depression? I now saw I had to change my ground; so I said I wanted to
liberate my wife (you see how far ahead of the times I was). What do

you mean, liberate her? he says, in the kindly stern manner a chairman ought to use with presumptuous youth. Why, said I, I want to liberate her from her job back to cookstove and cradle. A paradox, you imagine? A reactionary sentiment? No, quite literal. She—like Estelle Williams and others—was teaching five sections at three hours and thirty students each. I said to Tom, "If you could get the dean to give me $300 more, maybe we could scrape by without her $1,100." "What," said Tom, "you mean you are banking $800 a year?" There I was in the soup again, in my muddled way trying to face a clearheaded chairman.

Thus he kept me in the strait and narrow. But he intimated that he wouldn't mind tossing me a fleshpot or two if I could, so to speak, produce a little evidence. Evidence? asked I, wondering—I've seen many others do it since—whether he couldn't see pure intelligence and merit just oozing out of me all over the place. Well, he said—have you ever thought of writing anything? Why, I said, anything you want. What do you want me to write? (I cleverly stole this idea from a friend in the Government Department.) You know, all he did was turn red and not reply. He couldn't think of a single thing for me to write. It slowed my career down to a sub-jog.

Well, as you can see, surviving me and some of his other colleagues and the war problems and the budget problems meant a long rough induction into administration. In one sense the experience hardened Tom for the long haul. But it couldn't temper what wasn't there; it was really a testing period that did no more than reveal, and provide egress for, the inner talents that could and would make the long haul possible. With the latter stretches of the long haul I have less familiarity, but even at a distance I have been able to see the continuous hard work of maintenance and restoration, those carpenter's functions that year after year are at the center of the job. Losing the *Southern Review* and then finding it again. Losing the gifted editors, and in time coming up with new gifted editors. Always losing people for the honorable reason that one has made good-enough appointments for them to be wanted elsewhere, but then always replacing them in kind and keeping the department at its accustomed high level. Finding the kind of junior men that you can bring along because they know how to grow up and become supports of the structure.

Maybe it was a foreknowledge of this career that led Raymond Dexter Havens to refer to Tom as "Saint Thomas à Kirby." But, much as I like Tom, I have to say that this characterization seems a little incomplete. However, the instruction to be appropriate prevents me from going into this any further.

iv

Obviously I look back with affection to a stimulating and exciting university life, and I like to think of Tom's long term in office as, among other things, a symbolic continuation of a fine past through the subsequent decades. Now in that time past I want to look specifically at one element which I do not think has been pointed out: we had a certain historical or cultural good luck that later academic generations have not had. Now keep calm and think before you hiss or rise to a point of order: I do not say we were brighter, better, or purer than the youth of later times; I only say we were luckier. Since the saddest of mortals are those who weary us with stories of their bad luck, I hope that you will positively cheer someone who will boldly say "We were lucky."

Our luck was not freedom from plagues, earthquakes, and energy shortages; after all we did have a depression and a war. No, we were free from a much less spectacular kind of bad luck, and therefore a more insidious kind of bad luck because it may not be spotted as bad luck at all. The bad luck that we escaped was living in an atmosphere that makes people habitually ask the wrong kind of question—the kind which is unimportant or unanswerable and yet takes so much energy that even if we answer it right we are too worn out to go on from there. Such questions have now been plaguing unlucky youth for a decade or more.

First example—right out of Kirby history. Kemp Malone once said, "I always told my students that if they wanted to be really educated, they had to spend a year studying in Germany. Tom Kirby was one of those who did it." My point is this. Tom did not have to ask, Is it worth it? Do I really want to learn that much German? What use of it, if any, will I make in later years? Will it do me any good? The luck was simply that those useless questions were not in the air and that one did not waste time and energy upon them. Unluckily for many people, these questions are in the air now, they are generally answered wrong, and as a result we have a first-time-in-history phenomenon—generations of students essentially imprisoned within American English, with almost no glimpse of the larger worlds opened up by even small linguistic windows.

Again, we were lucky not to have to ask, or to think of asking, Will it interest me?—where *it* is a period or a body of work or an individual literary work. How lucky a person is if he is able to proceed on the assumption that everything will interest him if he lets himself be open to it. The unlucky devil who must ask about interest is in a hopeless situation: he can't be interested in what he is ignorant of, and yet his ignorance has to decide whether knowledge, if he had it, would modify the lack of interest due to ignorance.

We were lucky in not having to ask, Is this important? How lucky a man is when everything seems important, and the only problem is to find time to get to everything. I knew various people—Tom and I were among them—who set out to read the whole of English literature. Very naïve, of course, but still a lucky kind of naïveté to be caught in; you fail, but you do get many more doors open than you would otherwise, many more hooks to hang things on. We were lucky enough to have none of the more recent formulae which leave people stuck with their latest emotions and whims as guides to what they may try to learn.

But we were still luckier than that: we never had to ask, Is it relevant? *Relevant* is the one word in the language that tends to make me favor obscenity laws: it should be prohibited in mixed or youthful company, by which in this case I tend to mean anyone under fifty. In brief, everything is relevant all the time, and it is the business of any amateur of literature, be he student or associate professor, to discover the true mode of relevance. When the unlucky people stuck with the meaningless question of relevance are students, they are thrown further into the dark by undergraduates on the faculty who can think up new relevance courses as quick as they read the papers or listen to broadcasts. I know one man in the profession who has offered courses in Violence in American Literature, Protest in American Literature, Confrontation in American Literature, and Liberation in American Literature, and I have no doubt he is now planning a course on Executive Privilege in American Literature. I have just learned with delight of a course in another university entitled "Like It Is In American Literature." "Like it is" brings the true vulgarity of the whole operation right out into the open. In such courses the student learns nothing essential about literature. But there is something about learning nothing that is peculiarly seductive to many unlucky students today. If this relevance instructor doesn't make it in his department, the students are sure to organize the usual parades and protests to save Dr. Hotlips Hooligan from the tenure mafia.

Finally, we were lucky because nothing in the air told us to ask that unanswerable question, Who am I? or to state, in the usual affirmative form, I want to find out who I am. Then right away comes the next question that we were little bothered with, What kind of work or study is suited to that person who I am? W. H. Auden once said, "How do I know what I think till I see what I've said?" Likewise all we can say is, "How do I know who I am till I see what I've done?" The sensible man goes ahead and *does* something—because he likes it or has drifted into it or because it is there or because there is nothing else to do—and in his way of doing it forms himself and creates an identity of which, in some later leisurely moment of restrospection, he might just be able to say, "I was so-and-so" or "I became so-and-so." But to do this, he has to be lucky enough not to ask unanswerable questions instead of devoting his energy to getting on with it, whatever it is, and that doesn't really make very much difference.

V

To be sure that I have not misled anyone, let me repeat my main point: I am not glorifying a past, or claiming special admirablenesses, virtues, or perfections for it. I am talking about luck. Now, just for clarity, two other points. What is more basic than luck, of course, is intellectual and moral talent, which tends to remain constant in all ages. Second, men may be born lucky and not take advantage of their luck. They may be lucky enough not to have to waste energy on pointless, foolish, or unanswerable questions, and may still not use well the much larger supply of energy at their command. In other words, if a man is born in what I have called a lucky age and comes up palpably deficient in spread of knowledge, in range of awareness, in that indefinable grace of mind that we sometimes call wisdom, his failure—ours, that is—is so much the worse. If he is unluckily born in an age which encourages him to waste his energy on useless questions, and yet despite this handicap comes around and surmounts the provincialism which is congenital in all of us, escapes from the prison of his own language and his own time and his own initial limited tastes and the poor little ego that contemporary habits encourage him to take too seriously, and thus to get some historical and critical balance—if he so shapes himself, then he has done an admirable and indeed heroic job of triumphing over a given kind of adversity of which we have simply been too little aware.

To return for a final note on the long chairmanship: perhaps in it we could see faintly symbolized, what shall I say, a certain continuity, a mild subterranean persistence, or a surfacing or rebirth of such kinds of good fortune as I have sketched. But I see I have got poor Tom all tied up in an infernal machine of mixed metaphors: a crossbreed of chromosomes, underground railroad, and phoenix. This will never do. But I can blame John Wildman for it. I was struck by a passage in his fine October letter in which, toying verbally with East Coker, he referred to this ending as a beginning. I have tried to pick it up in suggesting that this ritual ending today conceals a going-on or resumption or recovery, whether because the retiring man has maintained symbolically something that seemed gone or because he held on until an apparently built-in balancing mechanism in the race seems to rediscover more fruitful ways into the life of learning.

vi

But I must rescue Tom before he chokes and collapses under the indecent symbolic burdens which, in my reckless theorizing, I have thrust upon him. I must return him quickly and finally to his very large personal role as good old friend of the class of 1935, as non-musketeer, as teacher, as Chaucerian, as incredible survivor, as long-distance runner not lonely but likely to trip over the friends who are there too (running or jogging or walking part of the way), as a personal fusion—though this seems a paradox to some—of administrator and gentleman. It is at this end of the line, after one has formed a life by a longtime continuous performance of whatever tasks present themselves, that one might be entitled to ask, Who am I? But the question which early in life cannot be answered and should not be asked, but which now might be answered, does not matter now; one would toy with it only in a moment of quizzical retrospection. But if Tom were to discard such irony and for a moment were to seek a defining mirror, he would have only to look into the hundreds of faces here this evening. Ruth and I are most happy to join them in affectionately reflecting the bright record of the man in the job. Thus we all salute a history that, though it come to a kind of ending now, happily goes on in spirit to let us hint at other renewals and beginnings.

III
THING: Books

III.9

Spokesman and Seer: The Agrarian Movement and European Culture

(1980)

i

I don't know how many of the participants in this conference are non-southerners. At any rate, it is a little difficult for one nonsoutherner not to feel like an intruder in the dust. Someone said, "Oh, you are the token Yankee." But also I was once called, in print, a "fellow-traveler of the neo-confederate party." Even at that I hardly feel like an initiate. Perhaps, then, it makes sense to accept outsidership and to approach our theme thus—as an outsider with a history that has partly affected his responses to *I'll Take My Stand*. This will mean confessing to various kinds of naïveté. If I am lucky, these may be not merely eccentric marginalia. Anyway, in this brilliant company naïveté may be the only approach not preempted by other participants.

I am of Pennsylvania German—*i.e.,* Pennsylvania Dutch—stock that, as far as our sketchy family history goes, apparently farmed the fertile rolling country of eastern Pennsylvania since mid-eighteenth century. There is no record of anyone's starving or being driven to city jobs by hard times. There is also no record of anyone's becoming a large landowner or very much of a landowner. My father's father farmed mainly but also taught all grades in a small country school. My mother's father, once a miller, was in the years I knew him a tenant farmer and a farm laborer or "hired hand." Up into my teen years we regularly visited the Bechtolds at different country spots and had marvelous times playing in barns and fields, riding on plow horses, feeding

This paper was read at Vanderbilt University in October, 1980, at a conference observing the fiftieth anniversary of the publication of *I'll Take My Stand*.

chickens, gathering eggs, weeding the vegetable patch, liming the outdoor john, or stacking wood for the kitchen stove which was usually
the only source of heat in the house. My father and his four brothers
began hard farm work in very early years; then three of them gradually
worked their way into teaching—one in local public schools, two in
normal schools. My father actually taught Greek and Latin in a normal school (today it is called, of course, a state university, and it makes
neither language available to any aspirants there might be). Not until
he was over thirty could he take his divinity degree. During the years
from my age three to my age twelve, he was pastor of a four-church
rural parish. We lived in a town of a thousand; the parsonage was on
Main Street, but the backyard opened directly on ten miles of open
countryside that extended in a mild roll northward to the Mahantango
Mountains. From this low range, as we watched skittishly, thunder-
storms would darken the sky and rumble ominously toward us on
summer afternoons. So life at home was only a shade less rural than
we enjoyed when visiting the Bechtolds. It too was full of joys—
damming brooks, exploring creeks, taking long hikes cross country or
on dirt roads, skating on frozen patches of water, sledding on country
hills after a snow, chestnut hunting on the side of Berry Mountain just
behind our town to the south.

I make a point of these zestful pleasures because on the whole this
rural world came to seem one that could be improved on. In some un-
explained way we did not think of the scene as a permanent one. Many
country people spoke only Pennsylvania Dutch, a nonliterary German
dialect; and the English spoken was laced with Germanisms and en-
crusted with German accents. The tongue could claim no such honor
as that of being an Elizabethan residue. The classics, which we are told
were standbys of agrarian households in the South, had, as far as I
know, no place in agricultural Pennsylvania. The world of literature
was widely unknown. The country people could be very generous
hosts, tables piled high with all kinds of farm produce and pastries,
but the Pennsylvania Dutch were rather well known for a sense of the
cost of things which wavered between stern prudence and severe nig-
gardliness. Conformity in the smallest matters was taken for granted;
any deviation in dress or speech was derided. And all the richness
of the land, which I can appreciate now more than I could at the time,

did not mitigate the strenuousness of life on the soil. My Grandfather Bechtold's usual day was work in barn or fields, 5 to 7; breakfast, 7 to 8; work, 8 to 12, with maybe five minutes off somewhere for coffee; dinner, 12 to 1, with a little rest period; then work until 6, after which he was free for chores in his own vegetable patch, workshed, barnyard, or whatever. I have no recollection of his, or anyone else's, complaining about this workday. My father and his brothers spent a considerable number of years on such a schedule before they managed—and I still do not see how they managed—to make it to normal school or college.

So, despite all the genuine, indeed the passionate, pleasures of childhood play in that world of nature, country life began to seem enclosed and a little oppressive. I do not believe that this cloudy sense of things was ever condensed into a precise meaning that I can articulate now. Luckily we had never heard of the word *culture,* so we could not complacently enroll under that banner. It was just that, in an undefined way, better things lay elsewhere.

When I came to LSU in 1935—only the second member of the tribe ever to live outside of Pennsylvania, and the first to live in the South—I soon heard about *I'll Take My Stand,* and sometime in the late 1930s I did enough reading in it to get some idea of its general direction and specific proposals. I cannot recall much difficulty in ingesting revisions of the Civil War theory routinely presented to us in northern public schools, or in coming to terms with adverse criticisms of the North from mid-nineteenth century to 1930, for my filial pieties did not tend much toward regional defensiveness. Anyway, it was clear that antinorthernism was not a strict code among contributors; what came from the North was less to be rejected than to be held within limits; Tate wanted to play down the regional angle, and Warren wanted to make the book a weapon against communism. The big dose was rather the affirmative-action code: the assertion of the indispensable values of a way of life that in my experience seemed limited, constricting, and too taxing to promise much beyond a bare, hard-won subsistence. Industrialism was hardly reversible; the need seemed rather to find ways of living with it that would preserve values to which it appeared indifferent or hostile. Still, one was not ready to dismiss the Agrarian credo out of hand, as I heard many southerners do. The volume came from too many gifted people to be ignored or simply rejected. I remembered the situation in Meredith's *Ordeal of Richard Feverel,* when Sir Austin explained his new educational scheme to his very commonsensical lawyer Mr. Thompson. Thompson was flabbergasted by the eccentricity of it. Still, in his view, a man who owned as many acres as Sir Austin could not be guilty of "downright folly." Similarly the writers who possessed as much intellectual acreage as was apparent in *I'll Take My Stand* could not easily be cast aside as purveyors of downright folly.

The result was some self-questioning. (It may be that the spur to questioning was a major achievement of the book; hence, perhaps, the interest in it for many years before it was possible to do what many observers now do, that is, value it as predictive or at least prescient.) I had to ask: Was there some vast fundamental difference between the agrarian life presented by the twelve southerners, and the Pennsylvania version of it? Could they speak so warmly of a life of subsistence farming because in the South that life had achieved a quality simply missing in the Pennsylvania version? They stressed the force of tradition; with us there was certainly a handed-down way of life, but to the best of my knowledge it was never conceptualized or turned into an imaginative force which made the life more than the dogged repetition of inherited practices. Learning had no part in it; in Pennsylvania there was nothing of what Stark Young, with charming modesty of statement, calls "some gentlemanly acquaintance with the classics, a whiff of the poets" (349; references are to the LSU Press edition, 1977). On the other hand I did find much that was familiar in Andrew Lytle's wonderful evocation of actual daily life in the country (an evocation also partly achieved by John Donald Wade, and more thinly echoed by Henry Blue Kline). Certainly the *Gemütlichkeit,* if I may use that term, was something that I had known. But in the Pennsylvania scheme of things I took it to be rather the creation of especially amiable individuals than a regular accompaniment of daily life. Hence our tradition appeared to be a narrower one, stronger on the ascetic than the aesthetic. If so, were certain virtues and graces inherent in country life, or did they result from fusions of agrarian life with other influences not necessarily agrarian at all? Perhaps German country folk emigrating to Pennsylvania had never come under such influences, and so remained unamenable to them here. Not that the potential influences were totally lacking. In Pennsylvania, for example, there were some sixty colleges, most of them dating from before 1850, and from the beginnings to as late as fifty years ago serving as carriers of a classical tradition now, of course, gone down the drain. Still, they seemed to stand on the periphery of an agricultural heartland on which they had little impact. If I was correct in sensing sharp differences between the agrarianism of my ancestors and that described in *I'll Take My Stand,* was the latter then the final truth of rural life? Or a rather special product not really expectable of, or capable of being reproduced in, other parts of America? I have not answered these questions to my own satisfaction.

Another question came up: Was I, without knowing it, under the influence of slogans about industry and progress? Was I, without knowing it, simply running with the times? In thinking that Pennsylvania rural life was too limited and limiting, was I undervaluing a sustaining and even satisfying element in that life? Or was I responding to various elements in the air—urbanism, mobility, jokes about rustics, fear of provincialism, advertisements plugging for an increase of comfort and ease? If I did undervalue the life I came from, this was not, I know, because I consciously responded to recognized pressures. Though I was conventional enough, I had a fairly early suspicion of going clichés, and I cannot imagine my having got addicted to the idea of progress. Even a little listening to Irving Babbitt at Harvard would have strengthened one's sense of constants not amenable to improvement by social changes. One could anticipate a continuing distribution of saints and sinners; novel systems would not notably expand grace or reduce original sin.

One had two main options then. First, were there different agrarianisms that made it difficult to frame a master concept for use in social debate? Second, even in a country life that seemed deficient, were there virtues to which one was blinded by spray from the roaring stream of current history? Was one undervaluing an actual strength because of an inculcated hyperawareness of limits? But there was also a third option: that the Agrarian credo was symbolic rather than programmatic, a strong base for attack by firepower rather than a homestead for year-round occupancy. As one rereads the essays now, one feels that in some of them the assertion of rural salvationary power, if not so tame as a dutiful afterthought, still lacks something of the warmth and spontaneity that almost invariably enliven the attacks on the enemy hosts. At the time, opponents liked to point out that the theorists of agrarianism were rarely practitioners of it. This line was, of course, too easy. It ignored the role of agrarianism as a symbolic force, a symbolic challenge to slogans and beliefs long unquestioned. To use the word *symbolic* resembles the approach of Louis Rubin when in 1962 he called the volume an "extended metaphor," a characterization which he was to modify in 1977. Still it has some applicability. The contributors sought a new defense for old values; the Agrarian statement was a fresh way of symbolizing those values; which of course is not to say it was exclusively symbolic. We might call the book "conditionally symbolic." We might also call it "conditionally utopian." The essays are of course admirably anti-utopian; that is, they abjure idealizations incapable of becoming incarnate in earthly sociopolitical bodies. But perhaps we can apply "utopian" to the presentation of possibilities better for humanity than the current actualities that we take for granted, and that are even puffed up by the going terms of self-esteem which every system extrudes in catchy verbal formulae. The possibilities may exist as critique rather than as pure proposals, as reminders of pursuable betterments rather than as literal designs for living. By the "utopian-symbolic" I mean the sketching of a guiding excellence somewhere between an impossible ideal and an inadequate actuality. It is this function that William Havard has in mind when he describes the consistency of the symposium with the political doctrines of Plato and Aristotle.

ii

Given the utopian-symbolic component and the rural setting, agrarianism can easily seem an heir or mode of pastoralism. Of the invocations of the pastoral analogy that I have run into, the most interesting is the Voegelinian metaphysical analysis of the "pastoral moment" or "motive" by Lewis Simpson: the concept of Arcadia comes into being when man becomes aware of "being both a creature of the cosmos and a creature of history." Through consciousness of this symbol he seeks "redemption from history," that is, I take it, invokes permanence against change, or being against becoming (the dualism actually used

by Kline, 325); or, in other terms that I have found convenient, remembers the constants as a protection against the fluid, the con-
tingent, the relative. It is in this sense that the symposium is as much
strategy as program (or what in our present fashion would doubtless
be called "programmatics").

One of the only (or twinly) begetters of this conference proposed
that I explore the pastoral as a source or predecessor of Agrarian
thought. Without prolonged research I can offer only some impressions. They have to do with literary practices rather than metaphysical
implications such as Simpson deals with. Insofar as pastoral places
a good life in rural scenes and occupations, it appears to be on the
same wavelength as agrarianism. But the work which as far as I know
comes closest to the Agrarian statement is the didactic poem, Virgil's
Georgics, which, with its faith in and rules for husbandry, seems
hardly to be classified as pastoral. Virgil's *Eclogues,* deriving from the
bucolic elements in Theocritus' *Idylls,* work mostly in the conventions
of love and grief that were to have a long run in Renaissance literature
and to pop up now and then in English literature for another two centuries. The fact that we can spot the conventions divides pastoral
habits from Agrarian statements, which oppose the going conventions.
In general—there may be exceptions—pastoral existed as a form of
entertainment for urban or court audiences; rather than portraying a
real alternative life, it had something of the weekend spirit; it gave a
breath of what we call "R and R," or just escape, or rustic relief.
Granted, it could contain the elegiac, which in our death-dreading
days (our major incurable disease is thanatophobia) hardly seems an
R-and-R theme, but the pastoral version of this was formulaic rather
than an authentic land-grant affair. True, as in Spenser, pastoral could
portray a gallery of actual courtiers and other characters, with praise
or blame for personal and institutional ways of life, but surely this was
getting a new perspective on the familiar rather than designing an inherently better life. For the most part, then, pastoral exploited a pleasure in certain conventions (like the detective story in our own day) or
else achieved freshness by providing familiar experience with a different *mise en scène.* It was less a change of life than a change of costume,
less of heart than of venue.

A third possibility derives something from both of the first two. It appears in Lodge's *Rosalynde,* in Shakespeare's version of it in *As You Like It,* and in a way in his *Winter's Tale* and *Tempest.* The Forest of Arden, the Bohemian countryside, and Prospero's enchanted island are not much more than temporary refuges. In them the innocence of victims—victims are good by definition—has a chance to dominate life because the bad guys, having taken over, are all at court. Gentilesse in woods and fields is imported from the court, and the pure natives are less likely to be country gentlemen than risible rustics (the hick joke is one antithesis of the Agrarian spirit). And the gentles or good guys, and dolls, are by no means wedded to their Edens; their restoration to the large world of outer affairs is the usual end of the tale. This is not the Agrarian spirit.

Whether or not I am right in thinking that what separates pastoral literature and the Agrarian manifesto is more conspicuous than what allies them—and obviously I am skimming surfaces rather than plumbing depths—at least this brief comparative sketch may help place agrarianism in the family of works exploring what we might call locational values.

iii

If literary pastoralism does not offer a true model for agrarianism as a challenge to an overly worldly and busy urban life, there were actual predecessors, some with rural loyalties. Who does not think immediately of Wordsworth's "The world is too much with us . . . / Getting and spending we lay waste our powers: / Little we see in nature that is ours"? Or of his prose lament for "the increasing accumulation of men in cities, where the uniformity of their occupations produces a . . . degrading thirst after outrageous stimulation"? This came in 1800, a hundred thirty years before *I'll Take My Stand.* Or of Blake's "dark Satanic mills"? A Shelley poem describes Hell as "a city much like London." Ransom alludes both to Carlyle—we recall his scorn for the "Cash Nexus"—and to Ruskin, who inveighed against both luxury and poverty. Of the much-heralded railroads Ruskin said, "The valley is gone, and the Gods with it; and now, every fool in Buxton can be at Bakewell in half-an-hour, and every fool in Bakewell in Buxton; which you think a lucrative process of exchange, you Fools Everywhere." (He anticipates Lytle's nice deflation of the clichés on time-saving: yes, "but what is to be done with this time?" [223].) In *Unto This Last* Ruskin called for "Not greater wealth, but simpler pleasure," *i.e.*, not prosperity but subsistence and plainness. Ruskin and Morris both wanted to encourage handicraft work as an alternative to machine mass production. The aesthetic movement of the eighties was another kind of revolt against the industrial order, though rural well-being was hardly its pitch.

Most of these protests against the industry-dominated dispensation—research would probably quadruple the record—expectably came in the nineteenth century. I find it fascinating, however, that they, and hence the Agrarians, had very vigorous predecessors in the eighteenth century, even *before* the Industrial Revolution. Sam Johnson's *London* (1738) says that the city "Sucks in the dregs of each corrupted state"; here "all are slaves to gold," and "looks are merchandise, and smiles are sold" (97, 178, 179); but a lucky man might escape to "some elegant retreat" with a view "O'er the smiling land" (212, 214). (And I can't help including a couplet of especial contemporary applicability: "Here falling houses thunder on your head, / And here a female atheist talks you dead" [17, 18].) The attack on commercial-urban evils is allied with a lament for rural decline in Goldsmith's *Deserted Village* (1770), which paints a fairly concrete picture of village well-being that could be a sketch for Andrew Lytle's much fuller account of the plantation day. Everyone will recall Goldsmith's most famous couplet, "Ill fares the land, to hastening ills a prey, / Where wealth accumulates and men decay" (51–52), *i.e.*, in later idiom, "when factories multiply and men decay." Rural life was adequate: "every rood of ground" "gave what life required, but gave no more" (58, 60); but now "trade's unfeeling train / Usurp the land, and dispossess the swain" (63–64). The speaker is for "Spontaneous joys, where Nature has its play" (255). The "mournful peasant" is "scourged by famine, from the smiling land" (299, 300), and the "rural virtues leave the land" (398). He hopes that "sweet Poetry" may "Teach erring man to spurn the rage of gain" (424).

Finally, a basic line: "Thus fares the land, by luxury betray'd" (295). *Luxury* is really Goldsmith's key word for the central vice of the age. He uses it five separate times (see also 67, 283–84, 311–12, 385). What is striking about this is that it was a fundamental term of the day, denoting a concept that had a life of over two millennia, and was now a common term. Its history, as sketched in John Sekora's 1977 book, *Luxury: The Concept in Western Thought, Eden to Smollett,* is fascinating both for the complexity of attitudes toward the idea, and for the points of contact with twentieth-century life as seen in Agrarian terms. From classical and early Christian thought on, *luxury* was a basic term for vice, so inclusive as to be almost a synonym of *original sin* (students of literature will remember that in Tourneur's *Revenger's Tragedy* of 1607 the criminal lecher was named "Lussurioso"). The term had such a polemic value that all sociopolitical combatants wanted to claim it. Established orders defined luxury as violation of "necessity and hierarchy," *i.e.*, the grasping revolutionary spirit in the lower classes. In the eighteenth century, however, luxury began to be seen, by the not-well-to-do, as the vice of the well-to-do. Again, while luxury was traditionally materialism, self-indulgence, conspicuous consumption, etc., in the eighteenth century it began, on the other hand, to be esteemed as an index of general well-being, or what we now call "prosperity"—a *volte-face* which obviously had to happen before modern advertising could espouse "luxury" and "luxuries" as necessities for everyman. The eighteenth century, then, was a period of transition, and Sekora has dug up numerous combatants on both sides of each of the several fences that marked the complexity of the property. He presents Tobias Smollett, especially in his novel *Humphry Clinker,* as the last major voice defending an ancient tradition. Smollett often sounds like an Agrarian spokesman.

In the ancient tradition, reports Sekora, "the natural legislator had been identified in the man of the land whose birth, wealth, and intellect had elevated him to independence of other persons" (32). Cicero said, "The city creates luxury," the source of "avarice and all other crimes," whereas the "country life . . . teaches thrift, carefulness, and justice" (35). For the Greeks and Romans generally, "the model of civil polity became agrarian, paternal, and hierarchical" (54). By the sixteenth century, Parliament was striving to "preserve the sanctity of the country estate" (58). Locke was a foe, for his "redefinitions of legitimate authority seemed to cast natural law away from its ancient agrarian center" (73). John Brown's *Estimate* of 1757 "blames the *new* commercial interests" "For the evils of his age" (93). A modern English critic charges that the "British . . . were overtaken by hubris after

1763. Everywhere the theme was expansion." Sekora adds, "English victory [over France] seemed to indicate that at least one kind of human progress, the commercial, was attainable" (106). While Defoe praised "tradesmen" and "manufacturers" (the word is his [117–18]), Smollett's many volumes included the "most sustained attack upon luxury of the period" (136). "He regarded the land and its resources as the ultimate economic units of a society" (137). He "boldly and vividly" portrayed the "ruthless, disruptive effects of unbridled commercialism nearly a century before Carlyle. There can be no doubt of Smollett's foresight into the ravages of an industrial England. No one . . . can believe Smollett exaggerated the effects of unreformed capitalism" (138). He "indicated that, while progress was illusory, deterioration was an accomplished fact" (141). Vulgar men take over, while "men of true substance—'men of landed substance,' *not* 'mere moneyed men'—go into exile or retirement" (142). *Humphry Clinker* attacks "merchants and their morality of profit," though one of the idea-men in the novel, Lismahago, acknowledges that "commerce is undoubtedly a blessing, while restrained within its proper channels"—an idea of a balance of elements which appears, in one way or another, in Nixon (195ff.), Warren (261, 264), Wade (284), and Kline (322). Lismahago seems to have an early idea of disastrous business cycles, anticipating Nixon, and avers that a "glut of wealth" means "a glut of evils" such as "false taste, false appetites, false wants" (224). To Smollett's gentlemen, Sekora sums up, "luxury is a many-sided threat. With its vulgarity and prostitution luxury undermines grace, hospitality, and fine manners" (287).

Surely the language of these quotations makes clear enough the parallels between luxury-thought and the Agrarian thought of almost two centuries later. Two Agrarian obiter dicta use the eighteenth-century key term: Lytle's that "if he [the "money-crop" farmer] makes any money, it goes for luxuries instead of discharging his debt" (240), and Lanier's on the farmer's being "kept in poverty" by the "purchase of needless luxuries" made seductive by advertising (152).

Finally, it is fascinating to see how, in Smollett's scheme of things, Scotland plays American South to London's and England's American North. I quote: "London's demands for luxury are so voracious that it despoils the remainder of the nation" (277), and, "as London is plundering the rest of England, so England is plundering Scotland."

A visitor to Scotland asserts, "I have met with more kindness, hospitality, and rational entertainment, in a few weeks, than ever I received in any other country during the whole course of my life" (278). All agree that Scotland "represents a better because *older* way of living. Refusing to bend to the blasts of fashion from the south, the people and their institutions have kept fast the best of ancient traditions, remaining hardy and virile" (280). Sekora summarizes: "Smollett's vision of genuine worth did not project an *alternative* society. . . . Rather he posited the values of an *earlier* society—one where life was simpler and where order, station, and identity were more firmly established and respected" (286).

Needless to say, this notation of parallels is neither the literary game of source hunting nor a way of alleging that Agrarian thought is derivative. Rather it underlines the durability of certain concepts. *I'll Take My Stand* clearly belongs to a strong, nonlocalized tradition of dissent against the commercial, and then the industrial, dogma of well-being. This continuity is impressive in itself. But it is more than impressive. The long life of the value patterns espoused in Agrarian thought is evidence of their deep-rootedness, and surely it is this that accounts for the predictiveness or prescience which has been widely attributed to the 1930 volume. You have to start very deep if you're going to have a lookout high enough to let you see very far. Too, the deeper the roots, the greater the strength for a battle essential in every culture. I mean the attack on the clichés which, in our media-dominated world, are the chief currency of thought and are therefore likely to seem endowed with metaphysical validity. My sense of things is that the cliché of progress (*cf.* Young, 343) has been superseded by the clichés of change (that is, all change is necessarily beneficent) and of mobility as inherently advantageous; and the cliché of prosperity by the cliché of socialism. Of course agrarianism had attacked the cliché of socialism fifty years ago, and at least inferentially the clichés of change and mobility.

iv

Among the statements which have the dual role of undermining a cliché and affirming an alternative, the one of greatest resonance, I believe, is John Ransom's challenge of the view that our "destiny" is "to wage an unrelenting war on nature" and to "conquer nature," and his balancing assertion that man's true course is to work out "a truce with nature," so that "he and nature seem to live on terms of mutual respect and amity" (7). Back in the thirties this struck me immediately as both fresh and enlightening, and I never forgot the idea. Returning to the volume this year, I noted the echo of Ransom's thought in other essays. I have not time to quote, as I should like to do, but there are statements about the value to human beings of contact with nature, with earth, with land, with soil in the essays by Davidson, Owsley, Lanier (in that fine roll call of the philosophical generators of the idea of progress), Lytle, Wade, and Young, who sums up the matter when he refers to "the form of labor in which the mystery and drama of life—the seed, the flower and harvest, the darkness, the renewal—is most represented to us" (347). But Ransom's word *truce* is the key. You make truces only with doughty and worthy foes. Since nature is indeed a doughty foe, one misses, in the symposium, the consistent acknowledgment of the sheer difficulty and often hardship of farming life. Davidson and Tate make passing references to the hostility of nature, but only Lytle, who had firsthand knowledge, seems regularly aware of nature as a tough customer, as both "destroyer and preserver," if I may quote a not very fashionable poet. Then there is the nature of the preservative action, which is also left implicit. Obviously it is more than subsistence. One implication is that subsisting on the soil produces the human society of most worth, one that unites its members in a common cause lived rather than lobbied. Beyond subsistence and society there is also, it is implied, a sustenance of a nonmaterial or spiritual sort. One is tempted to use the word *mystical*. But that might mislead, suggesting Wordsworth or Blake—nature as affording an epiphany of truth or a symbol of ultimate reality. In Agrarian thought, however, the earth is rather a transrational communicator of moral or psychic well-being for which there is no other source.

If I am right in reading in these essays a faith in the beneficent impact of soil on soul—I bypass the large issue of ownership, of whether soil profits if it is not property, and whether as property it produces a good beyond property—then I have to wonder where we are now, when agriculture has become mainly an industry, and the man-land relationship of subsistence is, for individuals, families, and communities, much rarer than it was fifty years ago. Have we lost an ingredient essential to an adequate way of life? Does an unspoken sense of that loss inspire a reversal of a two-hundred-year trend—the reversal which we call, probably hyperbolically, the flight from the cities? The creation of "green belts" in urban areas? Living in outlying or rural areas that require long commuting trips for urban workers? Keeping small secondary homes, cottages mostly, at shore or in mountains? Amateur efforts at vegetable gardening? The more frequent efforts at flower gardening? Even the more recent architectural trick which puts green belts inside houses? Apparently we assume that, if we can't have two feet always on the ground, it is a good thing to be knuckle deep in dirt now and then. Is this our simulacrum of a truce with nature? If it is a fake, we are in a bad way. We may have to look with new seriousness at Oswald Spengler's dictum of 1918 that when man leaves the land, culture gives way to civilization and a chaotic way of life. And on the other side of the fence our recurrent urban brownouts (or blackouts) give a new substance to E. M. Forster's famous image of impending disaster for modern life, his short story "The Machine Stops." Its date was, fascinatingly enough, 1928.

V

Perhaps the greatest success of the book is that it makes us think about such problems. It bucked the clichés of its day. While undermining clichés, it posed counter values, as a critic must. At the same time it evaded the risk of falling into a simple melodrama of good and evil. The dominant theme is less "Chicago delenda est" than a balance of various regional values and of socioeconomic modes. The book lauds a traditional agrarian life without falling into the simplistic dogma of farmer Dagley in *Middlemarch;* Eliot alludes to his "farming conservatism, which consisted in holding that whatever is, is bad, and any change is likely to be worse" (Ch. 39).

Now the challenging of clichés without simply putting out a nest egg of counterclichés or anticlichés means a kind of general perceptiveness which pervades, underlies, and even stands apart from immediate polemic sorties. Many passages invite one, as it were, to take them out of context, for they are neither liberty turned crotchety, nor old saws dulled by overuse. Such passages are self-updating, that is, so rooted in cultural and moral realities as to survive for half a century and help upset our own tool-kit of handy clichés. They reveal a moral core that, uneroded by fashions, gave the program itself, whatever its literal feasibility, a strong claim to continuing attention and respect.

Sometimes the passages are aphoristic or apothegmatic. While the book defends leisure against a hyperkinetic busyness, and deplores a leisure become "feverish and energetic" (Davidson, 34), it also insists, rightly, both that an indefinite reduction of "labor-time" means "satiety and aimlessness" and that "the act of labor [is] one of the happy functions of human life" (Introduction, xlii, xli). Thus it counters a tedious cliché of our own day: the always-shrill abuse of the "Protestant work ethic" (an ethic articulated, unless my history of ideas is hopelessly skewed, not in the Reformation but in the *Nicomachean Ethics*). The clichés that literally rule educational practice today were deflated fifty years ago. Take the cliché that democratic education must be infinitely adjusted to all comers, like goods in a department store to all shoppers. Fletcher exactly describes our situation: the "unlimited range of disconnected subjects, all open as possible 'credits,' and the same lack of an organic curriculum" (116). Beyond that, the more fundamental cliché that education can do everything with and for men. As Lanier puts it, "Man is not a *tabula rasa* on which arbitrary patterns of conduct may be inscribed without regard to his natural propensities" (142), and, as Fletcher puts it, even more absolutely, "All that education can do in any case is to teach us to make good use of what we are; if we are nothing to begin with, no amount of education can do us any good" (93).

On art: Davidson criticizes the Imagists as romantics whose "art is exclamatory and personal [and] avoids synthesis and meaning" (45), and Kline rebukes artists who engage in "fruitless contemplation of their own beings" (312). Thus both reject the cliché of the artist as hemmed-in solitary whose subjectivity is his only resource, and hence that more general malaise of the 1970s that we now know as "narcissism." Too, Kline denies that the "purpose of art [is] to show the purposelessness of everything outside of one's own ego" (312) and declares the public airing of "pessimistic views" to be the "most shocking kind . . . of spiritual immodesty" (314). Aside from spotting proclaimed despair as a self-displaying on street corners, Kline catches long in advance a cliché so assimilable that it came to be rattled off by undergraduates everywhere—the cliché of absurdist existentialism. I think it fair to say that with us the word *rights* has become a cliché, that is, an unexamined slogan word applied indiscriminately to all sorts of desires. As Wade says of a critic of Cousin Lucius, "that bounding youngster . . . wanted, without effort, things that have immemorially come as the result of effort only" (292). As for deserts and rights, Wade makes a subtle discrimination that we rarely hear: "The practice of a perfectly sound 'right' often involves the practicer, and with him others, in woes incomparably more galling than the renunciation of that right" (289). Kline puts a finger on another kind of self-indulgence, that of "self-torturers . . . romantic idealists disillusioned by the sharp prick of reality, defeated by the unideal conditions of sensuous existence . . . wish[ing] not to shape a satisfactory environment but to escape the effort of adjusting themselves to any set of conditions whatever" (307). Thus they become, one might add, set-ups for the spiritual pigeon-drops of communism, communes, and instant communions cadged up by christomimetic fast-buck artists and self-deceiving charisma-peddlers.

The rigidity that rejects the going, imperfect world creates another cliché, the cliché of "sincerity" as absolute virtue. Young cuts sharply into this masquerade: "Such forms of sincerity are usually ill-bred egotism" (346), "a sincerity that consists of boorishness and peasant egotism" (337), and it is only "self-centered boors" who reject routine courtesies (346). Young's definition of bad manners has much use for us now. Besides, he combines the case for manners with the case for a true independence of judgment and spirit. This independence invariably bows to the rites of social intercourse, but does not bow to the pressures of popular opinion. "Politicians may flatter the masses. But the ignorant do not possess every man of any intelligence, who should love and despise rather than indulge them; . . . there will never again be distinction in the South [or anywhere else, I might add] until—somewhat contrary to the doctrine of popular and profitable democracy—it is generally clear that no man worth anything is possessed by the people, or sees the world under a smear of the people's wills and beliefs" (338). In a day when polls make policy, elections establish excellence, and the media mob the man in the street to mine his meditations on all matters, Young's antipopulist caveat should be broadcast daily.

Young boldly calls essential social virtues "aristocratic." Actually, he defines the word in a way that makes the quality available to all who will diligently court it. But courting it would mean, right now, having to resist several popular cliché attitudes. Aristocracy means, Young says, "an innate code of obligations"—obligations, not "rights." It means "self-control"—that is to say, not letting fly, in the name of freedom, with every random lust. Self-control "implied not the expression of you and your precious personality" (discipline, not the "self-expression" that our age takes for granted as a need and indeed a right), and not "the pleasures of suffering or of denying your own will" (that is, of masochism). Rather, Young goes on, "you controlled yourself in order to make the society you lived in more decent, affable, and civilized, and yourself more amenable and attractive" (350). Put these passages together, and you have the happy union of a thorough independence that does not degenerate into a privateering willfulness or self-proclamation, with a social sense and style that acknowledge the claims and existence of others. It joins a proper pride and a proper humility: freedom from others' minds, but subservience to their social comfort and pleasure. That is an aristocratic condition open to the earning. It undermines another modern cliché: the antielitism which is an increasingly serious danger to our culture. Antielitism is that egalitarianism in which a mask of distaste for unearned privilege hides a genuine dislike of earned excellence, not to mention native superiority. Young spots that failing too. In deploring a debased Puritan "whining on certain pious excellences," he attributes it in part to a "half-conscious jealousy of all distinction" (337). With us, that quiet under-the-skin motive can become a real curse. For antielitism is self-promotion, which figures in two other current clichés: hypertrophy of the accusatory instinct, and hypertrophy of discontent with human vulnerability.

The South condensed in *I'll Take My Stand* was to enjoy a victory—not indeed the victory of formal doctrine over social practice, but still the achievement of an end that is always voiced in the text, implicitly and sometimes explicitly. That end is the creation of morale, of a sense of regional worth which would eliminate vulnerability to condescensions from elsewhere. It was, if you will, the Trojan mode of triumph—another Aeneas, Anchises on his back, going forth from the ashes to help shape a new order. The ultimate victory was probably not foreseen in 1930. It was the victory of a literary flowering un-equaled, I believe, by any other regional phenomenon of letters in this country. But if "unforeseen" in 1930, still not wholly unguessed at. I have in mind a modest statement by Davidson: "I do not suggest that the South itself is about to become the seat of some grand revival of the arts—though such might happen. I do suggest that the South, as a distinct, provincial region, offers terms of life favorable to the arts" (56–57). Well, the creators of literary arts were, and are, there.

In this there is something of the sheer grace of the goddess Fortuna: there is no rational accounting for a bumper crop of raw talent, and then one crop after another. There comes to mind, also, Young's fine statement, that "the greatest, most luminous defense of any point of view is its noble embodiment in persons" (334). There have been some noble embodiments—obviously among the symposiasts themselves, and impressively in the crops of writers coming up steadily ever since. Still, such crops are never ripened by doctrine. *Point of view*, Young's term, must mean less dogma than insight. The apologist must meta-morphose into the free historian and the humanist who is at once syn-optic and deep-digging. How brought about? Who knows? I suspect that the nourishing soil is a contact with literal soil, but with soil that is also a place. It is a place with a meaning, a meaning, as Wordsworth put it, "Felt in the blood, and felt along the heart." The place is at once the provider of a concrete scene and an anchor of feeling; yet the writer's grasp of the concrete is allied with a reflectiveness which has, as it must, its own abstractions; and the place-bound stability of feel-ing, though never displaced, is modified by a mobility that brings in, as a source of creative tension, the stimulus of absence and of memory, and something of an altered sensibility. Loyalty is yoked to a sepa-rateness whereby, though one is of this place, one is not wholly tied to it; attachment is conjoined with a detachment that helps transform the spokesman into the seer.

And these words, I think, explain the longevity of the Agrarian manifesto: in the end the spokesman—the chosen, public role—is a lesser figure than the not so visible center of force, the seer. And in the literary flowering that came after, the spokesman faded away in the seer.

III. 10

Cleanth Brooks and *The Well Wrought Urn*

(1983)

i

A retrospective glance at one of the formative works of twentieth-century criticism is not a place to argue again the merits of the case. I happen to think that these merits are great, that they have had a strong impact, and that they continue to be felt in ways ignored by pulpiteers of current faiths who assert their own vitality, they believe, by pronouncing requiescats over *The Well Wrought Urn* and its author. My concern is rather with the educational-critical-literary climate in which Cleanth Brooks's positions were formed, with the reasons for their very great influence, with some tactical problems in the vocabulary by which, as all innovators must, he seeks to head off popular preconceptions, and finally with the noises of "Brooks is dead" (or ought to be). The homicidal tendencies of new aspirants to power remind one a little of the priesthood of Nemi, well-worn though that myth of succession is. But Frazer's tale is not really a model for us. At Nemi the succession was of individuals in an archiepiscopal chair astride an unaltering theology; with us the succession is of creeds themselves, though each overturn may require an execution of some old church fathers. And in this succession of credal reigns there is another kind of cyclical structure evident: there are affiliations between the pre-Brooks and the post-Brooks. In the pre-Brooks era the literary work had difficulty existing as a thing-in-itself that revealed itself by its aesthetic constitution; we saw it relativistically as a sort of by-product of historico-sociocultural forces that were the true loci of reality. For Brooks and, needless to say, many other critics with comparable but rarely identical views, the work itself was primary, an art object, not divorced from

diverse genetic influences, but transcending them through formal properties, not timebound, that determine its quality. In the most audible of
the post-Brooks manifestations the relativistic temper, revitalized,
surges on to something like anarchy. The work is no longer an entity, a
benevolent despot whose power is to be critically understood; rather
the text is a by-blow of the hypostatizing imagination, an insufferable
tyrant against which everyman acts as his own successful Robespierre
by recognizing that nothing is really there but a stimulus to any libertine excitability. So much for the contexts of before and after, which
illustrate the odd tendency of various approaches to literature to ignore or flee from or even deny the reality of the works themselves. The
earlier context will come in for some further comment.

As far as influence is concerned, *The Well Wrought Urn* (1947),
containing various essays mostly written earlier, can probably not be
altogether separated from Brooks's *Modern Poetry and the Tradition*
(1939) and from Brooks and Warren's *Approach to Literature* (1936)
and *Understanding Poetry* (1938). The latter two, of course, were
aimed at the young fry in front of the desk; the former two, at the pros
behind desks and typewriters. Still one may think of a single, though
many-channeled, stream of influence that fertilized various pedagogical and critical fields. Most of the contents of his own volumes, and
of his contributions to the two-author volumes, Brooks wrote in his
thirties, some earlier; this is true also of major critical works by I. A.
Richards, William Empson, Kenneth Burke, Richard Blackmur, and
T. S. Eliot, all of whom resemble mathematicians by innovating in the
more flexible years before shades of the prisonhouse begin to close in.
Still it seems remarkable that so much influence should have been
exerted by relatively young men. It is equally remarkable that a man of
Brooks's years should write with balance and ease; in his "revolutionary" voice there is no shrill contentiousness. He is capable also of
graceful self-modification, as appears in the extent to which the *Urn* is
responsive to others' responses to *Modern Poetry and the Tradition*.
Indeed the greater memorableness of the *Urn* is partly due to its revi-
sionary component. Brooks revises, not a basic position, but a presentation which, as criticisms of the earlier book revealed to him, gave an
opening or two to hostile parties who wanted to charge him, in his
support of Donne and the moderns, with ejecting all other English

poets from the temple of true art. So he rephrases, clarifies, and offers a few avowals and disavowals, and in his major step shows how his critical method is applicable to the very poets whom he has been accused of undervaluing—Augustans, romantics, and Victorians—and indeed is essential to a discovery of their actual merits. So the *Urn* contains, besides several theoretical chapters, essays on works by Shakespeare, Milton, Herrick, Pope, Gray, Wordsworth, Keats, Tennyson, and Yeats, not to mention passing comments on many other poets. In arguing for the applicability of his method to poems of different times and traditionally incompatible modes, he denies that this method is only a front for a sort of mafia effort to set up a new underground power and leave the old order with nothing but uninfluential respectability.

A convenient shorthand term for Brooks's critical principle is Horace's *concordia discors:* though it may imply a degree of harmony not always possible to a poem bringing sharply discordant elements into play, it focuses on the dramatic presence of clashing perspectives that prevent the simplistic solutions natural to ideology, cliché, stock viewpoints, and hand-me-down sentiments. One of Brooks's abilities is demonstrating the presence of this quality in poems traditionally taken to be univocal or uncomplicatedly straightforward. Of the various critical terms that Brooks uses to embody or extend or annotate the concept of *concordia discors—wit, paradox, irony, contradiction* and *qualification, symbol* (as a replacement, challenge, or complication of the literal)—only *wit* in this special sense has not caught on. The rest have all so thoroughly penetrated critical discourse that 1) we easily forget their relative novelty in the 1930s and 1940s, and 2) they have actually taken on something of the air of clichés themselves. For the time being they are probably used less than some very popular successors: *metaphor* and *metonymy, perspectives, reflexive,* and all the *semioticalities* and *theoreticalities.*

ii

The most obvious reason for Brooks's influence was the widely felt insufficiency of the historical approach to literature that still dominated, as it long had done, the graduate schools and hence much of undergraduate teaching. This issue is so old that one almost blushes to mention it again. But it is one in which there has been so much misunderstanding and misrepresentation, so much inability or unwillingness to see the facts, that one more attempt to set the record straight may not be amiss. The irritatingly perverse criticism of Brooks, repeatedly made, is that he is against historical aids in general and regards diachronic and sociocultural illiteracy as the fundamental gift of the true critic. Many people acted as if he had said "Let's do away with history" instead of "Let's see what else there is besides history." In the *Urn* he reveals shock at this sort of response and emphatically asserts the importance to literary study of all historical matters that can shed light. Many people in the profession continued to ignore such an assertion. Like the man in the street, academics can take gossip for fact.

Brooks was, by both training and temperament, the possessor of wide historical knowledge and a strong historical sense; indeed he had some of the makings of the antiquarian, with an occasional amusing hint of the pedant. For such a person to say that history is not all is a rather different thing from an ignorant B.A.'s thinking that history is nothing. Furthermore, Brooks took for granted the presence of comparable historical knowledge in the profession generally: naturally scholars and critics would use it, and to suggest its limitations, I am sure he assumed, could not be mistaken for a denial of its utility or a proposal that it be abandoned. No humanist could be seriously taken to be antihistorical. I add an assumption of my own: to declare the literary work self-contained or autonomous was less to deny its connections with the nonliterary human world, past and present, than to assert metaphorically the presence in the poem of suprahistorical uniqueness along with the generic or the hereditary or the culturally influenced. Nevertheless the effort to assert the ahistorical or metacultural quality was repeatedly translated into an insistence on radical unrelatedness. This led to metaphysical problems that Murray Krieger addressed long ago and, more recently, to extraordinary accusations of begetting and proliferating the vice of nonreferentialism. Ironically, of course, the nonreferentialism once supposed to be a vice or at least a problem has now been made into a dogma by certain theorists, though compelled to coexist with an even more fashionable dogma about the work, self-referentialism.

But such matters lie outside my present assignment. *The Well Wrought Urn* spoke movingly to everyone in the profession who, without being antihistorical at all, suspected or felt or recognized the short-comings of the historical discipline in which all of us had been brought up. Our profession called great works "timeless" but treated all works as products of given times: there was no critical way to distinguish between Shakespeare and Glapthorne. Critical discrimination seemed to be a gift that went with the Ph.D. diploma; the degree was a license for aesthetic obiter dicta which had to be right because issued by one who had learned so many facts. But Brooks offered a way of distinguishing between Shakespeare and Glapthorne—that is, a way of treating the work as art object instead of merely as cultural artifact. Here was a way of talking about it as art, of looking at the inner reality instead of merely recording circumstances, of moving toward the center from the periphery which was the domain of graduate seminars.

A second liberation contributed to the impact and influence of the *Urn*—its introducing of critical standards different from the old habits and attitudes originating in the impact of romantic and Victorian poetry. In general we were to admire the romantics for some vague sort of lyrical exaltation (clouds, skylarks, west winds, nightingales, Alps, and other such instruments of altitudinizing) and the Victorians for a solid, sober, somber enunciation of the verities. Brooks's strong reliance on the craft of the metaphysicals—on the devices of *concordia discors,* to repeat my chosen shorthand term—simply opened eyes to possibilities of understanding that we had hardly thought of using. One need not think of Brooks's tools as absolutes to see that, innovate though they did, they went beyond the innovative and opened better ways to the heart of the matter. One could now think about poems as well as respond to them simply as the world seemed to; one could perceive in them the operation of intellect as a dramatic force rather than as a controlling deviser of suitable messages; and one could see imagistic language as structural contributor rather than old-school-tie embellishment.

A third reason for the power of the *Urn* was the inclusiveness of the operating field: poems from three centuries. (Incidentally this permitted devotees of the romantic and Victorian to continue to have their cake; indeed, if they tasted the cake properly, they would find it better than they had thought.) The effect was to form a literary realm out of disparate and indeed discordant states. Brooks sought out "what the masterpieces had in common" (the phrase *in common* is used repeatedly). Here again he spoke persuasively to a large audience weary of history—not of historical study as such, but of the accepted view that in literary study history was all. History is differentiating, and differentiation can finally destroy the concept of a literary domain, or a domain of literary excellence that has, whatever the diversity of its parts, an essential unity. (For example, Virgil and Milton both belong to that domain: one cannot be segregated in Augustan Rome, or the other in Commonwealth England.) Brooks's work nourished the important, but threatened, awareness of a suprahistorical realm of literary quality. He probably slowed down, if only temporarily, a differentiating habit of mind that has since gone on to wild new exploits of disintegrating and even atomizing effects. They reduce a term like *universality* to near meaninglessness or a cheerleaders' cliché.

A fourth reason for the influence of the *Urn:* the analyses of the individual poems were not only new but interesting, not only interesting but enlightening, not only enlightening but generally persuasive. If not always wholly convincing, they were sound: they were the product of a well-filled and perceptive mind that, if one did not go all the way with all its conclusions, still held attention and exacted respect. Brooks's sensitivity to the extraglossarial impact of words, and of their juxtaposition, constantly opened things up. The analytical drive of the essays was not a substitute for taste but rather an instrument, or even a proof, of it.

Finally Brooks's style was one to win the unwilling rather than, like some styles, to repel even the willing. By style I mean both the general demeanor vis-à-vis other critics and students and the specific management of expository prose. Brooks was that rare creature the gentleman as critic, always ready to explore understandingly alternate hypotheses about poems, always quick to acknowledge the merits of opponents, to grasp the central points of objections, to seek common grounds with others, to attribute others' misconceptions to his own failure to communicate successfully, to make the pacifying self-deprecatory gesture; always able to make the forthright riposte, but still to disagree without being disagreeable. There is never a hint of the boorish self-assertion, the rude putdown, the self-righteous and vulgar polemic, and the self-serving brattishness—the McEnroe-ism of literary discourse so likely to rule metropolitan exchanges of dogma and rectitude. The persistent courtesy appears also in a verbal style that is unfailingly considerate of the reader—easy, exact, diaphanous, unpretentious, never gesticulating or calling attention to itself. In its discipline it is in contrast with the accident-prone clumsiness or the swishing in-house jargon of the downright scholar, and with a worse evil—the egotistic-opaque that beclouds current exercises in theory (the concepts with which I deal, says the theorist in effect, are too difficult and profound to be reduced to public language). But a central sweet reasonableness is no bar against the firm, the crisp, the epigrammatic. Some critics have felt, he notes, "that the unravished bride of quietness protests too much." The quality of a poem is "a positive unity, not a negative; it represents not a residue but an achieved harmony." We mistake "certain remarks which we make *about* the poem . . . for the essential core of the poem itself." "The dimension in which the poem moves is not one which excludes ideas, but one which does include attitudes." The unity of a poem is dramatic, not logical; "it represents an equilibrium of forces, not a formula." The word the poet uses is "not . . . a discrete particle of meaning but . . . a potential of meaning, a nexus or cluster of meanings."

iii

The recent tendency to read an R.I.P. over Brooks and his work is to some extent an expectable reaction against his popularity and influence over two or three decades. The characteristic drift from vogue to vogue in our society (the media push it, whether they originate it, since news has to be new, or just respond to a singular lust for novelty in our culture) makes it possible to act as if a critical method, however valid it is, is still no more than a fashion to be used a while and then discarded—a neophilia which, incidentally, can hardly aid the humanities, whose low estate Brooks was lamenting forty years ago just as we do now. Critics may share the fate of novelists and poets who, when they have been very successful, often undergo eclipse and oblivion, to be followed, if they have the strength for revival, by a gradual restoration to whatever their permanent status is to be (*e.g.,* Johnson, Coleridge, Bradley). Just as they get tired of being good, so people get tired of using a good thing, especially if they have made very great use of it. There is a sense in which Brooks was too popular. Readers of journals got large servings of close reading; if you weren't writing that sort of thing, a younger colleague who wasn't writing that sort of thing told me, evidently quite believing it, you couldn't get published. Brooks's method looked easier—more available to, and appropriable by, anybody—than it really was. It succeeded for the reasons I have described, but many of those who took it over did not notice that it was used most successfully by practitioners who had a great deal of literary knowledge, historical and otherwise, and experience. Anybody who could spot an image or sniff out a paradox rushed into the explication business, without qualms or a full look at the human models whom he was adopting. The rage for "criticism" in the graduate-school atmosphere produced so much loose or rigid close reading that in the one degree program with which I had something to do I, who was taken to be above all a promoter of criticism, sought a renewal of emphasis upon graduate school as a place for gaining information rather than as a do-your-own-thing gymnasium for free-wheeling critical adventurism.

A surfeit is a surfeit: a good thing may have a hard time surviving its epigones. Meanwhile the unconverted remained outside the tent, ears attuned to any reassuring disturbances within. Old historians remained impenitent, and indeed have made a comeback, some with novelties that render the "old" inoperative. Old appreciators never did cease thinking of Brooks as conducting a vendetta against old favorites: after all there was something dubious about a man who could say that Samuel Johnson sticks to the "critic's proper job. He inspects the poems—he does not emote over them." The American-culture fraternity never liked aesthetic analysis anyway; nor did the ideological critics, for whom all art must subserve dogma, and for whom—simple of mind or disingenuous?—any allegation of complexity is only a secret plug for The Ugly American System. There arose the Freudians, who could perpetrate reductive simplicities surpassing those of all other naïve interpreters. And perfectly disinterested critical readers of Brooks could of course find grounds for disagreement with both theory and practice in the *Urn*. Other critics have disagreed sharply with Brooks's readings, notably those of the imagery of *Macbeth* and of "Ode on a

Grecian Urn." Their words have of course been good news to various dissenters and competitors.

I have not asked Brooks whether, if he were doing or redoing the *Urn* now, he would change any of his tactics. Some of his emphases probably gave openings to those who were glad to have openings. Though the formulation is not used regularly in the *Urn*, it may be that the a-poem-should-not-mean-but-be view (words by MacLeish) gets enough play to put off or mislead people not necessarily ill-disposed to the critical operations they saw going on. To seem to exclude a quest for meaning may have come across as a harsh rejection of an aesthetic impulse a little too universal to be quite written off as naïve. On the other hand there may be a delicate concession to that impulse even in Brooks's emphasis upon structure rather than content, on the poem as taking a both/and course rather than seeking a golden mean, on imaginative coherence, on the poem as drama: such emphases less rule out *meaning* than imply a subtler version of an essence that still cannot be reduced to a *message* and that yet, like a whole that is greater than its parts, is a little more than a total of formal properties. If it is not that, then dissatisfactions with the formulation are expectable. If, on the other hand, what we have learned from Brooks now makes his original battle against *statement* seem a little emphatic and prolonged, then we need to be reminded of a triple context not felt, and probably not known, by anyone whose adult life came after the 1930s. First there were the traditional academic simplicities about poetry as a mediator of the good, the true, and the beautiful (Brooks notes the defects of such old descriptive terms as *lyric simplicity* and *thoughtful meditation*). Then, and more scary, because it had a wave-of-the-future look, came the great influence, in artistic and intellectual circles, of a Marxism which wanted all art to be "committed"—that is, an agent of ideological dogma. Finally, attackers of modern poetry, a poetry which Brooks saw needed a better-equipped audience, were prone to damn it for lack of straightforwardness. Such pressures, especially the leftist type, may have made the new apologist for poetry (Krieger's term) a little heedless about the risks inherent in caveats against meaning and against the introduction of external standards in literary judgments.

In inveighing against paraphrase Brooks was not, as he makes clear, denying the instrumental utility of paraphrase; he was simply trying to make the point that even the best paraphrase was a poor approximation of the poem and should not be mistaken for its equivalent. To make that point, however, the term *heresy* seems a hyperbolic alternative to *fallacy*, already rendered commonplace and therefore unthreatening through pathetic fallacy (with intentional fallacy and affective fallacy just appearing on the horizon), or to *inadequacy* or *deceptiveness*—a hammer blow instead of a firm nudge. Be that as it may, heresy gives an opening to a frequent kind of modern mind. Heresy implies a theology, theology implies a religion, and that will not do in an age which makes a religion of irreligion. We're threatened with an inquisition, citizens: let's get the tumbrils rolling.

iv

Since it had an unusually wide circulation, as books of criticism go, *The Well Wrought Urn* functioned as a channel through which the works of other critics flowed to wider academic and critical audiences. Brooks relies on, follows up, or argues with Ransom, Tate, Burke, Empson, and Blackmur. Of Blackmur, Russell Fraser has surprisingly said, "The method called New Criticism was pretty much his invention. . . . Blackmur & Co. focused attention on the text itself." One is not sure who the "& Co." is. Blackmur went to Princeton in 1940, and he may well have inaugurated focusing on the text there (though Allen Tate was already on the ground), but Brooks had been doing this at LSU since 1933. As far as books are concerned, Blackmur and Brooks are pretty much exact contemporaries: Blackmur's first books appeared in 1935 and 1940, Brooks's in 1936 and 1938 (with Warren) and in 1939. And if "invention" includes persuasion, as in traditional rhetoric it may, and if we look beyond the local campus scenes, where two strong personalities were equally compelling, Brooks has a stronger claim to effectiveness: his considerate, urbane, and disciplined prose won readers easily, while Blackmur's opacities put off all but the most tenacious. A more significant issue is that the "invention" was less a private achievement than a cooperative affair. The final formulators in part weld together various opinions, insights, implications made in analyses of individual works, and refinements or extensions or modifications of ideas in the air; and by addition, alteration, and new contribution give a coherent position the stamp of individuality. For Brooks that stamp is best indicated by my shorthand term *concordia discors,* which points to the centrality of structural tensions. Given that fact, it is not source hunting or an allegation of derivativeness to identify various contributors to the invention. Brooks, for instance, made some use of Empson, but without any of Empson's hyperingenuity and ideological bias. In the *Urn* Brooks's most frequent references are to Eliot and Richards and, beyond them, to Coleridge and Johnson; he used these predecessors in different ways—finding support, altering the emphasis, veering away. A final word on chronology and on what it reveals about the cooperative aspect of the invention of a new critical mode: Richards' five volumes that included literary criticism, centrally or incidentally, appeared between 1923 and 1934; five volumes of Eliot's essays, many of them literary, appeared between 1920 and 1936; Empson's two famous volumes in 1930 and 1935; and Burke's first two in 1931 and 1935. Close reading of "the text itself" was a product of evolution rather than instant creation, but it succeeded conspicuously when Brooks made an art of it and showed the wide efficacy of the tools he had developed.

In the *Urn* he engages more or less regularly in a dialogue with slightly earlier predecessors and with contemporaries. He often imagines what else, besides what they have said, they might say. He is a master of good-tempered argument. He urbanely explores differences with Winters (an amusing irony: a Winters product has long coedited the revived *Southern Review*) and Ransom. He replies fully but gently to attacks on his work by Donald Stauffer and Herbert Muller, and does a lovely *reductio ad absurdum* of his friend Frederick Pottle's relativism. Pottle survives as Boswell's admirable Boswell, not as a critic, though a relativism of which he was one voice has become epidemic. I hope it is no very finical asperity to note that Stauffer and Muller are pretty well, as current argot has it, into oblivion; likewise the quasi-Aristotelian Chicagoans, those old thunderers against critics, including Brooks, who paid attention to images and symbolic structures.

But the demise of old antagonists does not mean the end of the tribe. New ones arise. Against some of these Brooks has defended himself with acuity, skill, and customary courtesy (*Sewanee Review*, Fall, 1979). What the attacks say, of course, is that there is still a live party there to attack; by now there have been so many attempts to refute Brooks that they almost confer upon him an air of irrefutability. Still they are distressing because they are tediously repetitive; perhaps the worst that can be said of Brooks's criticism is that it generates so many clichés in the hit squads: those old, old stories that he ignores history, meaning, and relations to the world of men (persons, that is), ignores everything but the tiny fibers of technique (a way of trivializing, out of incomprehension or tactics, the concept of structural tensions). It is as if, after the first wave of antagonists, none of the others had read anything but that first wave; as if they had, indeed, stayed away from the *Urn* lest it corrupt their tools of attack.

Two kinds of anti-Brooksism were in the air of the eighties, and, as might be expected from the habits of our profession, they directly contradicted each other. One was that Brooks was alive and evil; the other was that he was quite dead—gone with the wind of progress, as it were. It takes a pretty impressive person to be so contrariously mauled. The belief that the evil men do lives after them posits an unbroken line of descent from one generation to another in the New Haven seminary. What, from the brisk, gentlemanly, and lucid prose of yore to the punitively laborious riddling of now? From the literary work as organic reality, to be understood, yielded to, and modified by, to the work as hypothesis or mirror or insubstantial nodus of psychological interactions and linguistic compulsions? It won't wash.

Since *de mortuis nil nisi bonum*, accusations of evil do tell us that the defendant is alive. Of that aliveness there is no doubt: the study of poetry will not revert to the mix of historical annotation and vague appreciation that held the field before the new ways of doing things persuasively exemplified in the *Urn*. If some of Brooks's tools became overpopular and were bound, then, to partial retirement, still they cut too close to the heart of the matter to be permanently shelved. As a matter of fact some of them remain in wide use, often by people who do not know their origin and so take them for old standard equipment in literary study. The words that best describe what Brooks stood for and, subject to the limitations upon improvement imposed by human inconstancy, accomplished are those of René Wellek's splendid summary definition of the achievement of the New Criticism:

> The New Criticism has stated or reaffirmed many basic truths to which future ages will have to return: the specific nature of the aesthetic transaction, the normative presence of a work of art which forms a structure, a unity, coherence, a whole, which cannot be simply battered about and is comparatively independent of its origins and effects. The New Critics have also persuasively described the function of literature in not yielding abstract knowledge or information, message or stated ideology, and they have devised a technique of interpretation which often succeeded in illuminating not so much the form of a poem as the implied attitudes of the author, the resolved or unresolved tensions and contradictions; a technique that yields a standard of judgment that cannot be easily dismissed in favor of the current popular, sentimental, and simple. The charge of "elitism" cannot get around the New Critics' assertion of quality and value. A decision between good and bad art remains the unavoidable duty of criticism.

Some "scholarly" or "documentary " evidence that Brooks is alive, and alive in a quarter where his survival might be less expected, appears in a 1981 volume by one of the best Shakespearians—*Shakespeare and the Problem of Meaning* by Norman Rabkin. After making certain demurrals and exceptions, Rabkin says that he shares the New Critics' "paradoxical interest in scrutinizing the ways in which a literary work means while insisting that the meaning cannot be adequately paraphrased. My approach . . . will make clear my continuing debt to critics like Cleanth Brooks." Rabkin is in contrast with the unknowingly indebted who nonetheless announce or allude to the demise of Brooksian criticism. Direct: "It is dead." Indirect: "Now that we have got over all that." There tends to be a cycle in such matters: from awareness to forgetfulness; from influence to imitation to competition to repudiation; or, if you wish, Fortuna's wheel speeded by the winds of modishness; or, if one can risk seeming a psychophant of the oedipenpals, from filial piety to parricide. At any rate we have seen more than one Antony come to bury the old maestro, not to praise him. Here one detects another movement, which we may call Browneian. The funeral directors may think to have the last word against one who seemed to threaten the republic of letters with a dictatorship. After all, he challenged the *religio doctoris* (if I may shuffle the genitives a little) and laid bare a number of *pseudodoxia academica*. Hence what better putdown than a well-wrought *Urn*-burial? But if Brooks is, as I suppose, not yet *pulvis et umbra*, there will be a comeuppance for the hydriotaphics. Brooks goes on—one would like to say forever for the ring of allusion; but the truly durable needs not the puff of hyperbole.[1]

1. The reviews of *The Well Wrought Urn* are interesting. (I have seen photocopies of some twenty of these deposited with the Cleanth Brooks papers in the Yale University Library.) The reviews appeared in 1947 (American Edition) and in 1949 and 1950 (English editions). More than half of them are generally favorable, some enthusiastically so: "uncommon sense" (New Orleans *Times-Picayune*); "brilliantly demonstrated," "masterly exercises" (New York *Herald-Tribune*); "finest critical tact," "one of the foremost American critics" (Philadelphia *Inquirer*); "brilliantly argued defense" (*Books of the Month*); "substantial and admirable exhibition of [his] theory in practice" (*Tomorrow*); "brilliant and stimulating" (*Christian Science Monitor*); "finest example . . . of the newer criticism" (Chicago *Tribune*); "one of the most rewarding of American critics" (*New Statesman*); "fascinating and stimulating" (Melbourne *Age*). A few are generally unfriendly: those in the *Nation* and the *Saturday Review of Literature* in America, and the *Higher Education Journal* and the *Observer* in England; the latter two share with the *TLS* a sort of languid condescension to the colonies, while the American denigrators are grudging, grouchy, or downright foul-tempered. The influence that I have attributed to the *Urn* is foreshadowed by a debut on the whole markedly successful.

But the reviews do not much attend to the reasons for that success which occur to me, who was a university teacher at the time and who now, of course, have the benefit of hindsight. For example, what seems the primary cause to me—the release from the dictatorship of history—is hailed with enthusiasm by only one reviewer, Paul Engle in the Chicago *Tribune*. But S. C. G. Bach, in *Time and Tide*, does appear to approve of Brooks's antirelativism. Yet John Berryman in the *Nation* fears that Brooks's antirelativism will mean trying to compress all diversity within narrow borders; Vivienne Koch in the *New Statesman* believes that Brooks is misguided in seeking for the "universal" or the "absolute"; and Henry Wells in the *Saturday Review of Literature* calls Brooks "illiberal" for "exorcizing" history from the "sacred circle" of poetry as "profane" (this must have started that long-lived cliché).

Brooks's critical method is hardly seen as giving a new freedom from romantic and Victorian styles of evaluation, but to various reviewers it seems plausible in itself or useful in application. Some reviewers like the theory better than the application; perhaps more are on the other side. Henry Wells in the *Saturday Review of Literature* is pleased by neither: the theory, he says, consists of "innocent truisms," "generally acknowledged everywhere" (!), and Brooks "monotonously applies his formula," though somehow he does manage to say one or two good things.

My third point—that the wide operating field encourages a sense of a nonhistorical realm of literary excellence—receives a little attention, but not much. George F. Whicher in the *Herald-Tribune* credits Brooks with demonstrating that "successful poetry wherever found" has the qualities usually thought limited to the metaphysicals; Richard Blackmur says something comparable in the New York *Times*, as do Gaylord Leroy in the Philadelphia *Inquirer* and Paul Engle in the Chicago *Tribune*.

The effectiveness of the analyses of individual poems—my fourth point—is the subject most frequently treated in the reviews: it is of course praised by the friendly critics, and it is even acknowledged by some not favorably inclined. A few dissenters are crabbed. John Berryman (*Nation*) likes to tax Brooks with faulty readings. The *Higher Education Journal* thinks Brooks "lacks the sensibility of a critic" and refers to the "gulf between the excellence of the author's theory and the painful labor of his practice." Still he makes us "read afresh." Edwin Muir (*Observer*) says Brooks "has more intellect than sensibility," the "narrowness of the theory" results in "the inadequacy of the practice," and Brooks's readings of Gray, Wordsworth, and Tennyson are only case-making.

On Brooks's style, which concludes my catalog of his merits, there are some amazing negatives. Berryman (*Nation*) says Brooks apologizes too much and his "prose is troubling." Henry W. Wells (*Saturday Review of Literature*) thinks Brooks's style is inconsistent, being both too simple and too involved, and accuses him, of all things, of being "stridently dogmatic"! Quite opposite this is Edwin Muir's extraordinary allegation that "Brooks' worst fault" is "facetiousness." The *TLS* reviewer, on the other hand, sees "dullness," but strives to balance things up by asserting that Brooks "lacks equally the irresponsibility and the brilliance of Mr. Empson." But Brooks's style did receive due recognition. The *Higher Education Journal*, though almost entirely disparaging, terms the book "far from dull." Likewise the *New Yorker*: "Readable, and by no means an example of the modern dull, text-creeping school of literary analysis." Michael Thwaites in the Melbourne *Age*, crediting Brooks with "brilliant sanity," praises him for keeping "his technicalities well in check"; likewise Brooks "does not execrate the common readers' approach to poetry." Esther Willard Bates in the *Christian Science Monitor*, also using the word *brilliant*, states, much to the point: "Nor is he oracular. Freely he quotes other critics; freely and amicably he dissents." Finally Rex Warner in *Books of the Month* says "brilliantly argued" and rightly observes that Brooks "deals with his critics briskly, though with an admirable gentility." There could be no better finale to these citations.

Only one reviewer, Gaylord Leroy in the Philadelphia *Inquirer*, mentions, with a mild word of regret, a Brooks position that would later cause much uproar—his alleged antireferentialism. Five reviewers note that the "new" criticism is not exactly a novelty, and six name the major figures that contributed to the form. On the state of the humanities, which, as I note, Brooks deplores, Vivienne Koch (*New Statesman*) thinks Brooks is best when he "forgets his concern for the fate of the humanities." But George Whicher (*Herald-Tribune*) praises Brooks for a rehabilitation of poetry that is essential "if the humanities are to be restored to the place they once held in men's esteem and must rightfully hold again," and Harvey Curtis Webster (Chicago *Sun*) credits Brooks with "one of the most cogent defenses of poetry and the humanities generally."

III.11

Eudora Welty: *Losing Battles* and Winning the War

(1979)

i

On the face of it reading the long *Losing Battles* is like taking an extended ramble through a lush, variegated natural and human landscape in which there are many paths and so many enticements that one is constantly led off in new and unforeseen directions, always fascinated, often uncertain amid apparent aimlessness, and yet constantly suspecting the unclear presence of a controlling route, however camouflaged by the rich growths, vivid scenes, and surprising roadside attractions. Or it is like traveling in a canoe or boat moved and steered only by the current of a stream that is now an all-but-passive pool allowing plenty of time to look at tropical banks and multicolored bottom, now a languid eddy that turns us about rather than pushes us forward, now a short stretch of whitewater that brings on a tumultuous dash, now a sturdy little creek with a great deal of push, but most often a meandering flow that brings the craft to a succession of little stops and visits at dozens of logs, beaver dams, islets, gravelly promontories, sandbanks, coves, and inlets. No stop may seem to have much to do with where you're going, but then you aren't sure about the where, either; once a where begins to shape up, you may see the relevance of the stops in retrospect, or perhaps decide that some of them are there just for the fun of it. Occasionally what you sense as the prevalent drift may tighten up in a millrace drive taking you to a desperate pitch over a deep waterfall wave. But Welty may somehow slip around a danger spot hastily, or settle for an anticlimactic splash in an unforeseen pond, or just let motion die away strangely. Or the voyage through *Losing Battles* may be like listening to a perpetual-motion raconteur—drawling on breathless but always commanding, too full of stories even to stop for applause or a drink, dashing as if driven from one to another, knowing what their connection is but rarely bothering to make the connection explicit, seeming less to manipulate what is told than to be charmed by it as by an independent entity that the narrator barely touches on its way to an audience; getting from one episode to another by such devices (implicit only, never overt) as "You'd never guess what happened next," "I tell you, it was just one crazy thing after another," "Oh, I forgot to tell you what happened before that," "You see, there was this little thing in the past," "And by the way, that reminds me of another story," or "Now is as good a time as any to let Billy have his say," and so on. The surface impression, in other words, is one of haste, casualness, haphazardness, movement rather than direction, scattershot unselectiveness, of rushing ahead rather than rounding out, or of stopping short rather than keeping on, of ringing in the new before the old has been wrung out and hung clearly on the line of the finished and understood, of madcap tumbleweed hop-skip-jumping rather than of steady advance on a marked public route. This impression needs to be mentioned (a) because readers are hardly likely to escape it and (b) because the storytelling surface does not truly reflect the narrative substance. In brief, *Losing Battles* is a highly ordered book, but it does not wear its order on its sleeve. Perhaps Welty did what Sterne did in the parts of *Tristram Shandy* that he had time to polish: strove for an outer air of the accidental, the interrupted, and the inconsecutive (in Sterne, a formal mimesis of the psychological disorderliness of humanity; in Welty, a capturing of diversionary tendencies inevitable in a multitude of individuals even when they are seen as a group with a purpose). Perhaps she was simply the compulsive raconteur driven to transmit episode after episode, tale after tale, as they welled up in her imagination, and yet somehow mastering them with an instinctive grasp of their potential coherence. Perhaps she is basically a designer who worked out a governing pattern with great care, instituting a relationship of parts subtle enough, or letting them have enough of an air of spontaneity, to stir up a sense of the chancy, the lively but unselected, or even the willful. Whatever comes first, this is true: Welty digs deep enough to bring in a gusher, but she has an excellent supply of caps, valves, and piping.

The numerous ebullient parts are held together by personal and thematic relationships that I will try to spell out. A more visible kind of form is provided by typographic breaks: Welty divides the book into six uncaptioned parts and establishes most of these as logical divisions by providing them with conspicuous "closers." Jack and Gloria Renfro, the young couple just getting their married life under way, end Part 1 by leaving a family reunion to go on a family mission; the mission having taken a wholly ironic turn, they end Part 2 by returning to the reunion. Parts 3 and 4 end identifiable phases of the reunion, the latter involving Jack's startling return from another mission. Part 5 ends the reunion day: departures, bedding down, and several private excursions that look ahead to the next day. Part 6 includes the events of the next morning; again Jack and Gloria occupy the closing pages, affectionate but not unanimous about plans for the future. Jack is everybody's hero, and Gloria the hopeful young wife; still they are less a full counterpoint to the older generation than they are an accent. The central business is the revelation of patterns of living (feelings, values, attitudes) that are firmly established in the older reunionists. Jack and Gloria may alter, conform to, or even fall short of the family and village patterns gradually revealed through crowding episodes.

In each part we can discover an ordering of the materials that come at us through apparently rambling, scrambling, scurrying segments of conversational action. We can do this by the rather academic exercise of outlining the contents: thus we can see how Welty, through the surging hullabaloo of reunion talk, gradually introduces and identifies characters and issues, skillfully weaves in past events that generate emotions and speculations in the present, makes random chatter—greetings, cracks, claims or putdowns, in-house allusions, brief flytings—hover about major thematic concerns, and canvasses these concerns in a surrogate, a Chekhovian one carried to ultimate limits, for the linear plot or the special situation evolving toward a terminal point. I will simply assert this congruence instead of making the longish demonstration needed to describe fully the underlying order of any of the six parts.[1]

1. To detect an order, of course, is not to get at some ultimate essence of the novel. One keeps on and on describing constituent elements and their relationships, and still there is much that is elusive. The critic is only too well aware of the residual "mystery" that Eudora Welty has more than once said is lost sight of by reductive criticism. One

ii

The "terminal point" is arbitrary: the ending of the reunion, and the picking up of some of the pieces scattered by the windfall events of the occasion. The compacting of various lifetimes into a single day (this one of about thirty hours, from Sunday sunrise to Monday noon, with due time out for sleeping) is less of a *tour de force* than it was when Frank Swinnerton did it in *Nocturne* (1917) and Joyce in *Ulysses* (1922). The center of the reunion is Granny Vaughn's ninetieth birthday. Since her daughter and son-in-law are dead, the chief reunionists are half a dozen middle-aged grandchildren, the five Beecham men and their sister Beulah Beecham Renfro, plus many spouses and offspring. "Beechams' Day," to borrow a phrase from the Joycist world, is the first Sunday in August sometime in the 1930s. Welty gets the essential past into the picture through many flashbacks. These are rarely arbitrary moves of her own: they are rather stories told by reunionists who want, or have some good reason, to tell them (the old epic tradition of the inset story that covers more time without breaking unity of time). Welty manages these stories with great variety and verve: they may be long or short, the speaker may be called on or seize stage or struggle to hold it, he may repeat a twice-told tale ("Oh why does he have to go into that again?"), he will always face interruptions (questions, objections, pure irrelevancies, reactions to the history narrated), and at times a story comes as a group composition. If Welty is calling on a speaker only because the time has come to get some facts before us, she conceals the fact well; the narrated pasts seem to flow easily out of ongoing talk into present time.

What is told, like what goes on in the present, is not always clear; we may have to live with some fuzziness about the edge of motive, intention, relationship, and even historical or physical fact. Ultimately this may be due to Welty's conviction that all mystery and ambiguity cannot be washed out in the water of logical explanation; its immediate source is her basic technique of thrusting us plumb into the life of the reunion, submerging us in the flood of domestic doings and family

hopes to be inclusive enough not to be reductive, but even great inclusiveness cannot give one the sense of having got it all or of having got the right things.

feelings—partisan, predictive, philosophical, fluctuating between the casual and the intense. This is Joycean of course: the artist as distant divinity, electing an air of Olympian independence from all the scrabble and pother and sound effects he has plunged his readers into. He interprets nothing; readers intuit reality from its direct impact on their senses. They have no help from a Jamesian recording consciousness. But Joyce's management of our total immersion in actuality, his all-around-the-town odyssey, has an air of cool calculation in the library; Welty's is more like a flashing succession of on-the-spot interviews, a village neighborhood odyssey dashed off by a Dickens with Mark Twain as coauthor here and there. But unlike these lively recorders of community doings and spirit—mostly comic, frequently farcical, sometimes edging on the grotesque or the pathetic, and implicitly and in held-down ways, on effects rooted in still deeper feelings—Welty does no emceeing, no open steering of actors or audience; she provides no overt introductions, explanations, or transitions. She is directly present in only one way: she sets up scenes with marvelous fullness and concreteness of detail, naming with utmost ease all kinds of flowers, fruits, vegetables, weeds, trees, animals, soils, terrains, articles of clothing, household objects, dinner dishes, parts and shapes of bodies. At gifts-for-Granny time she lists and gives quick reality to sixteen presents (287). Perhaps no other modern novel would yield so massive a concordance of nouns and adjectives. Yet there is nothing of the relentlessly encyclopedic; Welty never lingers, caressing a scene or a detail of it (as George Eliot does at times); she seems always in haste, sensory images pouring out as from an overturned cornucopia, yet giving life rather than making a mess. Her pictures flash by with a cinematic fluency that makes them almost elusive.

Dialogue must occupy 90 percent of over four hundred pages. It looks uncontrolled, uncentered, and often irrelevant. Yet through it we have to learn virtually everything significant—identities, moral and mental natures, the feelings and ideas that inform life in the town of Banner, old events that influence life now. In other words, far more than most novelists Welty is using the techniques of drama. A dialogue that must be plausible in itself must effect an immense exposition of past and present for a reader who has none of the information possessed by the speakers, and must produce and sustain a tension about what is going to happen in two hours or two weeks or two years. The writer of novel-as-drama has one advantage over the writer of drama-as-stage-play: he is not bedeviled by limits of time. Hence Welty can let go on anyone who wants to talk, whether to get attention, to defend or attack or correct, to yield to a compulsion, or just to let us know what we need to know (in a very effective scene Miss Lexie Renfro, kneeling or squatting, repairs damage to Gloria's skirt while telling us about what she did as companion or nurse to a key figure, Miss Julia Mortimer, the schoolteacher who has just died; what with interruptions, Miss Lexie goes on for fifteen pages [271–86]). Welty makes excellent use of the figure convenient to both dramatists and novelists, the newcomer who must learn what others know. This is Uncle Noah Webster's new wife, Cleo, who not only comes from away but, in an endless itch of curiosity, never stops probing with questions that we too need to have answered. Yet Cleo is more than a prop, for Welty colors her questioning with something of a prosecutor's drive; Cleo comes in on a narrow line between an itch to puncture and put down, and the candor of a nonpartisan inquisitor whose quest for the complete and probably discreditable record surpasses her tact. Thus she contributes to dramatic tension; there are many little needlings between her and Beulah Beecham Renfro, hostess to the reunion and a lively tongued defender of Beechams. "Well, what's *he* got to hide?" asks Cleo about a Beecham urged not to "jabber," and Beulah replies, "Sister Cleo, I don't know what in the world ever guides your tongue into asking the questions it does! . . . By now you ought to know this is a strict, law-abiding, God-fearing, close-knit family" (343–44). But a moment's sharpness seems never to generate an hour's antagonism.

While she keeps clashes constantly going in the foreground, Welty is skilled in focusing on events to come and making the most of the characters' and our expectations: notably his mother's faith that Jack Renfro, the young hero of the family, will make it home for the reunion, and at length his striking leap into the scene. Meanwhile we have had to wait to find out where he would make it home from (the state "pen" at Parchman), how he got there in the first place, and how he got out and traveled home. All that done, we look ahead again: Jack's handling of a mission—to embarrass Judge Moody, who had sentenced him to the pen, and who is known to be in the Banner area.

Meanwhile various questions needing answers crystallize gradually from misty hints in the family talk: why Uncle Nathan's artificial hand, why his wandering life (Beechams stay put), why the biblical texts he plants about the country? What is Judge Moody's mission, once or twice mentioned quickly by the judge or his wife, in these parts? Who are the parents of Jack's wife Gloria, an orphan who was the local teacher before her marriage? What, above all, was the community role of Miss Julia, the legendary retired teacher who chooses reunion day to die? So the constant drama of questions awaiting answer joins the dominant dialogue to commit the novel to a theater way of doing things. It is still a novel, for it aspires no whit to the stringent selectiveness of drama; instead it clings to all the extrinsic constituents of full daily life that stage life cuts back ruthlessly.

Losing Battles periodically reminds us of several dramas of family life—Eliot's *Family Reunion* and Albee's *The American Dream* and *All Over*. Though the novel, like Eliot's play, explores some unclear but serious history that has an impact on the present, it vastly expands Eliot's farcical elements and cuts back and underplays the notes of pain and grief; and though it in no way minimizes rifts and tensions, the novel perceives reunion as a symbol of residual unity among country kinfolk rather than as an ironic recorder of disunity in a county family. Some resemblances to the Albee plays help set in relief the sharply different Welty mode. In *All Over* a family and various appendages await the imminent death of a father-and-husband, and they reveal themselves through their interchanges; in *Losing Battles* the death of the teacher releases a flux of commentary that is a principal means of characterizing the Beecham way of life. Otherwise all is different, notably the tone. In Albee everybody wields a hatchet of hostility or a stiletto of self-pity; aggression and self-defense or self-serving are everywhere; the scene is harsh, and the tone falls little short of disgust. Welty's people have a comparable candor, and it can be combative; but the various selfhoods are mostly held in check by a sense of the fitting, an unspoken acceptance of limited role, and even a talent for sympathy. Welty feels friendly amusement; Albee sneers bitterly. The contrast is made sharper by *The American Dream*, since major characters match: needle-tongued Grandma is paralleled by tart Granny, domineering Mommy by competently managerial Beulah

Renfro, downtrodden Daddy by misadventure-and-miscalculation-prone Mr. Renfro, and "The American Dream" Young Man by Jack Renfro. One brief look at the Albee monsters, their nastiness a filtrate of the author's malice, and we see the relative fullness of Welty's people, neither whittled down to allegories of human unlovableness nor without shortcomings; limited enough, but their limitations set off by saving spurts of energy, good will, good nature, devotion, or endurance. Albee is narrow-eyed satirist, Welty broad-gauge humorist.

iii

Banner people are often feckless, foolish, parochial, prejudiced, thoughtless, thickskinned, and rich in other frailties, and they can be petty, suspicious, tactless, or calculating; but we have little sense that their less glorious moments are seriously hurtful to others. Welty does not focus on the sly, the underhanded, the devious, or the malicious; and there is not a neurotic in the carloads of reunionists that come from away. Welty rarely makes us take sides between virtue and vice. I would almost bet, knowing as I do how such generalizations can ricochet against the maker, that the only true satirical passages are brief ones near the end. At Miss Julia's funeral several people, who sound exactly like Hardy conventionalists, sneer audibly at Jack and Gloria as a sorry pair, whose failings include not being properly dressed for cemetery rites. Here is the complacent snobbery that is an old target of satire. The pressure on the reader to reject false values is stronger when the sinner is known and acts as well as talks crassly. On each of two days Jack has spent laborious hours at the task of getting Judge Moody's Buick, which had leaped to a precarious perch high above road and river, put back on the road, towed into town, and restored to running condition. It is now funeral time, a long rain keeps up, and the road to the cemetery is all mud. The judge suggests giving Jack and Gloria a ride to the cemetery. Jack demurs; all muddied up, he may soil the Buick velvet. Mrs. Moody settles the matter: "They're young. . . . They can walk" (422). Here the priority of things over people, and people who have our sympathy, makes the passage strongly satirical. The episode lacks the sheer laughableness of a little earlier when, during the risky Buick-rescue process, the car door swings open, something pops out and is gobbled by wild pigs, and Mrs.

Moody mourns, "My cake!" (394); when a runaway truck crashes into a ditch and makes Miss Lexie cry out that it "splashed my dress" (395); and when, after drastic steps get the Buick almost miraculously down on the road again, Mrs. Moody complains, "You bring it to me covered with mud!" (396). Here are not the grossnesses that catch the eye of the censor, but the irrelevancies and anticlimaxes that appeal to the humorist. There are dozens of these.

The comic range is very wide: it extends from the ironic to the farcical. In a central irony Jack sets out to discomfit the judge by causing his car to go off the road; instead Judge Moody causes himself much greater trouble by driving his car off the road to avoid running down Jack's wife and baby. Welty often credits people with epigrams that we hardly expect of them, *e.g.,* Mrs. Moody's "Your real secrets are the ones you don't know you've got" (306). Numerous comic moments hinge on replies that suddenly veer away from created expectation (a traditional mode), as when Gloria reports that Miss Julia warned her against marrying into the Beecham family, and Beulah exclaims, "For mercy's sakes! Only one of the biggest families there is!" (251). Miss Julia rescues Rachel Sojourner from an apparent suicide attempt; since Rachel is cold and stockingless, Miss Julia strips off her own stockings, puts them on Rachel, and rushes Rachel to a doctor. Rachel gets the stockings off again, telling the doctor, "I don't care if it kills me, I wouldn't be caught dead in Miss Julia's old yarn stockings" (258). Brother Bethune, the aged parson, speaks defensively of his lack of descendants, "I ain't got a one. Now I *have* killed me a fairly large number of snakes. . . . [T]he grand sum total is four hundred and twenty-six" (213). Such incongruities in thought and values pour out from the Welty imagination. Parts of verbal games can be scattered over several pages. Jack fought Curly Stovall because Curly was "aggravating"; Jack then carried off Curly's safe, not to "rob" him but "just to aggravate him." At Jack's trial Judge Moody scorns Jack's plea that Curly was "aggravating" and finds Jack guilty of "aggravated battery."

Welty is brilliant in farce—in scenes where intentions are defeated by accidents, where coincidence and mishap crowd in to upset plans, where helter-skelter events keep up a dizzy pace, where people are prone to collisions and pratfalls but don't really get hurt, where objects themselves seem to conspire against order. She may describe an episode with the hyperbole natural to farce: "a crowd of his sons and their jumping children and their wives . . . poured out of the car," and then comes a "pickup riding on a flat tire, packed in behind with people too crowded in to wave" (9)—reminiscences of old dizzy movie scenes of dozens of people in a single car. Aunt Nanny seemed to have been "harnessed into her print dress along with six or seven watermelons" (10). In their "aggravated battery" brawl Jack hit Curly Stovall with a sack of cottonseed meal; it "busted" and "covered that booger from head to foot with enough fertilize to last him the rest of his life" (26). Next thing, Jack ties Curly up in a coffin made for Curly and lying inconveniently on his store floor. Curly later complains that he has been "pulled on by a hundred and seventy-five pound woman [his sister]" and "talked back to by a eight-ounce schoolteacher [Gloria]" (37). Jack lugs off Curly's safe like a farcical Hercules; it comes open and scatters contents all over the road; Curly never locked it because it was too hard to get open again. When it is brought into court at Jack's trial, it has a nesting bird in it.

When Judge Moody drives his car off the road to avoid hitting Gloria and her baby, Lady May, Welty could play for the melodrama of near-disaster. She does nothing of the kind. Lady May got on the road when Jack slid down a bank and fell into a ditch, and then failed to get to her because he ran into Gloria and fell into the ditch again— the pratfall series of the two-reeler. A moment later Jack whispers to Gloria, "Face 'em, from now on. Your dress is tore behind" (121). The car has stopped at a Chaplinesquely precarious spot on the edge of a small cliff, its motor still running. Its wheels are off the ground, for it is resting on a sign recently planted by evangelical Uncle Nathan, "Destruction Is At Hand," the balance that saves it depending on the weight of Jack's friend Aycock Comfort, who chased the careening car with his banjo and somehow got into it when it stopped, and who now has to stay there for nearly twenty-four hours. For half of a very hot and dusty Sunday, and several hours on a rainy and very muddy Monday, efforts to deal with the car produce round after round of farce, genuine risk though there is: everybody has contradictory ideas, advice and commentary are endless, potential helpers drive away, plans go wrong, towlines break and bodies pop in various directions, tires blow out, a dozen dogs bark assistance, Jack's baby kicks him in the eye, and then he is badly stretched in a tug-of-war with the escaping Buick (it gets away over the cliff and lands on a ledge on its "nose"), Jack's father makes a mess by dynamiting a partially obstructing tree ("with all its yesterdays tangled up in it now" [391]), and an unexpected secondary explosion not only tosses people and things about but brings forth Beulah's ironic observation on her husband's work: "Some folks' dynamite blows up once and gets through with it, but you don't reckon on that little from Mr. Renfro" (392). In this marvelous long-continuing zany struggle it is as if fictional life in the thirties were imitating the great two-reelers of the twenties.

Yet superabundant farce—and one could go on for pages describing it—does not supplant the comedy of events that come out of differences and inconsistencies of personality, or obscure the recurrent flickering presence of noncomic materials. There is much wit, ranging, as we have seen, from jeers to epigrams. The comedy that reflects humanity, in contrast with the farce that runs roughshod over it, usually has some share even in the most boisterous physical scenes. Some matters are wholly comic—for instance, the forgiveness theme. An annual reunion feature is a preacher's discourse which traditionally combines family history, humor, and homily—a task long carried out by the late Grandpa Vaughn, evidently a Mosaic figure, and this year committed to Brother Bethune, who is, Beulah says, "a comedown after Grandpa" and of whom Granny Vaughn asks, "Who went so far as to let him through the bars?" (175). The reunion alternately ignores him, interrupts him, helps him get things straight, and cheers him on as if he were the day's floorshow—a comic medley of attitudes. Various Beechams express the hope that he will officially "forgive" Jack, apparently for doing time in the pen, and discuss styles of forgiving; Jack feels that "nobody . . . would have forgiven" him for not making it from pen to reunion. As in drama, these quick references build up to a scene in which everything then goes quite unexpectedly. Brother Bethune suddenly directs his discourse to Judge Moody and declares, "We're going to forgive you." The judge is nonplussed; his wife says that they can't be forgiven for coming to the reunion, since Jack invited them. Uncle Noah Webster comments wittily that "hospitality . . . ain't no guarantee you ain't going to be forgiven when you get there," and the judge's growing annoyance catalyzes further forgivings for him—

"for bringing your wife" (Aunt Nanny), "for livin'" (Aunt Birdie), "for calling me 'old man'" (Brother Bethune). Brother Bethune urges him to "do like the majority begs and *be* forgiven." The comic irony of it is that the Beechams have unconsciously used "forgive" to mean "condemn" and hence have happily had it both ways. Moody is enraged at being "forgiven" for "being a fair judge at a trial." Beulah, politely passing cake to the judge, assails him with a lovely non sequitur, "Don't tell me, sir, you've nothing to be forgiven for, I'm his mother." Three good ironies follow. The first is that Jack, who was sentenced by the judge, strongly opposes all the forgiving; now immensely grateful to the judge for "saving" his wife and baby (by diverting the Buick), he seems to be apologizing for the family's tactlessness in practicing a needless and needling absolution. The second irony is that in thus seeming to draw away from his family, Jack is actually allying himself with them more strongly, but by a novel tactic: he springs a surprise by declaring openly that he will not forgive the judge, because the judge's unforgivable act was depriving the family of Jack's indispensable labors for eighteen months. The third irony is that the judge approves Jack's nonforgiveness, and judge and erstwhile defendant shake hands on it, each cherishing his own interpretation of the rite of concord. Beulah ends things by lamenting "this headlong forgiving" and helpfully suggesting to Mrs. Moody that she use a spoon to eat the "tender" coconut cake. This substantial scene (208–13) is not only prepared for, as we have seen, but is followed up by a number of brief variations on the forgiveness theme (321, 372, 427), the best of them the judge's witty "Forgiving seems the besetting sin of this house" (319).

Peeping through the regular crevices in the dominant farce and comedy are diverse touches of the somber, the pathetic, the disastrous, and even the tragic. Since she has a many-toned sense of reality, Welty is equally spontaneous in these noncomic notes, but she never, never holds them. Her rich sense of the wry does not diminish her sense of what goes awry, goes wrong, wreaks injury, but she does not linger over these; whether from stoicism or an instinct that does not crystallize as formal choice, she so manages human troubles that the reader may escape a solid sense of the real difficulties faced by the characters. The very energy of the tireless dialogue somehow denies the power of events over the characters, singular in apparent hope-

fulness or gift for survival. The Renfros say little of their poverty, of
their losses during the time when Jack, in jail, could not help them; it is
from the cracks of others that we learn that their farm has become almost a wasteland (drought now, against dangerous floods in the past).
It is never called so overtly, but the new tin roof is a pathetic disclaimer
of defeat, a chin-up welcome to Jack as he returns to serious farm
problems. Miss Julia's death makes a picnic excursion for other teachers, but at the news "Gloria stood as if she had been struck in the fore-
head by a stone out of a slingshot" (157). She had been Miss Julia's
successor and special protégée, but then we learn of their troubled split
over Gloria's marriage to Jack. Most touches of pathos are lightning
quick. Lifted to a table top, Granny does a determined little dance routine: "She danced in their faces"—not only visibility, but a little de-
fiance. She starts absentmindedly to walk off the table, is caught by
Jack making a cinematic split-second entry, and in her "eyes gathered
the helpless tears of the rescued" (308).

In the past there were destructive fires as well as floods; the Beechams'
parents were drowned in strange circumstances; the woman whom the
Beechams take to be Gloria's mother attempted suicide and, though
prevented, died of the aftereffects; Gloria's years at an orphanage and
teachers college were bleak ones; the most admired of the Beecham
boys, Sam Dale, died young; much neighborhood damage, as well as
losses for the Renfros, was due to a piratical transient named Dearman
(possibly Gloria's father). We see Uncle Nathan's artificial hand, then
the stump of his arm, and we assume a self-dismemberment as the center of a lifelong penance (wandering endlessly and putting up religious
signs). Suddenly he blurts out the reason: "I killed Mr. Dearman with
a stone to his head, and let 'em hang a sawmill nigger for it" (344).
The death of Miss Julia on reunion day brings forth many reminiscences of her zealous pedagogical career and quotations from her. The
key one is "All my life I've fought a hard war with ignorance. Except in
those cases that you can count off on your fingers, I lost every battle"
(298)—one source of Welty's title. Her dying words were, "What was
the trip for?" (241). The implicit despair, quick hints suggest, also has
a place in Judge Moody's inner reflections on her career and last
months; dying, she had to make heroic efforts to mail letters through a
strange barricade by Miss Lexie Renfro, a nurse-companion who had

mysteriously become a kind of jailer. The funeral of Miss Julia is the penultimate episode; it is followed only by a short tender scene between Jack and Gloria.

iv

Yet all such actions and effects are contained within the comic framework: the pattern is survival within a world in which one accepts, makes do with, a prevailing disparateness where much is out of whack with logic or desire. The diversity of narrative materials, however, does not imply a diversity of style. Not that a uniformity of manner disregards heterogeneity of matter: "each face as grief-stricken as the other" and "Ella Fay Renfro in front tossing a sweat-fraught pitcher's glove," which are only two lines apart (288), use different vocabularies, and even so few words reveal difference in tone. But both are brief absolute phrases; they suggest, without proving anything, that Welty likes certain basic syntactic arrangements. Ordinarily she does not write very long sentences or use complex structures; she coordinates a good deal; she has almost none of the involutions (such as parentheses within parentheses) of Faulkner, and she does not draw on different traditions of style as much as K. A. Porter does. To say this is to identify a difference, in no way to assert a shortcoming. Welty does not make much use of the logical, analytical, judicial manner (she uses very few abstract nouns) and the comedy-of-manners style (wit framed in syntactic formalities) ideally represented in Jane Austen and at times equally available to Charlotte Brontë (who thought Austen trivial) and George Eliot—Brontë with her unique emotional intensity of vocabulary and rhythm, and Eliot with her dual at-home-ness in a concrete natural world and a reflective or philosophical one. Porter likewise can combine sensory concreteness with an Austen wit and a sort of combed-out, almost Jamesian thoughtful hovering. Welty has an enormous idiom of homely actuality, domestic and rural; she is still more earthy than George Eliot, handicapped by neither the Victorian reticences (Eliot could not have an Aunt Nanny say to a spelling-bee victor, "You got it spelled but wet your britches" [289]), nor by the chic vulgarities now often mistaken by the naïve for proofs of vitality, liberty, honesty, etc. A varied and rampaging actuality of animals, natures (weather, earth, growing things), and even objects is what her bounding style throws us into; though the resulting atmosphere is occasionally sharpened by witty observations, on the whole it is rather suffused by humor, a tireless sense of incongruities, human fallibility, the grotesque, and the jokes of circumstance, even when disaster may be dimly underfoot or just around the corner.

Welty's language falls into two not wholly distinguishable categories—her own words when she acts as scene-shifter, and the speech of her characters. The vast extents of dialogue are never flat; they rush on colloquially like the freshets of spring, splashing with expletives, exclamations, loose connections, pronouns without antecedents, verbs without subjects, and now and then a local vocabulary. Syntax can be enormously compact. Jack: "Here's Papa something to open" (31), and, of the new roof, "I could see it a mile coming" (73). Granny: "I'm in a hurry for him back" (51). Lexie: "I listened hard to be asked for and I wasn't" (337). Uncle Noah Webster of the jail-keeper: "Drunk and two pistols. Makes his wife answer the phone" (50). Verbal or prepositional phrases may hold off stubbornly or hang on loosely. Willy Trimble: "Told him better to stay put with who he's with" (154). Beulah: "Cleo, what in the name of goodness did you think we ever started this in order to tell?" (39) and "Vaughn's got the teacher to tell he's misput the bus" (373). Miss Lexie, of Miss Julia's retirement: "So, where she had left to go, when they put her to pasture, was across the river" (296). The colloquial may substitute for an expected solemnity, as in two comments on Miss Julia's coming funeral. Uncle Homer to Brother Bethune: "And you can have your whack at her. I think you can look for a good crowd" (339), and Brother Bethune, "I'm just good enough to get her into the ground" (351). Scores of such locutions, unhackneyed and unpretentious, make for wonderfully lively speech.

Willy Trimble, who found Miss Julia's body, likes his phrase for her demise and uses it twice: "Down fell she. End of *her*" (162, 230). This is clipped and unsolemn, but instead of tumbling out, it is patterned. Likewise Beulah can put words into more of a pattern than we expect in colloquial style: "Well, you have to trust people of the giving-stripe to give you the thing you want and not something they'd be just as happy to get rid of" (243). Frequently speakers use phrases that have a slightly more formal (or even bookish or archaic) flavor than the context suggests. Some instances: Miss Lexie, "I at present call Alliance my home" (18); Uncle Noah Webster, "Cleo, I wish it had been your privilege to be with us our day in court" (51); Jack, referring to the late Grandpa Vaughn, "I miss his frowning presence just as I get myself ready to perform something" (102); Jack to his father, "What brought you forth?" (138); uncouth Curly Stovall, "I'll come back and see what story the night has told" (152); Mr. Renfro, a "thing surpassing strange" (294); Uncle Nathan, "I must needs," followed first by "be on my way" and then by "not stop to take comfort" (375); and Jack again, "Mr. Comfort elected to put in his appearance" (418). Some repetitions go beyond the casual: Beulah, "She run-run-run down the hill . . . followed behind 'em trot-a-trot, trot-a-trot, galloping, galloping" (217), and Miss Lexie on Miss Julia, "pencil racing, racing, racing" (283). Beulah can combine singular precision and balance: "I'm ashamed *of* her and *for* her" (296). Often speakers use so organized a locution as the series, from Jack's quick summary for his jailer—"I got my daddy's hay to get in the barn, his syrup to grind, his hog to kill, his cotton to pick and the rest of it" (44–45)—to Beulah's remarkably shaped "But the truth is you don't know, nor I don't, nor anybody else within the reach of my voice, because that ring—it's our own dead mother's, Granny's one child's wedding ring, that was keeping safe in her Bible—it's gone, the same as if we never had it" (40). Beulah uses such series in describing Gloria (69) and her late brother Sam Dale (221), Jack in picturing the beleaguered Buick ("singing along, good as gold, fighting along against the laws of gravity, and just daring you to come near her" [150]), Gloria of the normal school, "Not enough of anything to go round, not enough room, not enough teachers, not enough money, not enough beds, not enough electric light bulbs, not enough books," setting off the catalog with a quick irony, "It wasn't too different from the orphanage" (245). Mostly the series provide compact and speedy summaries, as in Vaughn's list of the bonds holding together the parts of the tow-train at the end, "Trace chains, well rope, Moody towline, fence wire, and Elvie's swing" (399), but a series can produce a pounding intensity à la Brontë, as in Miss Julia's last letter: "Something walls me in, crowds me around, outwits me, dims my eyesight, loses the pencil I had in my hand. I don't trust this, I have my suspicions of it, I don't know what it is I've come to. I don't know any longer" (299).

Welty can have characters speak in antithetical form, as in Judge Moody's "I'm not asking for a Good Samaritan, I'm asking for a man with some know-how" (125); Gloria's double antithesis that has almost an Austen ring, "Jack, I don't know which is worse. . . . What you thought you were going to do, or what you're ending up doing. For the sake of the reunion you were willing to run Judge Moody in the ditch. Now for his sake you are just as willing to break your neck" (126); and Mrs. Moody's exclamation over their fate, "To be saved from falling to the bottom of nowhere by getting blown sky-high with a stick of dynamite!" (140). Others can generalize with the pith of the epigram—Beulah's "You can die from anything if you try good and hard" (279), and Aunt Beck's "Feelings don't get old! . . . We do, but they don't. They go on" (346). And Miss Lexie can annotate an epigram with a series: "But they die . . . The ones who think highly of you. Or they change, or leave you behind, get married, flit, go crazy—" (272), another quick touch of the occasional pathos. Beulah can manage a paradox: when a night-blooming cereus produces, though "not a drop of precious water" was ever diverted to it, she comments, "I reckon it must have thrived on going famished" (349).

Welty has been praised for her "listening," for her "ear." No need to reaffirm that, or dispute it. Yet the passages that I have just been quoting, with their air of the formal or the formed, have a tone or orderedness that is created by the rhetoric of a self-conscious controlling mind rather than that of lay talkers letting fly with native woodnotes wild. To say that Welty has an ear, then, is not the same thing as to say that she is a human tape recorder whose authenticity in dialogue would be confirmed by a linguistic survey of the region where her characters live. We have rather to say that she composes dialogue which has an impressive air of authenticity. Now it may be that certain locutions and that even certain parallelisms and antitheses do come out of a heard speech, but I suspect that Welty is hearing—what? a probability rather than a going practice of speech. That is, given the feelings they have and a rhetorical impulse (rather than a contentment with an unplanned dribble of words about the things to be expressed), the speakers might speak as she makes them do. The special orderings of words symbolize an element—a mood, an ambition, perhaps even a parodic sense—not lacking or unimaginable in these characters. In making such a surmise I am seeking an approach to the authenticity, as I have called it, of unexpected elements in colloquial style.

A writer with a good ear for regional or dialectal speech has of course other sources of style. Hardy can suddenly shift from a fluid Wessex idiom to a heavy-weather cumbersomeness and even the pedantries of the autodidact. Welty, however, has not a trace of the academic or the inadvertently pretentious. She does not philosophize, as Hardy does; as I have already said, she is rarely analytical or interpretative. Hence she has little need for the kind of logical language used by virtually all nineteenth-century novelists, who were constantly doing formal commentary. In her nondialogue passages she rarely shapes sentences up by balance, symmetry, counterpoise, and so on. She characteristically uses a series not to control the materials but to hurry over them unsentimentally, as Meredith often did. Jack pursues Gloria, she "rounding the bank its whole way around, swiftly past the piecrust edge, streaking by the peephole, clicking across the limestone, bounding over the hummocks, taking the hollow places skip by skip without a miss, threading serpentine through the plum bushes, softly around the baby, and back to the tree, where he reached with both hands and had her" (111).

Choice and ordering of words both serve an antisentimental effect. Granny "put kisses on top of their heads like a quick way to count them" (10); Jack "bounced kisses on . . . cheeks and . . . chin" (228); Uncle Noah Webster "kissed [Beulah] with such a bang that she nearly dropped" his present (12). There are unexpected combinations: the boy's "stubborn voice still soft as a girl's" (8); the moon "going down on flushed cheek" (3); the honey's "clover smell as strong as hot pepper" (11); a "stinging veil of long-dead grass . . . hid cowpats dry as gunpowder" (98); Brother Bethune's fingers "rainbow-colored with tobacco stain" (106); and the busload of funeral-bound schoolteachers "rainbow-dressed" (157); and Gloria's phrasing of her devotion to Jack: "I love him worse than any boy I'd ever seen" (320). Visual images abound, fresh in themselves or in combination. A single abstract word adds a note of mystery to an early morning scene:

"Mists, voids, patches of woods and naked clay, flickered like live ashes, pink and blue" (4). Several strong-action verbs and an engineering simile picture the hairdos of Renfro females: they "raked their hair straight back, cleaved it down the middle, pulled it skintight into plaits. Miss Beulah ran hers straight as a railroad track around her head" (7). A special eye appears in many visual images. Once there is a "wall of copper-colored dust" (8); later "bales of dust tumbled behind" a truck (153). Welty distinguishes "solid" mud like "the balled roots of a tree out of the ground" from a "thinner, fresher mud like gingerbread batter" (395). She can do the quick snapshot—"She prisses to meet him" (30)—or the more painstaking camera study, as of the child's eyes "open nearly to squares, almost shadowless, the blue so clear that bright points like cloverheads could be seen in them deep down" (47), or make what sounds commonplace very suggestive, as in hills "near but of faint substance against the August sky" (99). Some effective verbs: "The baby . . . peep-eyed at Judge Moody with the puff of her sleeve" (141); the wagon "tunnelled into the shade" (229); the "cutting smell of coal oil" (347). Auditory images can be very original: "the air shook with birdsong" (46–47); the mockingbird was "singing the two sides of a fight" (22); a man's "thready voice" (22). The numerousness of "loud" words for speaking—"screamed," "shouted," "shrieked"—gives point to the ironic "again quiet threatened" (340). A subtle and often beguiling use of the auditory appears in synesthetic metaphors, which more than once define the seen by the heard, as in "A long thin cloud crossed [the moon] slowly, drawing itself out like a name being called" (3); dresses "rattling clean" (8); a quilt looking "rubbed over every inch with soft-colored chalks that repeated themselves, more softly than the voices sounding off on the porch" (46); a burning caterpillar web made "an oval cottony glow, like utterly soft sound" (348). Once Welty interprets the olfactory by the tactile—"a smell, more of warmth than wet" (3)—and a sound by a striking use of the visual: a "female voice, superfine, carrying, but thin as a moon-beam" (359). Welty then goes on into a rare lyric description of the night as perceived by twelve-year-old Vaughn Renfro, a passage that might have a place in *A Midsummer Night's Dream*. In this, she has a flux of images for the moonlight: it had "the thickness of china" (362); the world "had been dosed with moonlight, it might have been poured from a bottle" (363); Vaughn "waded through the moonlight"; the flowers "looked like big clods of the moonlight freshly turned up from this night" (366). Then, in contrast with this viscous, palpable light: "Lightning branched and ran over the world with an insect lightness" (367). She can get the same kind of speed in the one long sentence in the novel (about 175 words) by a quick succession of relatively short syntactic units joined by ten *and's* (407–408).

Welty has another stylistic device which amplifies the sense of vibrant life: she uses verbs that imply will, intention, and feelings in animals, plants, and even inanimate objects. The dogs "tried to bark [the teetering car] on over as fast as possible" (120), one dog "barked the truck off the road in spite of a dozen hounds" (381–82), and dogs along the road were "barking everything on past" (403). Stovall's pair of oxen would be a dubious rescue team since they are, Mr. Renfro alleges, "as set on mischief as they can be . . . as you'll know if you can read the glints in their eyes" (140). Plant life can be libertine or co-operative. The cactus "grew down in long reaches as if trying to clamber out of the tub," and Beulah is sure "it's making up its mind to bloom tonight" (18); when it does, Aunt Birdie claims, "We scared it into blooming" (349). The Renfro-dynamited tree exposes a mass of roots, "bringing along their bed of clay, as if a piece of Boone County had decided to get up on its side"; Jack says it's "clinging. . . . Waiting to see what's the next thing to come along," and Welty adds a brilliantly imaginative note, "Nothing but memory seemed ever to have propped the tree" (378); when it finally falls over the edge, Gloria interprets, "Mrs. Moody scared it down" (393). A cyclone animated many objects: "our stove, waltzing around with our lunch pails, and the map flapping its wings and flying away, and our coats was galloping over our heads with Miss Julia's cape trying to catch 'em. And the wind shrieking like a bunch of rivals at us children!" (237). The wind ruined the Methodist church but spared the close-by Baptist church; Mr. Renfro concludes, "I'll tell you something as contrary as people are. Cyclones" (238). When a tire on the stranded Buick blows, Jack has a recipe for saving the others: "let the air out of the others before they start copying" (142). Jack is sure that the car is "just breaking its heart to go over" (148); Beulah says that someone is "going to have to coax that car *down*" (199); and Gloria's analysis of the situation is, "I scared it up. . . . I only wish it was in my power this morning to scare it down again" (with that elegant moving forward of "this morning" from the final spot where it would normally clomp down: one of these occasional modifications of ordinary run-on speech by a special control over some part, 377).

In trying to describe Welty's style—with its speed, bounce, freshness, and frequent unexpectedness, and with its creation of a sense of movement and life in all the elements of the world—I have saved last place for her most frequent rhetorical device: her comparisons. She uses *like, as, as if, as though,* and *as*-adjective-*as* almost seven hundred times (a casual count induced by my own curiosity and claiming only approximate accuracy); of these, almost four hundred are similes with *like*. Welty instinctively—perhaps obsessively, provided the word is not used pejoratively—presents people and things by means of resemblances. She may portray one element more sharply, bring quite different things together into one existence, or heighten attention by surprise or shock. She wars against clichés and the hackneyed; she makes familiar life take on newness from striking or even thrilling comparisons. To show the range, here are three different sensory effects on succeeding pages: visual—"her vaccination scar shone at them like a tricky little mirror" (13); olfactory—"white organdy, smelling like hot bread from the near-scorch of her perfect ironing" (14); auditory—"four yards of organdy that with scratching sounds, like frolicking mice, covered all three steps" (15). She can make an old taste new—"fall plums . . . whose sucked skins tasted like pennies" (101)—and give unusual reality to an embrace by means of a surprising tactile effect: "Their hearts shook them, like two people pounding at the same time on both sides of a very thin door" (99). A machine may be pictured through the animal—"The truck sprang up like some whole flock of chickens alarmed to the pitch of lunacy" (392); the animal through the human—hounds "loudly sniffing, like ladies being unjustly accused" (142); and nature through the human—"whirlywinds of dust marched, like scatterbrained people" (21).

Visual surprises are constant: "The distant point of the ridge, like the tongue of a calf, put its red lick on the sky" (3–4); "trees . . . lit up, like roosters astrut with golden tails" (4); "butterflies . . . whirling around each other as though lifted through the air by an invisible eggbeater" (30); "hair . . . red as a cat's ear against the sun" (47); dust "climbed . . . in clouds like boxcars" (105), "went up like a big revival tent with the flaps popping" (153); "There stood the moon, like somebody at the door" (286); "The moon, like an eye turned up in a trance, filmed over" (367); a part of the truck "motor . . . glistening like a chocolate cake" (402); a "horse ran lightly as a blown thistle-down" (434). Auditory images have the same novelty. Watermelons, "spanked" by Mr. Renfro, "resounded like horses ready to go" (63); the tin roof made a "sound like all the family spoons set to jingling in their glass" (71); the "song of the locusts" was "a long sound like a stream of dry seed being poured into an empty bucket" (271). Welty can impute a palpable body to sound—"a sound . . . thin as that of a veil being parted" (118); a mockingbird "threw down two or three hard notes on him like a blacksmith driving in nails" (119); to light— the "substance fine as dust that began to sift down . . . was moon-light" (311); "lights hard as pickaxe blows drove down from every ceiling" (312); as Jack and Gloria came into a shady spot, "the final glare dropped from them like a set of clothes" (99); to smell—"The smell of the cloth flooded over them, like a bottle of school ink spilled" (78); to atmosphere—a "shaft of heat, solid as a hickory stick" (4). Welty can be ironic—insect bites make the baby look "like she's been embroidered in French knots" (358)—or playful and fantastic: a cake of ice is "dense with ammonia, like fifty cents' worth of the moon" (184).

The similes that increase the liveliness of an already pulsating and bounding prose by declaring or hinting the likeness of unlikes (numerous metaphors do this too) may also hint at thematic elements which are not much articulated openly. "'I bet you Banner School had a library as long as your arm,' cried Aunt Birdie, as though she saw a snake" (274). The "as though" clause tells us something about the local state of mind that makes the scene a trying one for teachers. The high heels of Gloria "tilted her nearly to tiptoe, like a bird ready to fly" (19); later we learn that Gloria would take Jack and fly away if she could. But we already have got, and continue to get, figurative hints about such aspirations: "flickered the yellow butterflies of August like dreams" (20). The same image and idea soon surface again: "Out there with her [Gloria] flew the yellow butterflies of August—as wild and bright as people's notions and dreams, but filled with a dream of their own; in one bright body, as though against a headwind, they were flying toward the east" (39). Again, "The old man came . . . climbing the path like a rickety ladder of his dreams" (103–104). If Welty does not openly interpret man's fate, such figures give a furtive imaginative clue to her sense of how things go.

The encyclopedic quotation in this section is risky. I can only pro-test that I have been highly selective, so much so as constantly to feel that I am not adequately communicating Welty's rich campaigns that win stylistic wars. But quoting and quoting and quoting, be it too much viewed one way or too little viewed another, can alone give a sense of literary reality. The other alternative is the critic's abstract words of identification and praise, words which cannot absent them-selves for a long while but which at their best remain a large distance from the objects they strive to account for.

V

Welty's natural tendency to juxtapose, and often unite, diverse mat-ters—many local stories of past and present, farcical and disastrous events, dramatic dialogue and novelistic description of scene and tone, and above all the sharply contrasting materials brought together in the comparisons that gush forth inexhaustibly—appears more in her themes than in her characters. There is a very large cast of characters, too many to distinguish fully: we tend to be more aware of their com-mon elements as members of a community than of their individualiz-ing traits of personality. They all adhere to the same basic ideas, cus-toms, rites; they have the same general emotional contours. The four married Beecham brothers and their wives can hardly be separated without special effort. Yet no characters are ciphers; virtually all of them have great general vitality; the Dickensian humor that I men-tioned earlier appears in the characterization. We see types, key mo-tives, psychological colorations providing the felt life of reunionists and others. Granny is frail, forgetful, and free to mow down anybody at any time. Mr. Renfro is the born loser—his mishaps with the dyna-mite to which he is addicted symbolize the way things go with him—who still manages a singular equanimity. His wife, Beulah, the reunion hostess, is an energetic manager, immensely talkative, sharp on occasions, ironic, an immense admirer of her son Jack, but able to say of him, since he wrote no letters during his eighteen months in the pen, that he "never did unduly care for pencil and paper" (16) and to "hope" that his Grandpa's death will "help him grow up a little" (69). Aunt Beck is regularly identified as "gentle," Aunt Nanny as ballooning and hearty. Aunt Cleo is blunt and disparaging: of the hometowns of the reunionists, "Never heard of any of it" (18); of Gloria's wedding ring, "What'd you have to do? Steal it?" (48); of Jack's having a truck, "You-all [the Renfros] don't look like you was ever that well-fixed" (67). Vaughn Renfro, aged twelve, is a bit jealous of the heroic stature that all attribute to Jack, and can show considerable competence in the tasks he takes on. Gloria, the teacher who married into the Beechams, passionately longs not to be a Beecham; in marrying Jack, she chose "feeling" over a teaching career and over Miss Julia's opposition; she is aloof but not rude, and can be strong at key moments. Hero Jack is strong, lively, helpful, fond of the hill country, devoted to the family, tender and affectionate to his wife and daughter; he takes charge of the Buick rescue but is not very effective except for one astonishing strongman feat; normally considerate, he surpasses himself in thinking of his imprisonment as a kind of penance for the murder committed by Uncle Nathan: "maybe it's evened up, and now the poor old man can rest" (431). Judge Moody and his wife have tasted a thin slice of a larger world, and their occasional ironic remarks have a shade more of self-consciousness and knowingness; the judge goes beyond the others in a mildly sad reflectiveness upon the human state as reflected in Miss Julia's career and demise. Mrs. Moody fluctuates between a narrow-gauge ordinariness and occasional sharp insight, as when she says of Miss Julia, "A tyrant, if there ever was one. Oh, for others' own good, of course!" (325).

But even with certain identifying marks that help us keep Jack and Jill, or Tom and Dick, apart, the individual psyche is not quite the business of the novel; individuals may have idiosyncrasies, but basically they participate in the group consciousness—the style, the attitudes, the mores, the traditions of their time and place. The men and women enact parts in the myth that orders their lives. We are not centrally held by the problem of how individual experiences are going to turn out; for the most part we know, or at least are allowed to think we do. There are no demanding plot lines to make us focus on the development of relationships or the resolution of conflicts. But in the medley of passing actions and endless talk that embrace an annual ritual, a social day's trivialities and serious moments, and a few hours' recollections of past crises that helped shape present life—in these there is a kind of plot of meanings that, though we may be incompletely conscious of it, is what holds us. These people's assumptions and values appear, sometimes explicitly but often only implicitly, in thematic strands woven into a quite variegated texture.

Of the themes that operate through gossip, jest, remembered events, and domestic and roadside small movements, the chief one is that of community. To take a fairly obvious phase of this first: Banner is a "Christian community." No one is antichurch, church talk is frequent, a reunion needs a preacher-orator, and nobody works on the Sabbath, especially if work means helpfulness. But what Welty finds underneath this is a kind of secular ecclesiasticism: denominational allusions make us picture the rivalry of clubs or lodges. The Methodist and Baptist churches are across the street from each other, and it is doubtless equally symbolic when they are brought closer together by a cyclone which "picked the Methodist Church up all in one piece and carried it through the air and set it down right next to the Baptist Church!" (238). When Brother Bethune rambles on in his reunion discourse, Aunt Beck demands, "Can't you make that church rivalry sound a little stronger?" (193). Mrs. Moody is sure that Curly Stovall, who has a phone in his store, can be got to open up even on the Sabbath; she argues, "I'm sure he's no more than a Baptist" (128). On the other hand, when Grandpa Vaughn, a "real, real Baptist," went to a Methodist revival and unexpectedly found "infant Baptism" going on, he gave unequaled "heartfelt groans" (182). Rachel Sojourner, Gloria's presumptive mother, may have got into trouble, it is proposed, when she "took to going Sunday-riding with call-him-a-Methodist." Aunt Beck annotates, "Well, you know how Baptists stick together. . . . They like to look far afield to find any sort of transgressor" (265). The style of both Baptists and Methodists leads Mrs. Moody to declare, with the candor that nearly all practice, "I'm neither one, and gladder of it every minute" (406). When a churchful of Methodists, homeward bound after service, indifferently drive by the stranded Buick, Mrs.

Moody comments, "I'd just like to see a bunch of Presbyterians try to get by me that fast!" (134). She is a Presbyterian, and she wishes that the graveside service for Miss Julia were in charge of a "down-to-earth Presbyterian"[2] instead of a Catholic priest, once a student of Miss Julia's who, observers declare, "worshipped himself, didn't he?" (430). Several years before, Uncle Noah Webster had identified Judge Moody as a Presbyterian because "the whole way through that trial, his mouth was one straight line" (61). Aunt Beck approaches closest to tolerance of Presbyterians. Miss Julia, she says, "was a Presbyterian, and no hiding that. But was she deep-dyed? . . . There's a whole lot of different grades of 'em, some of 'em aren't too far off from Baptists" (277). "Deep-dyed" beautifully conveys the sense of an alien other which, however, may not descend as far into gross error as it might.

Though ecclesiastical affiliation is an important bond, the Bible behind the churches enters the story in only a few casual allusions.[3] (There are, I think, no allusions to classical myth.) Of these, three are used to illustrate Brother Bethune's fuzziness: he calls Jack, just home from prison, "The Prodigal Son" (105, 107); he calls the reunion dinner "Belshazzar's Feast," remembering only belatedly to add, "without no Handwriting on the Wall to mar it" (177); and he alludes to Granny Vaughn and her late husband as "David and Jonathan" (184). One biblical allusion, rather funny at the moment of utterance, may have some value as a pointer. When Jack resolves to use main strength to bounce the Buick off its nose into a more functional position, his mother Beulah "cried frantically," *i.e.*, with ebullient pride, "Now watch! Reminds me of Samson exactly! . . . Only watch my boy show the judgment Samson's lacking, and move out of the way when it starts coming!" (394). Jack does—double success. We recall this passage in the final scene when Jack and Gloria look at all the problems that still do not cancel hope. Jack says, "And I've got my strength" (434) and again, "But I still got my strength" (435). Gloria is no Delilah to his

2. Despite all their setbacks and her husband's ironic attitude, Mrs. Moody has a persisting faith in a Providence attentive to their needs (142, 145, 149, 151, 165, 207).

3. To Lucifer (81), the Crack of Doom (129), the book of Romans (183), the Flood (250), Job (404), the parting of the Red Sea (406), Solomon (432). There are a number of references to the family Bible, mainly as the container of the family record of births, marriages, etc.

Samson; indeed, rather than enslave him to another people, she would save him from what she takes to be bondage to his own.

If churches provide some of the ritual forms of local life, place and family appear to be more fundamental sources of community. All the Vaughns and Beechams are, or once were, Bannerites; Aunt Cleo's rude inquisitiveness seems to be that of an alien; and the condescension of the Moodys from Ludlow is less a valid judgment than outsiders' instinct for shortcomings. Jack's love for this hill country, drought-stricken though it now is, is the aesthetic affirmation of local loyalty. What an unsympathetic outsider might call provincialism also comes through as a unifying sense of place. Yet this is several times managed humorously rather than solemnly. When a "boy cousin" thinks that Jack, not yet arrived, may be in Arkansas, Beulah exclaims, "Arkansas would be the crowning blow! . . . No, my boy may be in Parchman, but he still hasn't been dragged across the state line" (70). The sentiment arises even more emphatically when all learn that Jack and Gloria may be first cousins, who according to a recent Mississippi law may not marry, and when Judge Moody suggests that they could avoid legal trouble by heading out to Alabama, "not over a few dozen miles" away. "'Alabama!' cried Jack, a chorus of horrified cries behind him. 'Cross the state line? That's what Uncle Nathan's done! . . . [L]eave all we hold dear and all that holds us dear? . . . Why, it would put an end to the reunion'" (321).

The reunion is the preeminent symbol of family feeling. In fact, to lack the symbol is to lack right feeling, the substance that earns respect. Uncle Curtis finishes off the Comfort family: "The Comforts don't know what the word reunion means" (60). The Beechams won family honor because Jack's trial "drew" large crowds from all the villages that Beechams live in. Uncle Curtis provides consolation for the family's temporary loss of Jack to Parchman: of his nine sons, he says, "maybe not a one of 'em had to go to Parchman, but they left home just the same. Married. . . . All nine! And they're never coming home" (66–67). Beulah sums up the Beechams as a "strict, law-abiding, God-fearing, close-knit family, and everybody in it has always struggled the best he knew how and we've all just tried to last as long as we can by sticking together" (344). The day ends with "the joining-of-hands" as they form a circle, sing "Blest Be the Tie," and hear Brother Bethune's benediction (348–49). The reunion even provides a metaphor for the feelings of Vaughn Renfro on a moonlight mission: "the world around him was still one huge, soul-defying reunion" (363).

Behind the esprit de corps, which of course does not eliminate sarcasms and clashes, lie certain patterns of thought and feeling which govern family style and actions. Before Jack arrives on stage, all the talk about him builds him up as a heroic figure—a man of charisma and with the talents of the culture hero: he can right wrongs and solve problems such as those of the drought-ridden farm. When he crashes in, there are epic signs and portents—dogs barking, people screaming, the new roof "seemed to quiver," "the floor drummed and swayed, a pan dropped from its nail in the kitchen wall" (71): half great hurrah and half parody. With little delay a new large task is imposed on the hero. In thumbing his way back from Parchman, he had got one ride by clinging to the spare tire on the rear of a car. When the car went into a ditch, Jack was there to play Hercules as Good Samaritan: "Put shoulder to wheel and upped him out" (79). Now he learns that the driver was the very Judge Moody who had sentenced him to jail, and everyone censures Jack for rescuing an enemy (81ff.); the consensus is that he must retaliate. As Aunt Birdie puts it, "Now you can make a monkey out of him. . . . That's all the reunion is asking of you" (86). Family feeling develops the spirit of the feud; it gets to Jack, and all the men (with dogs) happily prepare to set off on an anti-Moody skirmish without any clear plans. Jack insists on his "family duty . . . to get Judge Moody tucked away in a ditch like he was in" (103) and "announce myself to him" (117). But the feudist spirit of getting even is not unanimous; Beulah sees only trouble in the plan, Gloria votes her "common sense" (112) against it (we remember the women in *Coriolanus*), Aunt Beck is "always in danger of getting sorry for the other side" (293), and Jack's father a little later takes "a shine" to the judge (359). What finally aborts the feudist foray, however, is wonderfully ironic, as we have seen: not a change of heart, but a combination of farce and melodrama in which the judge is a victim, not of a Beecham plot, but of his own humanity, running his car not down into a ditch but up on to an impossible perch. Jack promptly turns retaliation into gratitude because the judge "saved my wife and baby" (198), and shifts his role from wrecker to rescuer of the car.

The theme of the feud is thus metamorphosed into two other themes. The first is the most amply developed of the biblical materials—the story of the Good Samaritan. There are several roadside scenes in which helpfulness is possible, and Welty's pictures of human responses are always partly ironic. Hitching rides home from jail, Jack was helped by several Good Samaritans but wearied of the pious discourses to which they treated him. Then he hopped onto the rear of the Moody Buick, reporting that "Judge Moody was one and didn't know it" (196). The judge's unconsciousness of role is contrasted with Jack's great consciousness of his; referring to his various roadside efforts, he quite likes to call himself a "Good Samaritan" (125, 149, 163). He in turn is contrasted with other passersby who are indifferent, unhelpful, or profit-seeking, and then his good will with his overall competence, so that the judge can wish for expertise instead of Good Samaritanism (125). Thus Welty provides several perspectives on the myth.

While the ethic of the feud is reversed in the Good Samaritan theme, it is continued in another theme implicitly present—that of chivalry: in both, life focuses on recurrent combat. Welty introduces substantial, if subtle, suggestions of the chivalric, this in a village scene where subsistence problems are onerous: another mark of her originality. The relations between the Beechams and Curly Stovall are basically feudist, clearly. But then when Curly and Jack meet, they fall into each other's arms, pound happily on each other, and trade amiable insults; Jack calls Curly "skunk" (146), "rascal," and "greedy hog" (148)—all this in the tradition of frontier humor. But they have been opponents in a way that keeps reminding us of tournament competition; the initiating action of the novel was a duel of theirs in the past, and near the end there is another. In each of these the take-off point is a little interchange between Jack's sister Ella Fay, sixteen, and Curly; thus Jack is not too distant from the traditional defender of womanhood. Further, in a flashback narrative in midnovel we learn that a duel broke out when Curly aspired to the favors of Gloria—a battle that came "close to taking the cake," even though Jack "got beat" (205). A truck has the status of a tournament prize, so that uncertainties over its ownership lead the uncles to happy anticipation: "*Now* we've got a war on that's like old times! Jack and Curly buttin' head-on again!" (206). The final duel has interesting ramifications. After

Jack knocks Curly down, Ella Fay hints that she may be engaged to
Curly, and this leads to some delicate considerations of decorum. At
first Jack sees a political marriage that will bring the opponents into
"one happy family"; then on second thought he backs off and ad-
vances a substitute motion: he will make Curly a "present" of the
truck "not to marry into us" (412). Curly is offended by the thought of
receiving a present from Jack (as by an antagonist's boast), and Jack by
the refusal; Curly swings, Jack is the loser again, and Curly cuts off his
shirttail (413)—a trophy of his victory in the lists. Though the word is
never used, what is at stake is "honor."

There are other intimations of an underlying chivalric code. Jack
constantly uses a formal "sir" in addressing men; he tells some yokels
to mind their language, since "there's ladies present" (132); he imagines himself disciplining an unwilling helper of the judge by "setting
on his chest where I could pound some willingness in him" (143). Curly
doesn't want to play second fiddle while Jack "save[s] one more lady"
but insists, "*I'm* going to go ahead and save her while you watch"
(151). Shortly after Jack's returning home, he and his brother Vaughn
got hold of a "pair of dried cornstalks" and "jousted with them" (72);
"every day" in the pen Jack and his friend Aycock Comfort called
Judge Moody "Sir Pizen Ivy" (83), a soubriquet repeated several times
later (116, 117, 130). Jack has a chivalric sense of obligation; first he is
"beholden to the reunion . . . to meet that Judge . . . [and] sing him
my name out loud and clear" (112)—a symbolic throwing down of the
gauntlet; and then he is totally committed to saving the Buick of the
driver who saved his family (130). He craves the glory of single combat: when Judge Moody wants to call in his garageman to help with
the Buick, Jack responds with "a stricken look" (128; *cf.* 134). Perhaps his nicest touch of honor appears in his escape from jail one day
before the end of his sentence. "Today was my last chance of making
my escape. . . . One more day, and I'd had to let 'em discharge me"
(360). Discharge on schedule: the commonplace routine of the law
rather than the heroic romance of escape.

vi

These low-key hints of the chivalric add charm to the character who is
primarily the strong man, the culture hero, and the affectionate family

member. Yet there is no case-making for Jack: he is not a magically successful competitor, the legal or political or actual may supersede the chivalric at any time, and both his mother and his wife think Jack not altogether grown up. Telling him about the lost shirttail, Gloria positively forbids a resumption of jousting with Curly. Against Jack as agent of Beecham feudist feeling, Gloria sets out to "pit her common sense" (112); she demands that he modify his Good Samaritanism by using "some of my common sense" (126); opposing Mr. Renfro's application of dynamite to the Buick problem, Gloria insists that all the help Jack needs "is a wife's common sense" (140); and if she does not name her common sense, it is implicitly present in her urging him to give up tilting with Curly (153) and to forget about his pet truck—"a play-pretty. . . . A man's something-to-play-with" (425). But there is no case-making for Gloria either; of the competing values, none is espoused as an absolute. Jack is ironically ambivalent about Gloria's common sense. When Gloria tells him about her split with Miss Julia over her marriage to him, Jack asks, "Wouldn't she pay regard to your common sense?" (171). On the other hand, Jack can allege that his first Buick-rescue scheme failed because "Gloria run in too quick with her common sense" (140), and on another occasion Welty makes a deadpan comment that Jack "gave a nod, as when she mentioned her common sense to him" (172).

If Gloria wants to detach Jack from the youthful heroic games that add zest to community life, she wants even more to detach him from the Beechams. "When will we move to ourselves?" (111) she asks him soon after they are alone for the first time, and her last words are "And some day . . . some day yet, we'll move to ourselves" (435). In part this is the conventional desire for a private "little two-room house" (431). But it is also Gloria's revolt against the old community, the pressuring Beecham way of life. Symbolically, she sits outside the family group at the reunion. She presents herself—an illusion? a part truth?— as trying to "*save Jack* . . . save him! From everybody I see this minute! . . . I'll save him yet! . . . I don't give up easy!" (198). Again, "I was trying to save him! . . . [From] this mighty family!" (320). She never articulates the Beecham shortcoming; she perhaps believes that they take rather than give. She tells Jack, "The most they ever do for you is brag on you." But Jack insists that, despite her book learning, "about what's at home, there's still a little bit left for you to find out" (137). Near the end they have an argument, both of them affectionate and tender, but both holding to their positions; the summary lines are "Honey, won't you change your mind about my family?" and "Not for all the tea in China." She adds, "You're so believing and blind" (360).

Miss Lexie declares at one point, "The world isn't going to let you have a thing both ways" (280). But the author says, in effect, that you can't help living with it both ways: in this central action we see Jack clinging to two loyalties—to old family and new—and feeling them as equally valid. The two communities are mutually jealous. Gloria's worst moment comes when an old postcard message indicates that her father may have been the late Sam Dale Beecham. Being a Beecham is "ten time worse" than anything else. "Welcome into the family!" cries Aunt Nanny, and they force Gloria through an initiation rite which is a mixture of farce and humiliation. It is a baptism by total immersion— in the watermelon hyperbolically provided for the reunion. They rub her face in it and order her to say "Beecham," but she keeps on denying the identity (268–70). Later Jack says it was just a family welcome, but Gloria bitterly harps on one detail that may be symbolic: "They pulled me down on dusty ground . . . to wash my face in their sticky watermelon juice" (313). "Pulled me down": the rite was various things, and leveling was clearly one of them. The outsider, the teacher, the individual who felt apart, must be cut down to community size. Community survival would demand that.

The matter of Gloria's identity—her actual parenthood remains at least partially speculative, as if facts themselves partook of the "ambiguity" which Welty has recently said is the nature of life—is thematically relevant to her would-be secession from the Beechams. Jack wants her to have only a present, not a past, identity: "She's Mrs. J. J. Renfro, that's who she is" (346). Gloria spells this out more fully: "I'm here to be nobody but myself, Mrs. Gloria Renfro, and have nothing to do with the old dead past" (361)—her version of a recurrent human dream. She is not merely bucking Beechamhood; in general she treats the present not as a residue of the past but as the genesis of a future. Her "common sense" is mingled with a visionary tendency: she constantly looks ahead expectantly, just as she did in settling on a teaching career (47). "All that counts in life is up ahead," she says (315). "That's

for the future to say," she says on two occasions (65, 320), on the second of which she falls into romantic prophecy, "We'll live to ourselves
one day yet, and do wonders." Another time she humorously modifies
her teacher's aspirations: she would no longer "change the world" but
"just my husband. I still believe I can do it, if I live long enough" (356).
One episode is funny and painful and symbolic. Jack is in his tug-of-war
with the Buick, and there is this exchange between Gloria and him:

> "I don't see our future, Jack," she gasped.
> "Keep looking, sweetheart."
> "If we can't do any better than we're doing now, what will Lady May
> think of us when we're old and gray?"
> "Just hang onto my heels, honey," he cried out.
> "We're still where we were yesterday. In the balance," Gloria said. (390)

The moment of doubt enriches a picture that is mostly in another
color. Once Gloria says that Lady May is "our future" (358); throughout the Buick ordeal she "tried to keep my mind on the future" (421),
and at the end she promises, "I'll just keep right on thinking about the
future, Jack" (434).

So there is thematic significance in the clashes between the hereditary community—the embracing Banner-Beecham world summed up
in the reunion and its rituals—and the small new community that lives
only in the imprecise visions of the orphan-teacher-young wife. But the
only is inaccurate. For Gloria is carrying on, in her own way, the tradition first voiced by Miss Julia Mortimer, the by now mythical figure
whose career was an espousal of values different from those that rule
the local scene. She dies on reunion day, the very day when her protégée Gloria starts her life with Jack, just home from prison; Julia was
"in love with Banner School" (294), Aunt Beck says (we also learn that
Julia was attractive enough to have suitors), while Gloria, over Julia's
protests, has married a Beecham. Different arena, but same battle, as
key words show. While Gloria eyes the future but no longer seeks to
"change the world," Miss Julia writes, just a little before her death, "I
always thought . . . I could change the future" (298). Or, as Gloria
puts it, Julia "didn't want anybody left in the dark, not about anything. She wanted everything brought out in the wide open, to see and
be known" (432). Gloria still hopes for some success; Julia reports

that she herself has failed. But through Judge Moody we also learn that she has had some spectacular successes: she coached good pupils and pushed some of them into careers of note, and, early mindful of what we now call the "delivery" of professional services, persuaded the young lawyer Moody to stay in his home county—for which he "never fully forgave her" (305)—instead of following her other protégés into a larger world.

Though we learn much about Miss Julia from her deathbed letter to the judge and from his account of her, the heroic antagonist of the local status quo is presented mainly by a technical tour de force: the memories and commentary of ex-pupils who thus portray both themselves and their relentless quixotic challenger. At times they praise her for having taught them all they know, for having made them what they are; more often they portray her as a tormentor, a dragon, a fiend to be escaped. Julia and later Gloria put teaching above everything; it had to go on, come cyclone, flood, fight, angry parents, or local spectacles. But Miss Beulah says that no children of hers can be kept "shut up in school, if they can figure there's something going on somewhere! . . . They're not exactly idiots" (27), and she promises a chastised child, "And for the rest of your punishment, you're to come straight home from school today and tell me something you've learned" (374). Many such remarks give body to Gloria's assessment of Julia: "All she wanted was a teacher's life. . . . But it looked like past a certain point nobody was willing to let her have it" (294). Having heard some of the facts of "that teacher's life," Jack is sure it sounds like "getting put in the Hole [at the pen]! Kept in the dark, on bread and water, and nobody coming to get you out!" (312). Miss Julia, reports Gloria, "saved me from the orphanage—even if it was just to enter me up at Normal" (316)—an inadvertent picture of the education of an educator. Jack nicely sums up the local view of education when he says he's "thankful I come along in time to save my wife from a life like hers" (313).

This world is not an easy one in which to spread light. Miss Julia was independent, solitary, single-minded, respected, feared, a thorn in the flesh of the community, a Quixote with longer career, more bite, less laughableness. Perhaps in retirement she was a little mad; perhaps it served the ends of Miss Lexie, her attendant, to think her so; or more likely Miss Lexie did think her so. Miss Lexie imprisoned her, "tied her. . . . Tied her in bed" (278), and Miss Julia had to be desperately heroic to get letters out to Judge Moody. At the funeral her former student Dr. Carruthers says briefly, "Neglect, neglect! *Of course* you can die of it! Cheeks were a skeleton's! I call it starvation, pure and simple" (430). It is entirely possible that, through a nurse unimaginative enough to treat illness with tyrannous severity, Welty is satirizing a community for callousness amounting to cruelty. And yet the main drift of her art is not in that direction; the fate of Miss Julia, important as it is, is not made a predominant issue but is one of many matters presented in many tones. Welty does not tend to discover goodies and baddies. She is not bitterly condemning viciousness but rather symbolizing a neglectfulness that may, alas, crop up in any human community.

Miss Julia is the spokesman for one value, not an allegory of an ideal. Nor, on the other hand, do the three B's of folk life—Banner, Baptist, Beecham—simply define a culpable crassness. If this life is limited, it still has its own virtues of clan solidarity, humor, hopefulness; it has been molded by a succession of disasters which in the chatter and clatter of a busy day's doings we may almost lose sight of but which surface now and then in flickers of distressed awareness. As Mr. Renfro says on one occasion, "It's all part of the reunion. We got to live it out, son" (211)—the reunion as not only jolly get-together but as shared reexperiencing of many troubles. His wife, Beulah, puts this still more strongly after they have gone to bed: "I've got it to stand and I've got to stand it. And you've got to stand it. . . . After they've all gone home, Ralph, and the children's in bed, that's what's left. Standing it" (360). We can't help thinking of Faulkner's "They endured."

If Welty is not a satirist, she is even less a regional historian. A regional idiom she does use—the idiom of spoken style and social style. Yet it is a medium, not of local reportage, but finally of a wide and deep picture of American life. The dualism of this life—or better, one of its dualisms—is the larger reality implicit in the confrontation between Miss Julia and Gloria on the one hand, and Banner and Beechams on the other. On the one hand there is the family, the historical community, with its sustaining and unifying legacy of habits, customs, rites, and loyalties; its sense of actuality, its tendency to see the way things were as the way things are, its embodiment of "the system." On the other hand are the teachers—outsiders in Banner (the Ludlow belle and the orphan) and hence natural voices for alteration of the status quo. In them we see the side of national personality that turns away from the past and toward the future, places a high value on change, has unlimited faith in education, believes in "enlightenment," is full of aspiration, longs for a "better life," can become visionary and utopian, and may bring forth, to borrow from Mrs. Moody's description of Miss Julia, "tyrants . . . for others' own good." Still there are no allegorical rigidities; Miss Julia remains the lifelong prod from without, Gloria marries and hopes to bore from within. Her "future" may turn out to be no more than her small private acreage within the system; feeling superior to the Beechams, she must tearfully acknowledge, "One way or the other, I'm kin to everybody in Banner" (313). If the teachers are in one sense quixotic visionaries, still Gloria believes in her own "common sense," and she turns it against that other chivalry that Jack has imbibed from local tradition. "Family" and "future" both want to possess hero Jack; drawn both ways, he may embody an unresolvable division or foreshadow such reconciliations as now and then we come to for a time. He may refertilize the drought-plagued wasteland or simply duplicate the Beechams in a new Renfro family. Talk of the future though she does, Gloria can still sadly ask, at the very end, "Oh, Jack, does this mean it'll all happen over again?" (435).

On all this Welty looks with a vast, but never bitter, irony.

vii

In sketching the ways in which a Mississippi story plays variations on a central American myth—*variations* of course means hitting on innovations, altering patterns, mixing perspectives rather than taking sides— I am trying to communicate the sense of magnitude that this novel creates (as satire, which mostly gratifies prejudices, rarely does). The sense of magnitude is also served by the undercover wispy reminiscences of European myths and specifically of two wholly dissimilar works, a Greek tragedy and an English comic novel—Sophocles' *Oedipus* and Fielding's *Joseph Andrews*. To propose such analogies may seem pretty portentous, a laborious artifice of magnification, but since the resemblances came to me as a spontaneous overflow of powerful impressions on first reading, and since, recollected in tranquillity, they do not die away, I will take the risk.

During the reunion-day conversation, the talk occasionally takes a turn which Beulah tries to head off. In doing this, she somehow reminded me of Jocasta, who catches on to the truth before Oedipus does and urges him not to go further. Neither Jocasta nor Beulah succeeds. Just as Jocasta's son-husband had committed a murder in the past, so, we learn, had Beulah's brother Nathan; both men suffer self-mutilation and exile. Oedipus, coming to Thebes, returns unknowingly to his native city; so does Gloria when she comes to Banner (as Aunt Birdie says, in folk Sophoclean, "You was coming right back to where you started from. . . . Just as dangerous as a little walking stick of dynamite" [319]). Both are "orphans." Oedipus marries a woman who turns out to be his mother; Gloria marries a man who, it turns out, may be her first cousin, which would mean, at that time and place, statutory incest. Oedipus' mother-wife and Gloria's unwed mother are both suicides. Oedipus' horror at discovering his relationship to Jocasta and Laius is paralleled by Gloria's sense of disaster in the discovery that she may be a Beecham. The banishment undergone by Oedipus and Nathan is a possibility for Gloria and Jack.

The identity myth that starts with unknown parenthood and proceeds to a crisis of possible incest is an old romantic device that appears in Roman comedy and then resurfaces in moralistic melodrama in the eighteenth century and in comic form in Fielding's *Joseph Andrews* (which happens also to have a very fine roadside Good Samaritan episode). In the world there depicted, people have a habit of mislaying children, and the last of the vicissitudes that afflict the love of Joseph Andrews and Fanny (the Jack Renfro and Gloria of the story) is that they may be brother and sister. Before bringing in the prestidigitation of parenthood that removes the difficulty, Fielding, who is not given to the ambiguity that Welty elects even here, notes different responses to the possibility. Everybody believed it "except Pamela, who imagined, as she had heard neither of her parents mention such an accident, that it must certainly be false; and except the Lady Booby, who suspected the falsehood of the story from her ardent desire that it should be true; and Joseph, who feared its truth, from his earnest wishes that it might prove false" (IV, xiii). Aunt Beck says simply, of Beulah's response to the story that Gloria may be a Beecham, "if the right story comes along at the right time, she'll be like the rest of us and believe what she wants to believe" (267). The psychological comedy is the same as Fielding's.

Fielding, who revels in allusions, makes another joke about Joseph and Fanny: "They felt perhaps little less anxiety in this interval than Oedipus himself, whilst his fate was revealing" (IV, xv). Welty abstains from such allusions, but her plot does have its sketchy analogies to those of Sophocles and Fielding. Likely she never thought of either. The primary critical point is that in imagining human probabilities she fashioned experience in ways that bring to mind the situations developed by such predecessors. That is, she instinctively moved toward fundamental patterns of action that get at basic springs of human experience. Her materials are central rather than eccentric; or, to risk a rather overused word, they are archetypal. But I want especially to stress the fact that her management of materials clustering about the possible incest is reminiscent of *both* Sophocles and Fielding: that the tragic possibility is often just around the corner, or just under the surface, when the main lines of action in the foreground are comic and often, indeed, farcical. We are plunged into tall tales, folk humor, slapstick episodes of unruly persons and objects, all these mediating a life in which wit, non sequiturs, flashes of pathos and anguish, natural disasters, old patterns of feeling (feudist, chivalric, familial, partisan), and a dominantly good-humored, if not successfully channeled, energizing are kaleidoscopically reflected in indefatigable dialogue. Many tones, often side by side unexpectedly, emerge in this presentation of community: community with a time-created coherence that satisfies but constrains, that is filtered through moment-by-moment diversities of manner and positive inconsistencies of attitude, and that is always troubled by the periodic educational evangels with excelsiors that flicker for a while and then give off a dim persistent light. The characters enact the old modes of existence and the change-bound disturbances of them; the author says little. If she spoke from the shadows in which she remains, she might, we surmise, allude to the *comédie humaine*, pointing out that a wide spectrum of the laughable contains bits of the pitiable and the admirable; that *plus ça change, plus c'est la même chose,* that everyman comes to discover, like Gloria, that he is kin to everybody.

But Welty makes no such observations; she simply sets the scene and makes the actors talk their lives. She does both tasks with immense variety and vitality of style; most characteristically she brings apparent unlikes together. This central habit of style is a symptom of her overall method, which in *Losing Battles* conspicuously wins the artist's war against the chaos of tumbling history and sprawling experience—wins it even while camouflaging the victorious form in the multiplicity and miscellaneousness of the defeated antagonist.

III. 12

Style in Katherine Anne Porter's
Ship of Fools

(1962)

i

Katherine Anne Porter is sometimes thought of as a stylist. *Stylist* is likely to call up unclear images of coloratura, acrobatics, elaborateness of gesture, a mingling of formalism probably euphuistic with conspicuous private variations, like fingerprints. It might call to mind Edward Dahlberg's peremptory dense texture of crusty archaism and thorny image, a laboriously constructed thicket so well guarding the estate of his mind that it often becomes that estate. It is not so with Porter. There is nothing of arresting façade in her style, nothing of showmanship. Though on the lecture platform she could be all showman, and slip into the prima donna, in her proper medium both the public personality and the private being vanish from the stage. At least they are not easily detectable presences. In *Ship of Fools* the style is a window of things and people, not a symbolic aggression of ego upon them. It seems compelled by the objects in the fiction; it is their visible surface, the necessary verbal form that makes their identity perceivable. It seems never the construction of an artist imposing, from her own nature, an arbitrary identity upon inert materials, but rather an emanation of the materials themselves, finding through the artist as uninterfering medium the stylistic mold proper to their own nature. Porter is ruling all, of course, but she seems not to be ruling at all: hence of her style we use such terms as *distance, elegance,* and of course the very word for what she seems to have ceded, *control.* She is an absentee presence: in one sense her style is no-style. No-style is what it will seem if style means some notable habit of rhythm or vocabulary, some uninterchangeable (though not unborrowable) device that firmly announces "Faulkner" or "Hemingway." Porter has no "signal" or call letters that identify a single station or wavelength. She does not introduce herself or present herself. Much less does she gesticulate. She does not pray on street corners; wrestle with her subject in public as if she were barely managing to throw a troublesome devil; or lash her tail and arch her back like a cat demonstrating expertise with a mouse. She does not cry "Look, ma, no hands"; she just leaves hands out of it. Her style has neither birthmarks nor those plaintive rebirth-marks, tattoos. Not that she disdains embellishment; in her there is nothing of unwashed Kate in burlap ("I am life"). Nor, on the other hand, is there anything of frilly femininity tendering little dainties from a fragile sensibility ("I am beauty," "I am feeling").

ii

No-style means a general style, if we may risk such a term, a fusion of proved styles. Porter can do ordinary documentary whenever it is called for: the ship's passengers "advertised on little thumbtacked slips of paper that they had lost or found jeweled combs, down pillows, tobacco pouches, small cameras, pocket mirrors, rosaries." Here she sticks to nouns; yet she has no fear of the adjectives somewhat in disrepute now: "In the white heat of an early August morning a few placid citizens of the white-linen class strolled across the hard-baked surface of the public square under the dusty shade of the sweet-by-night trees." She relies without embarrassment on the plain, direct, ordinary, explicit. Veracruz "is a little purgatory"; Amparo decided "prematurely" that trouble was over. "Herr Lowenthal, who had been put at a small table by himself, studied the dinner card, with its list of unclean foods, and asked for a soft omelette with fresh green peas. He drank half a bottle of good wine to comfort himself."

On such sturdy foundations of style she can build in several ways. Without altering the everyday, matter-of-fact manner, she gets below the surface. Glocken, the hunchback, "scared people off; his plight was so obviously desperate they were afraid some of it would rub off on them." "Rub off": imaging casually a world of prophylactic finickiness. Captain Thiele paces the deck "alone, returning the respectful salutations of the passengers with reluctant little jerks of his head, upon which sat a monumental ornate cap, white as plaster." The commonplace comparison, dropped in without commotion at the end, unobtrusively deflates the large official figure. Of a shipboard Communion service: "The priest went through the ceremony severely and hastily, placing the wafers on the outstretched tongues expertly and snatching back his hand." The plain adverbs suggest a minor public official in a distasteful routine: "snatching," the fear of contamination. Mrs. Treadwell leaves a self-pitying young man: "If she stayed to listen, she knew she would weaken little by little, she would warm up in spite of herself, perhaps in the end identify herself with the other, take on his griefs and wrongs, and if it came to that, feel finally guilty as if she herself had caused them; yes, and he would believe it too, and blame her freely." The easy lucidity never shirks depths or darks, which to some writers seem approachable only by the involute, the cryptic, or the tortuous.

Using the kind of elements that she does, she can organize them, elaborately if need be, with control and grace. The local papers "cannot praise too much the skill with which the members of good society maintain in their deportment the delicate balance between high courtesy and easy merriment, a secret of the Veracruz world bitterly envied and unsuccessfully imitated by the provincial inland society of the Capital." Under the gentle irony and the rhythm that serves it, lie in easy and well-articulated order a remarkable number of modifiers—such as Hardy would have fouled into knotty confusion, and James, pursuing precision, would have pried apart with preciosity in placement. She manages with equal skill the erection of ordinary terms, both concrete and analytical, into a periodic structure in which all elements converge unspectacularly on a climax of sudden insight: "The passengers, investigating the cramped airless quarters with their old-fashioned double tiers of bunks and a narrow hard couch along the opposite wall for the unlucky third comer, read the names on the door-plates—most of them German—eyed with suspicion and quick distaste luggage piled beside their own in their cabins, and each discovered again what he had believed lost for a while though he could not name it—his identity." A compact sketch of outer world and inner meaning, it is never crowded or awkward or rambling.

Luggage as guarantor of identity: it is the kind of true perception regularly conveyed in terms modest and unstraining, but fresh and

competent. Of the troubles of boarding ship: "This common predica-
ment did not by any means make of them fellow sufferers." Each kept
"his pride and separateness within himself"; "there crept into eyes
meeting unwillingly . . . a look of unacknowledged, hostile recognition. 'So there you are again, I never saw you before in my life,' the
eyes said." Of David Scott's special capacity for triumph as a lover:
"Feeling within him his coldness of heart as a real power in reserve,
he . . . laid his hand over hers warmly"—with just a shadow of oxy-
moron to accent the reality without calling attention to itself. Jenny
Brown, his girl, had a "fondness for nearness, for stroking, touching,
nestling, with a kind of sensuality so diffused it almost amounted to
coldness after all": the plain tactile words preparing for the shrewd
analysis in which the paradox is not thrust triumphantly at one but
offered almost experimentally. There is a good deal of this relaxed
movement between the physical and the psychic or moral, each grasped
directly and surely. The Spanish dancers "would look straight at you
and laugh as if you were an object too comic to believe, yet their eyes
were cold and they were not enjoying themselves, even at your expense." The vocabulary is hardly more than elementary, and the words
are arranged in a classic compound structure, almost as in an exercise
book, yet they communicate a disturbing hardness. The next sentence
is of the same stamp but is trimmed back sharply to an almost skeletal
simplicity: "Frau Hutten had observed them from the first and she was
afraid of them." The fear is ours, but not through a tensed-up stylistic
staging of fear.

Porter can combine words unexpectedly without becoming osten-
tatious: for instance, an adjective denoting mood or value with a neutral noun—"serious, well-shaped head," "weak dark whiskers," or,
more urgently, "strong white rage of vengeful sunlight"; or sex words
with gastric facts—"They fell upon their splendid full-bodied German
food with hot appetites." She pairs partly clashing words: "softened
and dispirited" (of a woman affected by childbirth), "with patience
and a touch of severity" (of people waiting for the boat to leave),
"oafish and devilish at once" (of a nagging inner voice), "at once
crazed and stupefied" (of the air of a bad eating place); and gets inner
contradictions in sharp phrases: "this pugnacious assertion of high
breeding," "classic erotic-frowning smile" (of a dancer), "shameless

pathos" (of an angry face). She can surprise, and convince, with a preposition: a newly married couple's "first lessons in each other."

She has strong, accurate, but not conspicuous, metaphors: "soggy little waiter," "pink-iced tea-cake of sympathy," "hand-decorated hates," "making conversation to scatter silence," a "laugh was a long cascade of falling tinware." But metaphors are less numerous than similes, that now less fashionable figure to which Porter turns with instinctive ease, rarely without amplifying the sense or shading the tone, and always with the added thrust of imagistic vitality. She may fix the object visually: Elsa Lutz had a "crease of fat like a goiter at the base of her throat"; on her canvases Jenny Brown painted cubistic designs "in primary colors like fractured rainbows." She has a sense of how the inanimate may creep up on or take over the human: the steerage passengers "slept piled upon each other like dirty rags thrown out on a garbage heap"; or how a human attribute may be dehumanized: the Spanish dancers' voices "crashed like breaking crockery." When a woman, confident of her worldly knowingness, is publicly snubbed by the Captain, she first turns red; then her blush "vanished and left her pale as unborn veal"—colorless, unknowing, pre-innocent, pre-calf. When his wife bursts forth with a public expression of views contrary to his own, Professor Hutten "sat like something molded in sand, his expression that of a strong innocent man gazing into a pit of cobras." It is a complete picture of mood and man. Porter confers her own incisive perception of character upon Jenny Brown when she has Jenny thinking about David Scott, "I'll be carrying David like a petrified fetus for the rest of my life." Jenny's sense of rigidity and immaturity in her lover is really an echo of her creator's sense of many of her human subjects: she sees them with easy clarity and goes right to the point. Her images for them come solidly out of life; they are not stylistic gestures, literary exercises, but unlabored responses to need, responses from experience against which the doors of feeling and knowing have never been closed.

The difficulty of describing a style without mannerisms, crotchets, or even characteristic brilliances or unique excellences leads one constantly to use such terms as *plain, direct, ordinary, unpretentious, lucid, candid*. These are neither derogatory nor limiting words, nor words that one is altogether content with. The qualities that they name are not inimical to the subtle or the profound, to the penetrating glance or the inclusive sweep. Whether Porter's basic words are a multitude of documentary nouns or adjectives, are literally descriptive or pointedly or amplifyingly imagistic, are terms that report or present or comment or analyze, she composes them, without evident struggle, in a great variety of ways—in combinations of revelatory unexpectedness; tersely or compactly or with unencumbered elaboration, either in a succession of ordered dependencies or in structured periods where everything builds to a final emphasis; with an apparently automatic interplay of force and fluency; meticulously but not pickily or gracelessly; with a kind of graceful adjustment to situation that we call urbanity, yet by no means an urbanity that implies charm or agreeableness at the expense of firmness or conviction.

iii

Certain of Porter's arrangements disclose characteristic ways of perceiving and shaping her materials. She describes Veracruz as a "typical port town, cynical by nature, shameless by experience, hardened to showing its seamiest side to strangers: ten to one this stranger passing through is a sheep bleating for their shears, and one in ten is a scoundrel it would be a pity not to outwit." The traditional rhetoric—the triad series; the first half balanced against the second, which is balanced internally; the antithesis and chiasmus—is the instrument of clarity, analytical orderliness, and detachment. Porter has a notable talent for the succinct summarizing sequence; she often employs the series, which combines specification with despatch; through it a packing together of near-synonyms may master by saturation, or a quick-fingered catalog may grasp a rush of simultaneous or consecutive events. A dancer's "pantomime at high speed" to an infatuated pursuer communicates "pity for him or perhaps his stupidity, contempt for the Lutzes, warning, insult, false commiseration, and finally, just plain ridicule." A series may define by a concise anatomy: William Denny's "mind seemed to run monotonously on women, or rather, sex; money, or rather his determination not to be gypped by anybody; and his health." Such series remind one of Jane Austen, who can often look at people and things as logically placeable, sometimes dismissible by a quick list of traits, or naturally amenable to a 1-2-3 kind of classification. Porter has a marked Jane Austen side, which appears, for instance, in the dry summation of a girl and her parents: their "three faces were calm, grave, and much alike," with the anticlimax offhand instead of sharpened up into a shattering deflation. Porter's comic sense is like Austen's both in the use of pithy geometrical arrangements and in the presentment of observed ironies, sometimes suffusing a whole scene, sometimes clipped down as in neoclassical verse: Elsa Lutz spoke "with a surprising lapse into everyday common sense" (*cf.* "But Shadwell seldom deviates into sense"); Herr Lowenthal felt "he was living in a world so dangerous he wondered how he dared go to sleep at night. But he was sleepy at that very moment." (*Cf.* "And sleepless lovers, just at twelve, awake.") The irony is Austen-like when, though piercing, it is less censorious than tolerantly amused: "With relief he seized upon this common sympathy between them, and they spent a profitable few minutes putting the Catholic Church in its place." It may catch a social group, gently replacing the group's sense of itself by another: at the Captain's table Frau Rittersdorf "turned her most charming smile upon the Captain, who rewarded her with a glimpse of his two front teeth and slightly upturned mouthcorners. The others ranged round him, faces bent towards him like sunflowers to the sun, waiting for him to begin conversation." It may go beneath the surface to capture habits of mind, setting them up in a neat balance that comments on their insufficiency: Jenny Brown thinks wryly of "'the family attitude'—suspicion of the worst based on insufficient knowledge of her life, and moral disapproval based firmly on their general knowledge of the weakness of human nature."

Yet to a passage with a strong Austen cast Porter may make an inconspicuous addition that will elusively but substantially alter it. When Lizzi Spockenkieker runs carelessly into pompous Captain Thiele, he "threw an arm about her stiffly," and she, "blushing, whinnying, cackling, scrambling, embraced him about the neck wildly as if she were drowning." There is the Austen series crisply hitting off the ludicrous behavior, but there is more visual imagery than Austen uses, more of the physically excessive, and "whinnying" and "cackling," dehumanizing words, carry the joke beyond the usual limit of the Austen mode. It is more like Charlotte Brontë, who could often plunge into the comic, but was likely to do it more fiercely and scornfully. With Brontë, the absurd more quickly edged into the grotesque and even the sinister; she had an awareness of potential damage not easily contained within a pure comic convention. Porter is much closer to Brontë than to Austen in her description of Dr. Schumann when he catches the evil Spanish twins in another destructive practical joke: he "examined the depths of their eyes for a moment with dismay at their blind, unwinking malignance, their cold slyness—not beasts, though, but human souls."

Or consider this comment on a group of first-class passengers looking down on a steerage meal and feeling that the poor people there were being treated decently: "Murmuring among themselves like pigeons . . . [they] seemed to be vaguely agreed that to mistreat the poor is not right, and they would be the first to say so, at any time. Therefore they were happy to be spared this unpleasant duty, to have their anxieties allayed, their charitable feelings soothed." With the subdued ironic contemplation of the group, and with the series that dexterously encompasses their mood, this could be Austen's; and yet behind the smile-provoking self-deceit there is a kind of moral frailty, a trouble-breeding irresponsibility, and in the steerage sights a degree of wretchedness, that extends beyond the borders of the comic perspective. Here, as elsewhere, Porter's manner is reminiscent of George Eliot's—of a carefully, accurately analytical style that is the agent of a mature psychic and moral understanding. David Scott observes the nondancers: "the born outsiders; the perpetual uninvited; the unwanted; and those who, like himself, for whatever sad reason, refused to join in." The series serves no comic end, speaks for no rationally organizing mind; it makes nice distinctions among the members of a class, somberly, with a mere touch of restrained sympathy to soften the categorical lines. Freytag mentally accuses boat travelers, who "can't seem to find any middle ground between stiffness, distrust, total rejection, or a kind of invasive, gnawing curiosity." The general precision is especially notable in the fresh, climactic joining of the learned "invasive" with the common "gnawing," the latter used uncharacteristically of an external trouble. There is an Eliot-like perceptiveness in Freytag's discovery "about most persons—that their abstractions and generalizations, their Rage for Justice or Hatred of Tyranny or whatever, too often disguised a bitter personal grudge of some sort far removed from the topic apparently under discussion"—and in the matter-of-fact postscript that

Freytag applied this only to others, never to himself. Porter has repeated need for a vocabulary of emotional urgency, of tensions beyond comedy, as in Jenny Brown's concluding observation on the split with her family: "But that didn't keep you from loving them, nor them from loving you, with that strange longing, demanding, hopeless tenderness and bitterness, wound into each other in a net of living nerves." Here the terms for human contradictions are different in kind from those which present simply laughable incongruities. There is an Eliot note both in this and in another passage on the same page in which we are given a saddened sense of necessities which might, but does not, drift into bitterness: "She did not turn to them at last for help, or consolation, or praise, or understanding, or even love; but merely at last because she was incapable of turning away."

The language and syntax reveal Porter's eye for precision, specification, and distinctions. There is the same precision in the definition of Freytag's "hardened expression of self-absorbed, accusing, utter righteousness" and of a stewardess's "unpleasant mixture of furtive insolence and false abasement, the all too familiar look of resentful servility." Freytag himself distinguishes the phases of another personality: "overfamiliar if you made the mistake of being pleasant to him; loud and insolent if he suspected timidity in you; sly and cringing if you knew how to put him in his place." David prefers, he thinks, "Mrs. Treadwell's unpretentious rather graceful lack of moral sense to Jenny's restless seeking outlaw nature trying so hard to attach itself at any or all points to the human beings nearest her: no matter who." Porter confers her own flair for distinctions upon certain characters. Thus Dr. Schumann, planning to go to confession: "he felt not the right contrition, that good habit of the spirit, but a personal shame, a crushing humiliation at the disgraceful nature of what he had to confess." And it is near the end of the book that Jenny, the most sentient and spontaneous character, reflects upon her griefs over love that did not fulfill expectations: "—and what had it been but the childish refusal to admit and accept on some term or other the difference between what one hoped was true and what one discovers to be the mere laws of the human condition?" The clarity in words comes here from the character's clarity of thought, and this in turn from the writer's clarity of mind. Thus an examination of style in the narrower sense of verbal deportment leads, as it repeatedly does, to the style in conceiving—to the "styling" of, we might say—episode and character, and from this on to the ultimate style of creative mind: the grasp of fact and the moral sense.

We have been following Porter's range: from wit to wisdom, from the sense of laughable slip or flaw to the awareness of graver self-deception and self-seeking, and to the feeling for reality that at once cuts through illusion and accepts, among the inevitable facts of life, the emotional pressures that lead to, and entangle, fulfillment and discord. Now beside this central sober work of reflective intelligence and alert conscience put the gay play of the Captain's being driven, by a "lethal cloud of synthetic rose scent" at dinner, to sneeze: "He sneezed three times inwardly, one forefinger pressed firmly to his upper lip as he had been taught to do in childhood, to avoid sneezing in church. Silently he was convulsed with internal explosions, feeling as if his eyeballs would fly out, or his eardrums burst. At last he gave up and felt for his handkerchief, sat up stiffly, head averted from the room, and sneezed steadily in luxurious agony a dozen times with muted sounds and streaming eyes, until the miasma was sneezed out, and he was rewarded with a good nose-blow." This is farce, the comedy of the physical in which mind and feelings are engaged either not at all, or only mechanically: of the perversity of things and circumstances that render one absurd or grotesque with merely formal suffering, not the authentic kind that by stirring sympathy cuts off outrageous laughter. To say that it is in the vein of Smollett is to emphasize both its present rareness outside the work of committed funnymen and the extraordinariness of having it juxtaposed with writing of sensitiveness and thoughtfulness. Farce may have a satirical note, as in this note on Lizzi Spockenkieker's disappointment with Herr Rieber, her would-be lover: "Every other man she had known had unfailingly pronounced the magic word *marriage* before ever he got into bed with her, no matter what came of it in fact." A little earlier, Herr Rieber, a short fat man, having gone through suitable amatory preliminaries, decided that his hour had come and, "with the silent intentness of a man bent on crime," maneuvered Lizzi, a tall thin woman, "to the dark side of the ship's funnel. He gave his prey no warning. . . . It was like embracing a windmill. Lizzi uttered a curious tight squeal, and her long arms gathered him in around his heaving middle. . . . She gave him a good push and they fell backward clutched together, her long active legs overwhelmed him, she rolled him over flat on his back. . . . Lizzi was spread upon him like a fallen tent full of poles." Herr Rieber's passion for flesh and conquest is defeated, turned into grief, by the vigorous surrender that has swept him into unorthodox subordination, and he can get rid of his victorious victim, who is in a "carnivorous trance," only by gasping to her in agony that they are watched by Bebe, the fat and generally seasick dog of Professor Hutten. Bebe, only three feet away, "the folds of his nose twitching, regarded them with an expression of animal cunning that most embarrassingly resembled human knowledge of the seamy side of life." After all the modern solemnities about sex, this sheer farce—with the farcical morality of the dog as grave censor—is reassuring evidence that a fuller, more flexible, less doleful sense of sexual conduct can be recovered.

For a final note on Porter's great range, we can contrast this hilarious Smollettian jest with two quite dissimilar passages. One is the vivid imaging, in her visible gestures, of the inner unwellness of a Spanish countess: "Thumbs turned in lightly to the palm, the hands moved aimlessly from the edge of the table to her lap, they clasped and unclasped themselves, spread themselves flat in the air, closed, shook slightly, went to her hair, to the bosom of her gown, as if by a life of their own separate from the will of the woman herself, who sat quite still otherwise, features a little rigid, bending over to read the dinner card beside her plate." Though here there is a more detailed visualization of the symbolizing object, the feeling for the troubled personality is like Charlotte Brontë's. To this countess, Dr. Schumann feels attracted, guiltily. After seeing her, "He lay down with his rosary in his fingers, and began to invite sleep, darkness, silence, that little truce of God between living and dying; he put out of his mind, with deliberate intention to forget forever, the last words of that abandoned lost creature; nettles, poisoned barbs, fish hooks, her words clawed at his mind with the terrible malignance of the devil-possessed, the soul estranged from its kind." In the meditative element, in the imaging of a remembered frenzy, and most of all in the particular moral sense that leads to the words "soul estranged from its kind," the account is reminiscent of Conrad.

Range means contrasts such as these. Often, too, there is direct jux-taposition of different styles. Porter can write page after page of sono-rous periods—plausible, not overplayed—for Professor Hutten's din-ner disquisitions to a captive audience, and then shift bluntly to Frau Hutten's perspective: "He was boring them to death again, she could feel it like vinegar in her veins"—another trenchant simile. Here are two ways of commenting on intelligence: the cultivated irony of "[Elsa's] surprising lapse into everyday common sense," and, on the next page, Jenny's breezy colloquial hyperbole for the Cuban students, "The trouble . . . is simply that they haven't been born yet." David Scott solemnly claims a high disgust for sexual binges: "He had felt superior to his acts and to his partners in them, and altogether re-deemed and separated from their vileness by that purifying contempt"; Jenny retorts, with pungent plainness, "Men love to eat themselves sick and then call their upchuck by high-sounding names." Or there is the innocent, flat-voiced irony of Porter's comment on the "lyric prose" of newspapers reporting parties "lavish and aristocratic—the terms are synonymous, they believe"—and on newly boarded pas-sengers wandering "about in confusion with the air of persons who have abandoned something of great importance on shore, though they cannot think what it is"; and beside this the blunt force appropriate to a tactical thought of Herr Rieber's: "A man couldn't be too cautious with that proper, constipated type, no matter how gamey she looked."

iv

In their slangy vigor or insouciance, their blunt and easy immediacy, their spurning of the genteel, their casual clinicality, their nervous grip on strain and tension, some of these passages have an air that, whether in self-understanding or self-love, we call "modern." The novel has many such, and they evidence in another way the range of Porter's style. However, the modernity need be stressed only enough to acknowledge that the style, like any well-wrought individual style, cannot be wholly placed by comparison with well-known styles. My principal points, nevertheless, have been that Porter's style has strong affiliations with the Austen and Eliot styles, that its main lines are traditional rather than innovating, and that it is markedly devoid of namable singulari-ties, mannerisms, private idioms, self-indulgent or striven-for uniquenesses that give a special coloration. These points are interrelated; to some extent, they are different emphases of a central truth.

To claim for a writer affinities with Austen and Eliot (and to note, as evidence of her variety, occasional reminiscences of other writers) may seem faint praise in an age quick to think, in many areas, we have left all that behind us. The procedure does have its risks, and a disavowal or two may be in order. To note a resemblance in styles is not to make premature judgments of overall merit, which involves other problems not dealt with here, and which in the end must be left to history. It is not to suggest influences, imitation, idle repetition, failure of originality, or limitedness. On the contrary, it is a way of suggesting superiority in the individual achievement; here is a writer working independently, composing out of her own genius, and yet in her use of the language exhibiting admirable qualities that seem akin to those of distinguished predecessors. It is a way of proposing, perhaps, that she has got hold of some central virtues of the language, virtues whether of strength or grace, that tend to recur and that, whatever the modification of them from writer to writer, may in essence be inseparable from good writing. To say this is to imply a traditional style, or core of elements of style. To hypothesize a tradition is precarious, since the word seems likely to make critics either a bit solemn, seven-candled, and hieratic on the one hand, or, on the other, self-righteous, flambeaux-lighted, and rebellious with an anticlerical fervor. I venture the word, not to beg a theoretical issue or invoke a charm or scorn a curse, but to suggest figuratively a group of long-enduring ways of using the language, apparent norms of utility, representative workings-out of possibility. These would constitute a discipline of eccentricity but not a constraint on originality; to call a writer a traditionalist in style would involve the old paradox of unique personality seizing on the universal thing or mode.

It is in such terms that one must approach Porter's style. Though it looks easy rather than hard, it has a certain elusiveness that makes it not quite easy to account for. It would be difficult to imitate or parody, for what is most open to copying or travestying is the novelty, the idiosyncrasy, the raw ego in words that betokens a flight from or an inability to get hold of some persisting "nature" in the art forms of one's own tongue. Porter has a very wide vocabulary, but no pet vocabulary;

she has considerable skill in compositional patterns but no agonized specializations of order. She is exact and explicit; she eschews mystery in the medium without losing the mystery in the matter. The solidity of her writing, of the *how* that implies the *what*, we signify by naming her peers. Her variety appears in an obviously wide spectrum of tones and attitudes, rarely with the pen as pardoner of all, or the stylus as stiletto, but within these extremes modulating easily among the contemptible, the laughable, the pitiable, the evasive laudable, and, most of all, the ever-present contradictory—of face and heart, belief and deed, illusion and fact—that regularly compels one to look anew at all familiar surfaces.

III. 13

Salesmen's Deaths: Documentary and Myth

(1969)

"Well, Eudora Welty has already done it," the girl said severely over her drink. "And a damsight better."

This was in an exchange of prejudices about Arthur Miller's *Death of a Salesman*, then in its first flush of fame. Like others of its kind, this exchange brought forth more stiff-chinned insistence than high-brow discrimination, more temper than temperateness. I was drawn toward the girl's side. In this there may have been something personal, however vicarious. In Athens, Ohio, long before, I had been a friend of John Rood, who later published Welty's "Death of a Traveling Salesman," her first story to see print; I was a young instructor and Rood a young printer, and we had a sharp eye for the shortcomings of people not so young. Later, in Baton Rouge, I had known well Brooks, Warren, and Albert Erskine, whose *Southern Review* was next to publish Welty—three stories in a year. Now in Seattle I had been hearing a good deal about Welty's appearance at a writer's conference at the University of Washington several years before. Such threads, slender as they were, might have helped pull me to the Welty camp.

The girl was wrong, though—not in her admiration but in "has already done it." It's the *it* that's off. The Welty *it* and the Miller *it* ("thing," as we would say now) are not the same. The death of a salesman is likely to be one thing in a lyric tale, another thing in a very stageworthy play, of course. But the generic difference is not primary. Rather, the two deaths take place in different locales, and they speak for different themes. What's more, the themes are tied to the locales; the locale of either work could not support the kind of symbolic statement made by the other work.

"The Death of a Traveling Salesman" appeared in 1936, when Welty was twenty-seven; *Death of a Salesman* was produced in 1949, when Miller was thirty-four. Something might be made of the fact that hers was beginner's work, his the product of a fifth year of professional writing; hers prewar, his postwar. On double grounds her work ought to be more ingenuous, his sophisticated; yet beneath a formal simplicity her sensibility is very mature, and beneath theatrical sophistication, his sensibility is at times naïve. No profit there. We go deeper when we work with a more superficial contrast: he writes of New York, she of Mississippi; he of urban life, she not only of the country but of the backwoods. By *urban life* I do not mean the daily mores and habits of thickly populated areas, but a more deep-lying spirit or way of life that flourishes in megalopolis. The "lonely crowd" has become a cliché, and Willy Loman does talk several times of being "lonely." Partly this is a justification for having a hotel-room girlfriend; partly, no doubt, he speaks a literal truth. But loneliness is a minor motif; it is not Willy's real trouble. His urban malaise is centered in the dream of "success"; his ideal is Ben, "success incarnate," "rich" at twenty-one, master of an "authoritative air"; Willy's chief fantasy is of "friends," "contacts," of his own irresistible personality; he is sure that his boys will "get ahead" of others, "lick the world," move into "great things ahead," advance by a "very big deal"; for them, "the sky's the limit," and they "will end up big." For Willy, death is to be the last big deal; Biff asks, "What is this supposed to do, make a hero out of you?" Willy's life-insurance proceeds are to propel him into vicarious glory through Biff. There are verbal hints of a Faustian grab of divinity: Biff, as football hero, "looks like a young god," and in turn the insurance money, Willy thinks, will make Biff "worship me." Linda's inquiry is not much heeded: "Why must everybody conquer the world?"

The yearning is not merely to get ahead, but to get ahead of someone else; success must be conspicuous; others must bow. This is the urban form of what is sometimes called "The American Dream"— urban, because megalopolis alone provides enough others to triumph over, enough human mirrors to reflect triumph and thus prove it real. Glory-seekers always turn to the city. Frank Merriwells, Tom Swifts, and Alger heroes never achieve glory by farming.

This is why Miller is not doing the same thing that Welty did ear-

lier. We should not make too much of the chance resemblances, interesting as they are: that the leading characters are both salesmen, that
they fall easily into the routine verbal artifices of bonhomie, that both
are "lonely," that they feel ill or strange while driving, that their cars
seem not under full control, that the men die in or near their cars. R. J.
Bowman's crucial experiences all take place in the country, and this
wholly different world means a wholly different theme. One hero
grieves for an unachieved divinity, the other suffers from an unachieved
community. Loman would triumph, Bowman yearns to belong.

With Loman, the sense of failure is the door to death; with Bowman,
the onset of death is the door to a mute sense of failure. When I reread
the story, my first response was regret that death has so conspicuous a
role; it seemed to overload the story, create an excess of event, deflect
us from the thematic center to the spectacle of finality. I sensed it as the
product of a young artist's fear of inadequate substance. However, in
thinking the death gratuitous, I was of course wrong; it is so thoroughly woven into the fabric of the story, from the very beginning, that
what happens near the car on the road is simply the formal completion
of a pattern. During the drive toward Beulah, before we learn of the
pounding heart, there are repeated images of Bowman as victim, as
helpless, as dependent, as regressive—all suggesting a decline from
adult fullness of life. Clearly death belonged to the original concept of
the story.

In first thinking the death nonessential, clearly I wanted the story to
be about the salesman's soul and not his health. Thematic death and
thematic salesmanship seemed to pull in opposite directions (here I
was shifting my doubt from execution to "original concept"). If it is
the inner stirrings of imminent death that stimulate the long painful
awareness on which the story centers, the dying person need hardly be
a salesman; the subject is simply the response of consciousness, anybody's, to monitory signs in the physical being. If it is the life of the
salesman that is being assessed, this can be done without killing him
off; the physical and psychic debility begotten by a severe and not really
concluded illness can occasion an acute sense of nonmembership.

It is worthwhile recording my false starts, for the questions they
ask are answered specifically in the text. When Bowman is finding, or
imagining, a faint thread of emotional contact with Sonny's woman,

the text tells us: "But he wanted to leap up, to say to her, I have been sick and I found out then, only then, how lonely I am. Is it too late? My heart puts up a struggle inside me, and you may have heard it, protesting against emptiness." Here we have it: the loneliness is the primary reality, and it antedates the present crisis, which has the function of bringing it to consciousness. Loneliness, then, is the salesman's condition; the role of the salesman is the right one for the human figure seen in his capacity for isolation. The writer might stop at exhibiting the state of affairs; Welty takes a big step further by making Bowman's loneliness enter, however mutely or imperfectly, into his self-knowledge. Heart trouble, we may say, leads to the troubled heart. Yet in taking this step Welty is moved by an ironic sense that might seem to belong to a much older writer: what we come to know, we hardly know in time. "Is it too late?" The ultimate symbol of the too-late is death; death, then, is as intrinsic to the story as is the fact that Bowman is a salesman. Too-lateness is virtually a condition of learning, as in the tragic structuring of experience.

Welty's theme opens out. Miller particularizes his salesman; Loman is topical rather than transcendent. He is the salesman as salesman, a sociological specimen; we are invited to consider the problems of this mode of life; at the end Charlie lectures about the type, like the Doctor in a morality play. Bowman, as we have seen, "had" to be a salesman; yet his reality is not sociological but symbolic. Welty's salesman is everyman in a characteristic tendency toward the "casual" existence, in a secret commitment to flux. He is everyman as mobile, and hence unattached, and hence ultimately solitary; his is an apartness that is "human" because it derives from a strong element in our nature (not the special separateness of the saint or the perverse alienation of the sick person who affects outsiderism in rebuke of society and hence in praise of self). The habit of impermanence, of withdrawnness, may grow out of the life innocently chosen; conversely, the disposition to be on the move and to avoid human commitments may determine choice of life. Solitudinarianism is rarely absolute, though; if it totally masters a personality, it is hardly a subject for dramatic treatment. It is available for art when it is representative, that is, when it is accompanied by a grasping for ties. The tie half grasped at may be only the nexus of cash or charisma; Bowman mechanically, if not resolutely, reaches for both of these. But what is much more important is the tentative, hardly formulated, reaching out for essential communication, for a sense of membership.

From the beginning Bowman feels a cut-offness, a separating silence in the world. He is "angered" by "the road without signposts." He has not got "close enough to anyone" to ask the way. Then there comes one of the fresh and powerful images that appear throughout the story: "The stares of these distant people had followed him solidly like a wall, impenetrable, behind which they turned back after he had passed." He drives past "bare" trees, through "dead" leaves. "No one had been along this way ahead of him." Then, suddenly, the "shotgun house" and the laconic but not hostile woman: the transition from the impersonal, self-enclosed world to a human, tentatively accepting microcosm. However, this central experience of the story starts with striking errors by Bowman: he takes the woman who receives him to be "old," to be "fifty," to be "stupid." Why the mistakes? Surely their function is to be a subtle index of his cut-offness; he is not even in tune with the facts. His "humble motion, almost a bow" annoys him, "betraying his weakness": the relationship of routine courtesy, the acknowledgment of another, is a difficult step out of isolation. Once they are inside, he does not understand her style—the few words she speaks, "silently bestowing her presence on him." Then another of the forceful Welty images: his eyes, "stiffly wide," are "fixed . . . on the woman's clasped hands as though she held the cord they were strung on." The connection is mechanical, involuntary, not free and spontaneous. Bowman resents the resemblance between Sonny's hat and his own; Sonny's "seemed to insult" his. He cannot even "state his case." His incapacity is summed up: he cannot "appear either penitent or authoritative." He cannot be either humble or dominant, that is, practice even the one-sided relationships that substitute for a genuine mutuality.

Instinctively he acts as if what I have called the nexus of cash or charisma might hold. He falls two or three times into the hearty style of commerce, with "his old voice, chatty, confidential, inflected for selling shoes." "Fine!" he exclaims when help is offered, "Fine!" "Yes sir, you bet, thanks"—for the drink. If enthusiasm wins, money talks. "By paying the hotel doctor he had proved his recovery." He promises Sonny, "I'm going to pay." But Sonny refuses him "belligerently": "We don't take money for such." Bowman cannot buy what is given, be "authoritative" as a mode of, or substitute for, belonging. Welty is very skillful in having him, as he leaves, "put all [his] money" under the lamp; it is a final try for the lesser bond—the cash nexus—with the community to which he does not belong.

This after the painful sensing of, opening of consciousness toward, half-tasting of a special intimacy that betokens, not a private affair, but a shared community. Even in this apparently aging and dull woman Bowman is aware of a quiet vibrancy of being that releases urgent impulses in himself. "Perhaps he might embrace this woman." His heart "should be holding love like other hearts. It should be flooded with love." Yet this imagined leap into a new relationship is embarrassing to his habitual way of feeling: it disturbs him "that he might . . . have tried by simple words and embraces to communicate some strange thing—something which seemed always to have just escaped him." Hence with relief he anticipates departure; he "could feel . . . the readying of his blood for motion and for hurrying away." The counter-pull of the mobile and the casual ("motion" instead of emotion) appears decisive; he is sure he "would never speak to her now, for the time was past." But he still feels, if reluctantly, a possibility or openness in the immediate situation: "he hesitated to rise and stand beside her." It is "as if," in pointing to Sonny in the distance, "she had shown him something secret, part of her life, but had offered no explanation," as if "she had made a silent declaration equivalent to his own." But then he "felt how," when Sonny entered, she "went to the other man's side." Ironically, Bowman's pull inward works again: "he longed to stay." "Those people cherished something he could not see. . . . Between them they had a conspiracy." Yet he pleads, "Let me stay"; they should "know . . . his real need."

He is granted at least a pro-tem share in the community. His being taken along to get the hidden whiskey is almost an initiation into the mysteries. He is fed. He moves closer into the circle by seeing better: the woman is young, and she is Sonny's woman; he learns, "She goin' to have a baby." When there is no longer anything remote or mysterious, one is less an alien. And yet the very definition of the situation that makes it understandable may not make it penetrable: "The only secret was the ancient communication between two people." He had wanted to love and communicate; here are love and communication. They are inaccessible to him.

We remember all the dramatic signs of his nonparticipation. Heartiness had been of no avail, nor money. He had offered matches to start the fire, but Sonny had insisted on borrowing fire; the old rituals of the self-contained community were not to be broken in upon, nothing could be contributed from without. Bowman is now "through with asking favors"; asking implies membership, which is simply not open to him. "They had not meant," he realizes, "to give him their bed." But he cannot quell the yearning: "he wished that the child were his." Here would have been communication and continuity—alternatives to, and denials of, the casual, stop-and-go, disengaged life of episodes. The life of episodes ends in itself, sterile; it is the Negative Way that human beings often choose, but a secular Negative Way with no mystical union to crown the solitary journey.

I have asserted the importance of locale in Miller's play and Welty's story: the city for competition and conquest, the country for mutuality and community. The scenes are not interchangeable. The city displays crowds to be got ahead of, the country a society to be entered into. In one, man is the aggressor; in the other, the sharer. In one, society must belong to the individual; in the other, the individual must belong to society. Miller and Welty give us complementary pictures of the impulses toward relationship in men who have gone it alone—the obsession with glory, the yearning for membership. Though Willy might be a sort of Tamburlaine *manqué*, Miller cuts him down into the peddler and his problems, the peddler who in place of the old grandiose pursues the new tawdry, and who never knows it—as if the urban milieu itself shrinks men and their ends. But Sonny and his woman are the symbolic human family, at once domestic and societal; the rural no-man's-land becomes the world. And Bowman is an everyman, not a midget everyman, but a true everyman as solitary, and, above all, the most meaningful solitary—the one for whom, if only too late, solitude is not enough, and who knows it.

Sonny and his woman give Bowman a brief taste of partial communion as he passes from a long solitude to a still-longer one. Welty dramatizes, without clamor or inflation, what has since been inflated into a clamorous cliché—that man dies alone. It is an ancient theme:

we can see it five hundred years ago in the original *Everyman*. That Everyman was summoned to "a long journey": Bowman stops for a while during a literal trip that, when he comes to "the road's end," we see as a metaphorical journey. We think naturally of a pilgrim's progress; we recall that earlier Bowman "seemed to be going the wrong way" and it came to him that he "was simply lost," like Bunyan's pilgrim. But what reminds us still more of Bunyan is that the destination Bowman hopes to reach is Beulah. In *Pilgrim's Progress* the country of Beulah is at the end of the terrestrial journey "upon the borders of heaven." Welty, of course, may have in mind no more than the actual Beulah, a village in Bolivar County in northwest Mississippi. (In the 1930s it would have been accessible only by gravel road, and would the more have seemed a long and hot "fifty miles away from the last town.") In one sense, of course, Beulah has to be taken literally; Bowman has been there before. But if only some remote physical spot were wanted, many other Mississippi town names would have served as well.

Beulah cannot help being evocative, and the more it is so, the richer the ironies. It is difficult to forget Bunyan's Beulah, or alternatively those later and lesser offspring of the Protestant imagination influenced by Bunyan—the "Beulah Land" hymns. In Bunyan's Beulah the air is "very sweet and pleasant"; birds sing and "flowers appear" daily; Christian and Hopeful find "abundance of what they had sought for in all their pilgrimage." The "Beulah Land" of E. P. Stites and John R. Sweney is also "heaven's borderland"; it is a "land of corn and wine," "sweet perfume," and "flowers . . . never fading." The "Beulah Land" of Mary M. Hughes is a "beautiful land" with "meadows fair." Such images of delight introduce an initial irony: Beulah is indeed not what Bowman has found in erring to a cold and barren road's end. What is more, *Beulah* means "married," and in Bunyan's Beulah "the contract between the bride and the bridegroom was renewed": the enduring relationship alien to Bowman's way of life.

Yet the opposite irony is present too: if a geographical Beulah has eluded Bowman, he has at least had a glimpse of the spiritual Beulah of tradition. He has seen the "married" state and a kind of renewal of contract, and with painful longing he has half reached toward it; Sonny and his woman do offer him an "abundance" of what they can, literally of the "corn and wine" named in the hymn. So, like Christian and Hopeful, he "solaced [himself] there for a season." Now another irony dawns on us: the spiritual quasi Beulah, stumbled upon in place of the lost mundane Beulah, is entered only at a price. Here is the deepest resemblance between old tale and new: whatever of serenity or joy belongs to Beulah comes just before death—for both the Bunyan and the Welty pilgrims. From Beulah, Christian goes on into the river of death (in one Beulah hymn the speaker faces "the river's brink," in another "look[s] away across the sea"). It is hard not to think of this river of death when we read that Bowman "listened uneasily," "heard something," asked, and was told, "You might hear the stream" (the actual Beulah is not far from the Mississippi). And when he is preparing to leave during the night, "he heard the stream running, the fire dying, and . . . his heart beating"—the heart that is about to fail him. The final irony, only hinted at by the analogy with Bunyan, is the contrast between the older day's Beulah and its river beyond, and those of the present. Then, the dangerous crossing led to a glory visible in the distance; now, there is only a nullity by the car on the road.

Miller's drama of death drifts toward documentary, Welty's toward myth. The mythic is there only as it should be—an implicit presence that seems a casual by-product of far-ranging imagination rather than a consciously sought dimension, that enhances the moving power of the story as we respond to it spontaneously, and that we formally identify only when we go back and look a second time.

It is remarkable how well Welty's apprentice work holds up, how much of substance it has, how much of imaginative resonance and subtlety—and with how much sensibility and art it invites reflective rereading.

III. 14

All the King's Men as Tragedy

(1947)

In the history of English literature it is pretty much of a truism that by the eighteenth century, tragedy was in a state of polite decay and the novel was rising rapidly toward a long-lasting status as the preeminent literary form. Under the reign of neoclassicism, and of the following pre-romantic sentimentalism, something happened to the tragic sense—a something which included the growth of scientific rationalism, the pressure of prudential upon transcendental values, and at the same time a turning of the life of feeling outward toward the easily pitiable and away from the ironic discords that are the center of tragic life. In direction the novel was social or even sociological; its concern was less the troubled being than the troubles between people, and these by and large were soluble. The characters were for the most part whole and easily placed (some of Richardson's are exceptions)—Joneses, Allworthys, Brambles, Evelinas, the Bennet daughters, Micawbers, Beckys, Grantlys, Patternes. The perception and the imagination that produced such characters were excellent. But the tragic sense of things does not go away, however much Enlightenment we have, and since mid-nineteenth century various novelists have been moved by it. George Eliot, overly condescended to now, begins to cut back into the inner man; the later Hardy goes further; James, Conrad, and Joyce lay hold of inner obscurities, parts that do not match; and Faulkner seizes upon disruptive urgencies and intensities. Robert Penn Warren's *All the King's Men* is a significant element in the recovery, by fiction, of the tragic mode.

Recovery is probably the right word, for Elizabethan, and possibly Greek, tragedy has made a mark on *All the King's Men*. Shakespeare won the pit, and this novel is a best seller, which is to say that it has a level of dramatic tension more widely accessible than one expects in the philosophic novel. The plot involves public figures, but the record is finally of the private agony (as with Macbeth and Oedipus). The author begins with history and politics, but the real subject is the nature of man: Warren is no more discussing American politics than *Hamlet* is discussing Danish politics. Then there are the ironic intrafamily confrontations and injuries, the repercussions of generation upon generation, as with Hamlet and Orestes—a type of situation which, it may be observed in passing, Aristotle praises. As with the older tragedy, all this can look like steaming melodrama if one wants to stop at the deed as deed and simply forget about meanings. But as in the older poetic tragedy there is, beneath all the explicitnesses, a core of obscure conflicts, of motives partly clouded, of calculations beset by the uncalculated, of moral impasses in which both action and inaction may damn, and Oresteian duty be Oresteian guilt.

All the King's Men is the tragedy of incomplete personalities whose interrelationship is rooted, in part, in the impulse to completeness—in the "agony of will." Anne Stanton cannot find it in the uncertain, unfocused young Jack Burden, sardonic in a detachment closer to alienation than objectivity; by contrast the rude, better-directioned power of Willie Stark acts compellingly upon her. Dr. Adam Stanton, the man of idea, cut off, driving himself with ascetic, self-destructive violence, seeks, though apparently acting unwillingly, a liberating public deed which allies him with Willie Stark, the man of fact—the split between whom and himself, as symbolic modern characters, provides the explicit philosophic groundwork of the story. Jack Burden, the narrator, rootless, shrewd, speculative, but unintegrated, lacking, so to speak, a personality, gives his life an appearance of personal form by his close attachment to Willie, who has cohesion and aim and a genius for the action that organizes and excites—and that still calls up slow questions, questions which Jack, in evidence of his never-quite-blotted-out iota of grace, always keeps asking. Everybody's needs are ironically summed up in the grotesque gunman, Sugar Boy, the stutterer who loves Willie because Willie "can talk so good." Willie completes the others, whose need is a centering and a commitment; but Willie cannot complete himself. In a complex of polarities that are structurally important throughout the novel, Willie also seeks completion in them—an identification with idea and tradition, and with the asker of questions in whom he senses an entryway into a realm beyond facts. For in Willie, the man of fact, there is the paradox of action: action completes and yet is incomplete; action is necessary but is never pure; action begs to be undertaken but imposes its conditions. Adam cannot sufficiently accept the conditions of action, and Willie cannot sufficiently escape them. But if Willie cannot save himself from his gift, he can, as is needful in tragedy, understand himself; the man of action becomes the self-critic in action when, in every phase of the hospital drama, he actually, if not overtly, repudiates his working half-truths.

A plurality of heroes is one symbol of a riven world. There are in Warren's novel other partial men; there is especially Jack, whose story, he says, is Willie's story: he is the riven world which produces Willie and serves him and yet always keeps a last thin aloofness from him, and which through him comes to a possibly saving understanding—the note of hope, of spiritual discovery, which completes tragedy. Jack is a scarred Ancient Mariner telling what happened and what he learned; he stubbornly tells it in a style which re-creates things as they were to him, without benefit of the exceptions he might make in his maturity.

I have stressed Warren's belonging to the tragic tradition because his book has brought into focus a very disturbing situation—our sheer incompetence to read tragedy. A large number of critics have beaten Warren around the ears and cried that he should have written a political melodrama. He woos a long-neglected Melpomene, and is told he should be doing a carmagnole with an up-to-date Clio. He tries to give his readers the universal in the unique form which is the individual work of art, and they bawl at him for not sticking to social platitudes. He gives them metaphysics, and they call pettishly for sociology. Well, he does give them some social documentation, all right, but he gives it to them the hard way: he pictures for them the spiritual condition— the decline of tradition, the loss of an integrating force, the kind of split—which results in Willie-as-hero; he makes it still harder for them

by pointing out the kind of greatness Willie had to have to be to a society what he was. Warren says, I take it, that a universal complement
has to be a little more than a melodrama villain. But they do not want
understanding—because it involves the pain of self-scrutiny? They
know in advance that Willie, insofar as he is Humpty, is a bad egg who
ought to have had a fall; we should simply and happily hoot him. And
feel ever so warm a glow inside. But we can get a warm glow from
liquor or likker, and some prefer chemical analysis.

Most of the daily and weekly reviewers who tell America what to
read still have the simplified view of *belles lettres* deriving from the
eighteenth century. Of some two score of them whose reviews of *All
the King's Men* I have been able to see, precisely two have a complete
grasp of the work as tragedy: Henry Rago in *Commonweal* and Brain-
ard Cheney in the Nashville *Banner,* both of whom do brilliant analyses. Four others come close: Victor Hamm in the Milwaukee *Journal,*
Paul Engle in the Chicago *Tribune,* Granville Hicks in the *American
Mercury,* and Lee Casey in the *Rocky Mountain News.* Surely these
publications would not come to mind as the first six most likely sources
of critical light in America. But by their diversity and distribution
they establish the public intelligibility of Warren's novel; it is clearly
not a work for club members only. Besides these six, about fourteen—
in all, a little less than half of those I have seen—recognize that the
novel is of philosophic dimensions. George Mayberry of the *New Republic* and James Wood of the *Saturday Review* read the book very
intelligently; but the philosophic insight of others is often neither large
nor secure. Most reviews are laudatory, some of them grudgingly, and
others clearly uncertain why. The *Daily Oklahoman* headlines its review, "Nothing To Do But Like This Gay Old Cuss." From such a
journalistic cradle, presumably typical, it is, paradoxically, not too far
to the mature journeyman critics, a dozen or so of them, who provide the real problem for discussion. They are the ones who fear that
Warren fails to show the dangers of dictatorship, or who outright ac-
cuse him of defending or aiding fascism. If these were all journalistic
hillbillies, one could shed a tear for the darkness of the underbrush
and forget it; but they furnish part of the candlepower of some of the
stronger fluorescent lights in Megalopolis—the New York *Times, PM,*
the *Nation,* and the papers that subscribe to John Cournos and Sterling

North. Further, Fred Marsh of the *Herald-Tribune* fails so completely to understand the book that he finally hypothesizes that it may be "intended only as melodrama in modern prose."

It would be easy to compile a florilegium of critical quaintnesses. Only two reviewers, for instance, indicate awareness that the management of the religious theme at the end is more than a pious postlude. The *New Yorker* and the Chicago *Sun* both regard Jack Burden as an interloper; *PM* and Sterling North regard the Cass Mastern episode, which is of high structural importance, as an intrusion. Most of the commentators on style should go to Henry Rago of *Commonweal* for a lesson on the quality and functional role of the style. Of three reviewers who use the word *slick,* only Robert Gorham Davis of the *Times* adduces evidence—two sentences, both of which, he fails to realize, are indications of the attitude of Jack Burden; the second he particularly mistreats by lifting it, without explanation, from a bitterly ironic context. But what is one to think of reviewers' sense of style in general when he can find applied to Warren's writing two such beautifully irreconcilable judgments as those of Fred Marsh in the *Herald-Tribune* and Laban C. Smith in the Chicago *Sun?* The former's words: "elaborately stylized prose (since nobody ever either talks or writes like this)." Smith's comment on figures of speech: "most of them very familiar if not trite, and the full development of these figures and their repetition frequently corrupts . . . a strong and intelligent style."

But the heart of the matter is this: why can so few critics read tragedy, and what are the implications of this disability of theirs? In the muddling over *All the King's Men* we can see several main tendencies, overlapping and not always properly distinguishable; perhaps they are all facets of a central cultural phenomenon. As a group the reviewers exhibit certain habits of mind that have been familiar since the eighteenth century—habits which appeared as tragedy began to disappear and which, as long as they are general and uncorrected, are, without necessarily intending to be so, hostile to tragedy and to the insights made possible by the tragic sense. Perhaps the presence of these habits means simply the absence of the tragic habit of mind. Then the novelist faces the hard task of creating it for himself. The habits against which he will have to contend are the puritanical, the sentimental, the scientific, the social-topical, and the lotus-eating or slothful.

The puritanism that one finds in the reviews of *All the King's Men* is of the pale, literal, unhand-me-sir kind that, when Troy is falling, complains of, or even rises to a certain vice-squad petulance against, naughty words on the wall. Eunice Ross Perkins grieves, in the Macon *Telegraph,* that there is "no really fine" woman in the book and that Warren has not caught sight of the really very nice things in the South. The same obtuseness appears in two ecclesiastical organs, with which *Commonweal* is in encouraging contrast: Harold C. Gardiner in *America* abuses the book as blasphemous and immoral, and Daniel Poling in the *Christian Herald* regrets that Warren "goes into the gutter." Warren is trying to tell them about Troy, and they call for The Story of the Good Little Boy. A man's search for truth is too-tough substance for these sentimental hand-me-downs from a simpler day. A cousin of theirs, Ethel Dexter of the Springfield *Republican,* wonders how women can really fall in love with such a fellow as Willie. These are familiar cries for familiar pluckings of the heartstrings. Give the cries a political twist, and they become demands for praise of reigning dogmas, and caveats against inquiry into underlying truths.

The scientific mind turns from aesthetic problems to the provenience of the book, the man behind the book, the book's effect on society, etc.: a perverse factuality trespasses on the domain of the imagination. Certain reviewers cannot separate Willie Stark from Huey Long; some actually fear that Warren is not *biographically* accurate. Such minds cannot distinguish fact and fiction, the point of departure and the imaginative journey; they cannot realize that a few biographical facts are merely, and can be no more than, an alterable design for a mold into which the artist pours such dramatic body and such values as his insight permits. How can these people read Shakespeare? Some of them, self-consciously sharp, scream "special pleading"; Sterling North and Robert Davis consider the novel a personal apologia, an apologia, Davis says outright, for having edited the *Southern Review* at Louisiana State University. It may be remarked parenthetically that Davis' criterion, if applied with any sort of consistency at all, will deprive most universities of their faculties and most moneymaking periodicals of their reviewers. What is of critical interest, however, is not Davis' squinting detectivism, but the pseudoscientific, psychology-ridden cast of mind, with which he is obviously well satisfied, that makes it literally impossible for him to read and understand the literary evidence. He cannot tell what the story says; he simply cannot grasp the author's detachment and integrity.

This category of incompetence overlaps the next, where we find the science-and-society frame of mind. Historically, this kind of reader represents the main tradition of the English novel, which finds its tensions in social patterns, in problems of relationship in society rather than in the individual. But societies change, and with the evolutionary friction the social becomes the topical. To us, in our day, the social appears as the real, and atmospheric pressures tend to convince the writer that literature ought to be an adjunct of societal reordering. Now this concept, if taken as profoundly as possible, could accommodate high literature; Warren *is* concerned with society: his very subject is the split personality of an age. But the self-conscious practitioner of social consciousness does not want such radical investigations; he has already done the diagnosis, and all he wants is a literary pharmacist to make up the prescribed vitamin and sulfa pills.

The social-topical critics, bound by their inflexibly applied theory of literature, cannot read the individual work. But there are degrees of subtlety among them. Granville Hicks, as I have already said, gives so sensitive an account of *All the King's Men* that he does not belong with the table-pounders at all—except for one small point: he notes Shaw's and Steffens' insistence on changing a corrupt society, and adds that Warren says nothing of socialism. That is all; yet it suggests that Hicks wants the novel to do something which is hardly in its province. But he holds to his dogma with such tact that he is not blinded to the goodness of what has been done. It is quite a step down, therefore, to Saxe Commins, who in the Cleveland *News* pays formal tribute to Warren's various skills but goes on to express regret for Warren's indifference to Negroes and "the people who should be the concern of the state." Commins' social concern is familiar: he wants a conventional conflict developed by standardized dramatic symbols; he wants the novelist to be a one-man pressure group instead of a man of tragic vision. So, dogma-bound, he gravely warns that the novel serves to glamorize the man in the "bullet-proof limousine" and thus to "invite disaster." Diana Trilling of the *Nation* imagines that Warren is defaming Hegel's relativism and hence gets things so out of focus that she perpetrates an extraordinary series of misreadings. She calls Jack Burden's Twitch theory "embarrassingly maudlin"—and completely misses Jack's repudiation of the theory. She says that Jack's "moral awareness" is of "low quality" and that he has a fine eye but "no equivalent gift of inward vision." She utterly misses his long search for truth, his reflectiveness, his later understanding of Cass Mastern, his insight into the Adam-Willie cleavage. What must a man do to exhibit vision? Declaim the Bill of Rights? Trilling thinks the hospital is meant to establish Willie as a benefactor and that Warren approves of Willie because Willie is Jack's "hero." Even a strong commitment to liberal dogma seems hardly sufficient to explain, in a justly distinguished professional critic of fiction, such gross oversimplification of what a book says.

Dawn Powell gives the readers of *PM* little more than flippancies; but she closes with the warning that increasing regard for the strong-man legend may be paving the way "for a really successful Willie Stark." Sterling North's purely literary comments are too genuinely stupid to warrant mention; what he lacks in insight he makes up in insolence and malevolence. But is he, in his political and moral judgments, really the honest barbarian he looks? Beats there a heart of gold below the red neck? Or is he the slicker in the backroom who knows what the customers want? Are there pleasant little pills in the innocent, downturned palm?

Diana Trilling, Dawn Powell, and Sterling North—a pretty bedful. And when we find the somewhat primly schoolmasterish Robert Davis' head on the same pillow—he assures us that Warren is playing Parson Weems to Huey's Washington—the picture has a wonderfully satisfying completeness. For what do they all do but pull the covers up over their heads and refuse to listen to the real warnings about the society they are so preciously and loudly concerned about? They have taken the symptom for the disease, and they want the symptom denounced; out, out, dark pimple. When an artist takes the symptom and traces it to radical causes—and when he even shows the kind of consciousness that nourishes the causes and with a severely disciplined

hopefulness shows a possibly saving alteration in that consciousness—
they mistake him for a germ-carrier. The artist proceeds from the region to the civilization, and from the civilization to the dangers of dis-
integration implicit in human life; this is tragedy; but they cannot read
it, and in their confusion they are as complacent as if they were pro-
tecting Humpty down there under the covers.

Before we turn out the light and tiptoe away from this dormitory
and its fantasies, we need to note that, aside from missing what is in
the book, Davis prescribes a formula for contemporary fiction: that
"we fight men like Long with the utmost resolution . . . to preserve . . .
free, open, pluralistic societies." One may doubt whether *Macbeth*
would have been improved if it had been conceived as a recipe for the
curtailment of royal abuses. Davis makes the old confusion of citizen
and artist; but, what is far worse, he is apparently bent on imposing
upon the artist a topicality, and a predetermined point of view, which
must dull and destroy his insight. It is dangerous to read badly; but it
is a terribly serious matter when an elite itself—I refer to most of the
critics I have quoted—when this elite, as if moved by a devastating
self-distrust, calls for easy propaganda in place of the difficulties of
tragedy. It is easy to hate a villain; and it is usually the groundlings
who want life reduced to a manageable melodrama. What if all artists
give in?

In many of these readers of *All the King's Men* there is plain slothful-
ness—not as a personal vice but as a public habit which appears to
have grown since the eighteenth century, to have been nourished upon
and in turn to have insisted upon, a relatively simple, one-dimensional
literature. Not that there has not been difficult, complex, poetic writing;
but it has been exceptional, and, until lately, rather much neglected. It is
obviously not quite fair to pick Leo Kirschbaum of *Commentary* as
the sole exemplar of the well-intentioned, easygoing readerhood, for
he has tried not to be careless or casual, and has indeed worked hard at
his assignment. But in him the moral becomes beautifully clear: as a
sharp reader of Elizabethan tragedy, and as one who understands poetic values, he is precisely the person who ought to read *All the King's
Men* with especial discernment. Yet his trouble is that, as a man of the
long post-1700 age of prose, he somehow approaches the novel with
a totally different set of assumptions—an approach which is tanta-

mount to an abdication of his critical powers. As a modern work, the novel is going to be explicit, straightforward, resonantly in favor of the accepted goods, adapted to intelligent upper-middle-class sentiments, not too poetic, and with the philosophy, if any, prompting pretty audibly from the wings; and if the work draws its skeletal materials from modern history, it must stick faithfully to what we all know to be the truth about those materials. Now Kirschbaum would never read Shakespeare or Sophocles like that. He would unconsciously junk all these preconceptions and start with the text. But in his modern *acedia*—and perhaps it is the literary *acedia* of any age—he starts, alas without knowing it, with something else that the text is supposed to fit into. So he misses entirely the central theme—the split in modern consciousness; in Jack's unrelenting philosophical inquiry he finds only callow, even pathological insufficiency; and the complex attitude of Jack to Willie, which involves not only his being hypnotized by the genius of action, but also his sense of guilt and his paradoxical detachment and critical distance from Willie, Kirschbaum takes to be an "amoral and mystical approval of the American fascist Willie Stark."

It may be worth repeating, as we leave the reviewers, that enough of them glimpse the novelist's intention to establish his power of communication. Those who miss it are, in the main, not at all dull; but by some habit of thought, some cast of mind, which seems to come from the mental sets of the civilization, they are blocked off from seeing how the novel, as tragedy, works. Warren treats them as independent minds, able to slip away from societal apron-strings. In fact, he never condescends to his readers; those who would read him aright will have to work out careful patterns. It would have been easy to supply a chorus identifying Willie's half-truths as half-truths; but Warren does it indirectly by having Willie in effect repudiate—his attitude to the hospital denies his formal relativism—his own announced positions, and by having the implicit repudiation seen through the awareness of a Jack Burden who is himself experimenting with concepts. Jack could have underlined his reservations about Willie, but we only see those reservations nibbling at the edges of an apparently whole-souled commitment. In the midst of strenuous muckraking Jack tells Willie, "I'm not one of your scum, and I'm still grinning when I please," and thus we see both the split in Jack and the withheld area of self which differentiates him from the Duffys and Larsons. The split in Jack—that is, the split in an age—finds a symbol in half-truths, with which the difficulty is precisely that they are partly true. While striving toward a whole, Jack veers from half to half. In early years he is inactive, his personality is diffuse and amorphous. There is no imperative in either tradition or work; as a lover he ends—this is one of the most delicately managed episodes—in a hesitation which is in origin an echo of an old honor, thinned out now into a wavering sentiment, and which is in effect a negation. What Anne does not find in Jack she finds in Willie; what Jack does not find in himself he finds in Willie—resolution. But, riding on another man's activeness, Jack the doer is never free of Jack the self-critic; he justifies by half-truths, but: he also accepts half-truths uttered in judgment. The photographer says, "You work for Stark and you call somebody a son-of-a-bitch." He is half right, half wrong, Jack thinks, "and in the end that is what paralyzes you." Now the sense of paralysis is ironically a symbol of reorientation: Jack is trying to make his action and his idea cohere—a private parallel to his outward act of bringing Adam and Willie together. But the still-more-embracing irony, the irony which is all the preachment for which anybody could wish, lies in Willie's relation to this half-truth world. For his dubiety of his official philosophy is activated too late. For him the half-truth of acting according to the facts has been a whole truth; of the paralysis of others he is born; from the start he is always shown acting; and in turn all the spirit, the essence of action has somehow formed young Tom Stark. What is the end of Tom Stark? In the hospital bed he lies *paralyzed*—a fine climax to the counterpoint of kinesis and paralysis and a symbol of Willie's real failure. Willie, as Jack says, "could not tell his greatness from ungreatness and so mixed them together that what was adulterated was lost."

Who would read the book aright, we have said, must find the patterns. Jack, searching for a past, kills his father; Willie, searching for a future, may be said to kill his son. What Willie learns, there is not enough life left to define wholly; it is Lucy who seizes, in a quiet irony, the instrument of continuity into the future. Jack finds a truth, a basis for values, a faith. All this is part of a very complex theme of past-and-future, a theme which is really another way of presenting the split in the world. Here the split is defined chronologically; the separation of fact and idea is also man's separation from his roots, a separation which appeared extensively in *At Heaven's Gate* and which appears intensively here. Jack's separation from the past is so extreme that at first he cannot understand Cass Mastern's acute sense of moral responsibility; the essence of his inner development is his coming to terms with the past, knowing the reality of guilt, and learning, with Cass, that "the world is all of one piece." There is a skillfully managed irony in the ambivalence of the past: when it is no longer a nourishing tradition, it is a terrifying skeleton: *the* past is gone, and each man has only *a* past that he can be coerced with. The skeleton, the sterilizing past, is all that Willie professes to believe in (even while being drawn to the Burdens, who represent traditions, the fertilizing past); Jack digs up each man's past and discovers *the* past; from case histories he progresses to the meaning of history. He moves away from his old misvaluation of the past, of which the two faces are cynicism and sentimentality. "We can keep the past only by having the future, for they are forever tied together." "Only out of the past can you make the future." Faith is proved by deed, and fruitful deed comes only out of the long wisdom. He is, at last, prepared to face history, to enter "the awful responsibility of Time."

Shift a few pieces on the board, and the history-theme becomes the knowledge-theme, which can be traced from episode to episode and from reflection to reflection. "Life is Motion toward Knowledge," Jack argues. Willie's career is a progression in self-knowledge, and Jack's is a passion for knowledge that leads from factual to moral awareness. "All knowledge that is worth anything is maybe paid for by blood." Jack's self-criticism is important here—the innumerable passages in which he catches himself at lying, or self-deception, or histrionics; or understands his feeling that Duffy "had . . . like a brother winked at me." Or shift a few pieces again, and the action-theme becomes a study of participation and withdrawal, with its echoes in Jack and Adam and Hugh Miller, and the conclusion to which it leads, that there are no perfect choices: "there is always a price to make a choice." In one sense the body of the work is the regeneration theme: the variations range from a prefrontal lobectomy to the Scholarly Attorney's efforts with "unfortunates" to the acquisition of new insights by Cass Mastern and Jack Burden.

As the consciousness of an age, Jack also embodies its philosophic searchings. Jack appears first as an Idealist, and there is a nice implied contrast between his version of Platonism, which rationalizes away responsibility, and Adam's, which takes insufficient account of the facts. Then Jack plunges into pragmatism, but it is a drug and never a very efficient one; under the pressure of pain he falls into Mechanism—the Twitch theory. But eventually he rejects the world as Idea, the world as Act, and the world as Mechanism; these are the half-truths of a disintegrating order. What he envisages is a saving union of the idealist and pragmatist impulses of modern man; while the brilliance of Willie is his executive mastery of fact, his greatness, in which the others "must" believe—the margin between him and the ordinary political operator—is his emergent awareness of the inadequacy of fact. If they cannot believe in that, there is nothing left; but they can believe, for tragedy reaffirms the whole truth which measures the failure of the incomplete man. Humpty is Willie and he is also Jack—that is, the man who has broken into parts. Nor will men and horses, human intention and mere animal strength, reunify man. That is, reintegration transcends the secular; Jack moves, at the end, toward the deepest possible grounding of his world view, a grounding in theological terms. He assents, "in his own way," quasi-committally, to a metaphysic which accommodates evil, not to despair, but to define salvation. The reader recalls the earlier words of the Scholarly Attorney, "God is Fullness of Being." Humpty is partialness. The fall in the old rhyme becomes a version of The Fall.

Some such matters the critics may reasonably be expected to see. Let it be said, if it need be said, that no one expects them to do more than see the evidence. They need not like the evidence—a situation which, as we all know, *non est disputandum;* they need not consider the evidence sufficient to prove what the author wants proved. For various reasons they may not like the author's looks. If they think him unhandsome, that's their privilege; but, it may be repeated, they are wholly obliged to take a good, long, direct look at him instead of using one of those hasty city-street snapshots at twenty-five cents a peep. What contests he will win will appear in time. But those who have looked close enough to realize the intellectual and imaginative richness will know that they have been at least in the neighborhood of great-ness. There is room, perhaps, for further coalescence of the gifts that appear brilliantly in, for instance, the vitality of Willie, the ironic com-mentary of Jack, the Jack-Anne idyll and the weak spot where it is breached, the bursting fullness of image, the reflective probing. For the present reader there is room, still, for some reproportioning and for some filling-out, with the logic of feeling and motive and the immedi-ate concretenesses of man in action, of the immensely moving symbolic paradigms whose rightness carries one into wholeness of admiration and into all but wholeness of assent.

III.15

Tangled Web: Warren's *World Enough and Time*

(1951)

In *World Enough and Time* Robert Penn Warren again tackles the theme which was the core of *All the King's Men*—the failure of a private, subjective "ideal" realm to come to terms with, to be integrated with, to be married to a realm of public life and activity, the realm of politics and society and group action, of law and justice. Warren's fourth novel is less neat than his third (not that neatness was a prime virtue of it), in the sense that *Hamlet* is less neat than *Othello:* it is longer, and its length springs from a mind that overflows with its observings and recordings, and is relentless in its questionings and questings; the seams are strained by a redundance of plot; by the piercing, tireless images of outer and inner life; by the figures that qualify and communicate so substantially as to belie the initial innocence, or justify the initial shock, of the words; by the bursting intellectual action, the tracking down of motives, the search through the labyrinth of personality, the formulation and reformulation of meaning, the alternate embrace and rejection of theory which are the coordinates of moral and philosophic growth. Here is enfolded enough of the world and of time—enough for the young protagonists to come to the borders of self-knowledge, enough for the reader who would fix a little more clearly the outlines of the world and of self, enough to make an adequate definition of this work depend upon a great deal of studious rereading by many critical readers.

The immediate world is Kentucky and the time is the first quarter of the nineteenth century: Warren sticks to the central method of his other three novels, digging up a pretty well-preserved skeleton of action from recent history, covering it with the flesh of imaginatively conceived story, and giving it the life of human (suprahistorical) meaning. Such a literary anthropologist always runs the risk of a tap on the head from some errandboy of social science whose chief punch is: has he tampered with the facts? Of course he has. And only by doing so does he extend his anthropology beyond a museum operation and make it a proper study of man for mankind. Literary anthropologists have for a number of years been very active in Americana, and their re-creation and transmutation of various American pasts may be understood as an aspect of the development of an imaginative self-consciousness, of a feeling and yet critical awareness, the achievement of which might well let the artist reflect on his share in the forging of the uncreated conscience of his race. This throwing of a certain coloring of the imagination over the ordinary—and extraordinary—things of the past, however, may minister to different kinds of consciousness. The past itself may be used only as a new veneer for stock literary sideshows ("entertainment literature"). The past may be used merely to create a sense of the past (the standard "historical novel"). The past may be used only to create a sense of the present (the historical allegory). Or the past may be used to create a sense of both past and present, or of realities that are neither past nor present because they are both. This is the field in which Warren works brilliantly, though to the puzzlement and disappointment of all those whose expectancies have been nourished in fields one, two, or three. (Even among the professionals: read a review by an established historical novelist, and see the anguish seeping through; or one by a semiliterary slickster, and see what he sees—only an I-push-over-easy wink to Hollywood.) But if Warren's past is Everytime, there is no woozy timelessness or lack of ubiety in the drama; documentation is heavy. The dates are all there and can be checked in the record; the geography is meticulous, and can be checked on driving maps; many characters are given full biographies, and at least some may be checked in *DAB*. But calendars, court transcripts, diaries, maps, *DAB*, and all that take us only to the threshold of the work.

The narrative organization of the theme, despite the kinship between the two books, in quite different from that of *All the King's Men;* the earlier book uses a narrator, Jack Burden, who tells of tragically separated men of ideas and men of action and of his involvement with both, who duplicates within himself the split in society, and whose failure of understanding, until almost the end, is a major source of tension. In *World Enough and Time* the author tells directly the story of the conflict between Jeremiah Beaumont and the world in which he lives (his friend Wilkie Barron; his once mentor, Cassius Fort, whom he murders; and all the private interests and social and legal forces arrayed against him); then he uses Jeremiah's journal as a means of comment on Jerry's intentions and actions; and finally comments himself on both action and journal. Thus we have not only a level of action, which itself is very complicated, but two levels of comment. Since Jeremiah is made not only as articulate as Jack Burden but also, if no more wise, at least a more conscious searcher of motives and meanings, the element of reflection and inquiry is larger in the present novel. Jerry's frantic philosophic quest, which ranges from self-deception through various tentatively held views to new insight, rarely ceases. Yet at times it covers pretty well-worn ground so that, despite its intensity, it can let the story down into a stasis; and the tireless repetition of questions can become actually nagging. But the total effect is one of a manically exhaustive ripping apart of excuses, justifications, defenses, ruses, consolations; of a furious burrowing into ever-deeper layers of self-understanding until almost every clarity becomes a puzzle and every dependability a delusion. Characters who end their search for an author in Mr. Warren's fold come under a hardbitten taskmaster, who has an indefatigable eye for subterfuge, for the empty heroic, the phony benevolence, the slippery self-seeking, the concealed or direct malignity, the impulse to wound or sell or kill. Yet it is important to distinguish this deep-lying suspicion, this embracing skepticism, from a mechanically, doctrinally hardboiled way of looking at things; it is the difference between the maturely sensitive and the half-grown sentimental. Wisdom has its affirmations and its negations; here is the negative side of wisdom. The flaws and failures of men are wonderfully dramatized, and they are in every sense right; but the small acquisitions of joy or honor skim by thinly. Let us by no means undervalue the awareness of Lilliputian chicanery and Yahoo savagery; without them, narrative can't get beyond polite reassurance and good clean fun. And let us also keep in mind that, if affirmations are of the threshold, tentative, acquiring somewhat less of dramatic convic-

tion than the weaknesses, trickeries, malevolences so watchfully des-
cried, in our day the wisdom of negation seems almost the limit of the
possible, at least for the man in the world who will not live by cliché
and slogan.

Self-discovery is not an autonomous process, with the materials
yielding up their own principles of definition; rather it is the application to the self of the best-available categories of meaning and value.
The basic categories in *World Enough and Time* are "world" and
"idea," which, as we have said, are clearly related to the governing
concepts of *All the King's Men* but which certainly aim at a larger inclusiveness and are intended to put a finger on basic human motives.
Viewed neutrally, "the world" is simply the forum, the marketplace,
the scene of public activity; viewed ideally, it is the realm of the cooperative search for justice; viewed in terms of the dominant facts, it is
expediency, opportunism, flux-worship, deriving principles from polls
(private, unwritten, but nonetheless taken), spotting the winner. This
is the inevitable degenerate form of the cooperative principle: coopera-
tion unideally—without the "idea"—is getting on with, and getting
on with easily sinks into getting on, and getting on into getting. Warren
gives due play to all the potentialities of the world: at his trial for murder, Jerry is defended by two attorneys of radically opposed political
parties, emblems respectively of "worldly decency" and "unworldly
truth"; and Cassius Fort, Jerry's victim, who like the lawyers lives and
acts in the world and who has a due share of "human weakness," is
apparently actuated by political conviction. But the chief figure in the
world is Wilkie Barron (of whom we have already seen something in
Bogan Maddox of *At Heaven's Gate*), Jerry's friend and his Iago, the
Mr. Worldly Wiseman of the tale, who never backs the wrong horse,
fails to make the proper gesture, or falls into an unprofitable passion
(like the too-successful sea captain in *Lord Jim*, he finally commits suicide in midcareer). Among the men of the world, he must be the principal actor for us of the twentieth century, whose "every effort is to live
in the world, to accept its explanations, to do nothing gratuitously."
Finally, beyond clubman-competitor Wilkie in the range of worldlings
are the lesser and leaner fry of vote-sellers, perjurers, and cutthroats—
the success-boys with the makeup rubbed off.

Since for a novelist of Warren's stature the world is not big enough game, the book naturally belongs to Jerry Beaumont—to "idea." If one were a good positivist, he would scorn the idea; if one were a sentimentalist, he might present it as high nobility in itself; if a Platonist, he would define it as reality. Instead of doing any of these things, Warren is writing a tragedy of the idea—to paraphrase Hardy, "a tragedy of the unfulfilled idea." Jerry early discovered, he thought, "the vanity of the world" and yearned to "live in the pure idea." This was enough; he could renounce the world—retire from a legal career and create a private idyll (by taking up the cause of, and eventually falling in love with, a girl he doesn't know, Rachel Jordan—so excellent a symbol of both capacity for devotion and a fanciful separation from reality that one is loath to question the event and the way of its being brought about). But the idyll itself led back to the world, and Jerry found his unworldly motives mixed with worldly; so we find him trying to compel the world to "redeem" the idea (murdering Rachel's seducer, Cassius Fort, whom he had made into a symbol of the world; and by deceit striving to have the world, through its courts, declare him "not guilty" and therefore acknowledge the innocence of his idea turned into act). After the inevitable failure of this project, Jerry falls entirely into the world, accepting both a jailbreak appropriately engineered by Wilkie (for his own purposes) and a drunken and lecherous sanctuary among Yahoos in a wretched junk-strewn swamp controlled by an aged scoundrel whose last vocation in treachery was piracy on the rivers ("the blank cup of nature," Jerry calls it. Murder, said the pirate, "c'est naturel"— that happy phrase by which today we beatify so many cravings and indolences. There is a reminiscence of Edmund's appeal to "nature" in *Lear*. The episode is a biting parody of romantic naturalism, of innocence secured in Arcadia.). In Jerry's view there has been a necessary evolution from the first of these stages to the third.

The story has another representative of the "dialectic" of the idea— Percival Skrogg, a tubercular father-hater who pursues "the Justice in my own mind" by various means from demagogic journalism to political trickery and inordinately successful dueling—a killer who is eventually assassinated. But for years he had lived in fear, which in part superseded the "idea" and allied him to the "world."

What, then, is the "idea"? If I read the novel aright, Warren accords to the idea the same breadth of treatment which he gives to the world.

In one light it is aspiration, the sought nobility, the good dreamed of, the felt ideal of justice, the uncontaminated and holy thing. Rachel and Jerry read Plato, and Jerry once (from his accomplished murder) rides home in the style of a knight of chivalry. But the idea is held in the private mind, and it can become a purely private reality; yet it seems, in virtue of its withdrawn purity, able to claim general fealty and public obeisance. The idea becomes the *idée fixe;* the love of right, the sense of rightness. Impulse and uncriticized motive creep into the idea. It becomes will, drive, the compulsive personality, the doctrine without deviation or qualification, the end which claims all means. It becomes mania. It tries to compel history. Opposite, the Wilkie Barrons are only trying to ride history's coattails. One gives too little (to time, to humanity, to the world), the other too much.

If this sounds pretty simple, the narrative mass from which it is extracted is not simple. There are all the inner complications of Rachel and Jerry, in whom the author has discovered an extraordinary range of impulses; there are the fairly complete histories of various supporting characters (Jerry's and Rachel's parents, various politicians, the crooked lawyer Suggs Lancaster, Cadeau the pirate); there is the incalculable interweaving of private life with the public issue of Relief *vs.* Anti-Relief, New Court *vs.* Old Court; the immense detail of plotting and executing murder, of a trial in which state witnesses cross up each other and the prosecutor, and the defendant tries by suborning perjury to outsmart both the false witnesses and his devoted attorneys; of the slow unraveling of machinations and mixed motives and psychological and political maneuvering (a mass of ingredients best held together in the second half of the book, where the movement is far more sure and the action yields less to the impedimenta of explanation and discussion which have not fully surrendered to, or been forced into, the narrative stream). But above all this, the interrelationship of the parts is such as to yield an immense suggestivity of meaning; there is a confluence of diverse motifs and patterns; there are imaginative extensions, constant examples of what Richards calls felt depth and recession. The story can be read in the light of various ways of organizing experience. Cut out enough, and the rest goes neatly in psychoanalytic terms: the conditioning "trauma" in the lives of Jerry, Rachel, and Skrogg (only in Wilkie the worldling is adjustment hereditary, so to speak), the religion-sex short circuit in Jerry's life, the father-murder pattern in Jerry and Skrogg, the various scenes in Jerry's life where the return-to-the-womb is hinted. Cut out enough other parts, and the rest can go as a study of the relationship between a man and a woman, especially of the man's unwittingly forcing upon the woman a role which ministers to needs of his not clearly understood; a kind of study which makes possible the author's most complex and most generally successful portrayal of a woman. A more inclusive approach is through the traditional situations into which the story falls. For instance, the tragic mechanism of the family curse operates for both Jerry and Rachel, each of whom in some way duplicates a parental bias or flaw and so increases his burden of self-discovery. Again, Jerry plays Othello to Wilkie's Iago, in a variety of situations. More markedly, Jerry is Hamlet, the student, the questioner, plotting a revenge (in discoursing on which the author uses as his text "What's he to Hecuba?"), employing a literary mousetrap to secure the admission of what he already knows to be a fact, thinking that "nothing could repair the twisted time," refusing to kill Fort when the act would seem morally incomplete (Claudius at prayer), abusing his sweetheart and driving her mad, literally comparing a hoodwinked plotter to Rosencrantz and Guildenstern, near the end even listening to quips from a gravedigger. In Jerry is focused the action-contamination theme so frequent in Shakespeare: how mediate between a fugitive and cloistered virtue and the contamination inherent in the work that must be done (a theme of interest to Warren since *Night Rider*)? The juxtaposition of sex and death, in both act and reflection, recalls both a traditional association and the specific Elizabethan ambiguity in the use of *die*. The idea that hardens into will is a favorite George Eliot theme, and Jerry's attempted flight and unforeseen involvement may be set against the roughly comparable experience of Heyst in *Victory*. It of course does Warren no service if these comparisons are taken to imply that his work somehow includes all these others; all the analogies should suggest is the breadth of *World Enough and Time*. At the same time there is a general Elizabethanness of cast—in the combination of full and violent action (including a kind of helter-skelter finishing-off of physical lives) with rich rhetoric and overt philosophical investigation—that defines an important influence on Warren's imagination.

Or the story can be read as a myth of America. *World Enough and Time* is, like Warren's other novels, with their Kentucky, Tennessee, and Louisiana backgrounds, southern only in the surface facts; yet it comprises more of the American story and temper than do the others. Half the characters are "self-made" men, with the animus and drive generated on "the other side of the tracks." Their stories are "success stories" seen in tragic perspective. They have "dreams"—a word used just often enough to comment lightly on the "American dream." In the contest of Reliefers and Anti-Reliefers, both with clearcut twentieth-century analogues, we see the archetypal standpat and reformist tendencies. One characteristic passage neatly debunks a modernist-positivist debunking of dueling; any fight for an unseen, intangible, but felt value—a war for instance—is a duel. Most of all we sense the two "streams of American thought," the "idealist" and the "practical," with their contradictions and overlappings and ways of becoming corrupt. Jerry is obviously not defined as a national archetype, nor does he accidentally become one, but in him there is much that we can see in ourselves: the turning "from the victor to the victim," the conviction of inner rightness, the inconsistent dreams, the quickness to anger, the sense of injury, the accidental involvement, the self-deception, the contradictory impulses to withdraw and to dictate to others, the confusion about means, the desire to live by the private view and yet to have public justification, the passion and the calculation side by side.

There are other themes: the elusiveness of truth, however fanatically pursued; the enigma of self; the "paradox and doubleness of life" (the enemy as friend, the coexistence of incompatible motives, all the lies against Jerry combining to tell the truth); the seat of justice—in the heart or in the law? (Jerry wavers between the two positions.) There are the subtle comments on figure after figure: the pirate who betrayed the Cherokees had foreseen their end and "had cashed in on his investment while the market was still good." The rich dark-light imagery is a system of meaning in itself. Recurrency is structurally important, notably in the recollections of scenes and sensations—the picture of the martyr, the first sex experience, the enchanting music from the keelboat, the sense of oneness with nature—which establish links among different episodes in Jerry's life. There is a recurrence of the lives of the fathers in the lives of the children; there are a half dozen versions of the go-west-young-man dogma, most of them commenting ironically on the dream. All these kinds of communication will have to be taken into account in a final assessment of this book; nor is it an abjuring of the critical function to insist that the definition of a complex work of art depends upon a continued collective experiencing of it.

The book is all these things, but it is one book, and the author has indicated how he wants us to see its oneness. When we first glimpse "A Romantic Novel" on the bang-bang jacket, we automatically assume that Random House is bravely dreaming of some deception in the drugstore. But "A Romantic Novel" is also a subtitle, so that it is official as well as promotional. It seems to me that there are three ways in which *romantic* may be taken. At its simplest there is the "romance of adventure"—the almost-perfect crime, the pursuit of the suspect, the deviousness of the trial, the jailbreak, the love story, the attempted suicide, the quick gunplay and fistplay, the bravado and battles of wit. At this level it might all be out of Scott, and from Scott might have come a workable title—"The Tangled Web," which, despite the heavy moralism of the context, would pretty well describe the complication of physical and moral action. Yet all this apparatus of romantic melodrama, when qualified by a central tragic awareness, yields something more serious than a romantic-melodramatic effect. Again, *romantic* describes the kind of personality the book deals with: Jerry as Byronic hero is intimated by his and Rachel's and Fort's devotion to Byron. Indeed, *Childe Harold* is an arsenal of mottoes and epithets for Jerry: "self-torturing sophist," "I have not loved the world, nor the world me," "I have thought too long and darkly," "Wrung with the wounds which kill not, but ne'er heal." Jerry is hardly so self-contained as Byron / Harold imagined himself to be, but he is impulsive, suspicious, bitter, melancholy, devoted to an ideal, in search of the fine and noble, hoping for too much, disillusioned, attitudinizing, demonic, exacerbatedly sensitive, self-questioning, self-tormenting, self-deceiving, self-detecting, self-pitying, with all the anguish and despair and nostalgia for a happiness not accessible to the "dark" personality. (He even employs "romantic irony" in commenting on his venereal sore.) In "pure" romance he would be merely a suffering victim of the world, and indeed Jerry has a neurotically active sense of betrayal by the world; but this romantic hero is seen in perspective. Compared with Wilkie's entire devotion to self-advancement, Jerry's dedication to the gratuitous act is impressive; but all his dedication does not dissolve the corruption which encrusts the act itself. The second and final stage in the tragic transformation of romance is Jerry's coming to understand and to reject his earlier self. At the end he does not stand off and gesticulate. He judges himself.

At the third level, then, the book is a study of a basic kind of impulse to action. Jerry calls himself guilty of "the crime of self"; he speaks of having acted from "a black need within me." We have already spoken of the tendency of the "idea" to become "uncriticized motive" and "compulsive personality." The kind of human motivation defined in Jerry is suggested by such terms as *the self, the personality, the subjective;* here we find the private sureness, the inner insistence, the confidence in the rightness of the heart (as in Hitler), the intransigence of the will, the flight from discipline, indeed the very summation of individualist pride. This "kind of impulse" may lead to both scorn of the world (which may range from simple retreat to challenge and defilement) and effort to subjugate the world: Jerry ultimately comes to see what Rachel had seen earlier, that he had "tortured" her into crying for Fort's blood and thus providing a factitious moral imperative as veneer for an almost instinctive drive.

The human pattern exhibited in Jerry, and with variations in Rachel and Skrogg, is universal. If I am right in judging the ultimate applicability of *romantic* to be to the "kind of impulse" which moves Jerry, then the author is describing the timeless by a time-word, using a term of specific historical relevance as a means of concretizing the issue. Time and the timeless meet when, in the failure of an ideal tension among impulses, one or another enjoys a temporary historical dominance, as did the Jerry-impulse—the basis, really, of the cult of the individual—in the "Romantic" period and indeed in most of subsequent American history. Whatever name one might give to the antithetical and equally timeless impulse—the Wilkie-impulse—it is clear that its period of dominance was another one; Wilkie has affiliations both with Lord Chesterfield and with the President of the Junior Chamber of Commerce to whom the author refers in a double-voiced choral comment near the end. The problem of these contending im-

pulses, which provides the intellectual framework for the drama of
Jerry, really finds its analogy in Coleridge's epistemological doctrine of
the subjective and the objective, which in perception reciprocally modify each other. So in moral life a "subjective" and an "objective" view
of reality, of innocence, of justice—intention and deed—must inter-
penetrate, lest the idea or the world run mad. This is not the "practical" principle of compromise—the doctrine that *the* truth is the sum
of many half-truths, or the political expedient of the committee swollen
into a metaphysic—but the insistence upon a recognition of all the impulses and of the problem of finding a unity. (Extremes can compromise and even cooperate in a remarkable way; mania and success can
sleep together comfortably. Skrogg as idea and Wilkie as world always
collaborate politically. And Skrogg—the idea as gangsterism—has a
couple of thug bodyguards, a fine concession to the way of the world.)

The conception of the romantic here advanced in the name of the
author may grieve professional peddlers of romanticism, at least those
whose style is that of a stockholder with an investment to protect. But
in many ways it need not do so. Warren has written a study, not a tract.
Jerry always aspires; he has the Ulyssean character—to strive, to seek,
to find. He is always played off against the positivists; his chief error is
to try to be positive—to guarantee the future. He comes to grieve at,
not to rejoice in, the "cold exile from mankind" which results from an
attempt at a purely private ordering of life. The theme of alienation—
that seclusion which emerges from and punishes the crime of self—is
always present and is explicitly central in Jerry's final self-analysis.
Whether this be regarded as the summit of the dialectical progression
of a romantic, or the saving modification of a romantic credo, Jerry
puts it this way: "There must be a way whereby the word becomes
flesh. There must be a way whereby the flesh becomes word. Whereby
loneliness becomes communion without contamination. Whereby contamination becomes purity without exile." In these words of longing
for what is impossible in life yet must always be sought if life is to have
order, Jerry speaks a religious, in part even a biblical, language. This
way of speech, which is natural in the character that Jerry has been
shown to be, serves not only to communicate the meaning of the moment but also to pull together strands of suggestion that have run
throughout the story. Early in life Jerry had been under the influence of

one of those evangelists "who got their hot prides and cold lusts short-circuited into obsessed hosannas and a ferocious striving for God's sake," and for years he was obsessed by a remembered picture of a female martyr in flames whom he could imagine himself either rescuing or helping to destroy. He declares himself an unbeliever but tends always toward a religious comprehension of experience. He thinks of his campaign against Fort as a "mission"; he thinks first that his idea will "redeem" the world, later that the world must "redeem" the idea. Honest trial witnesses make him "as reborn." He is passionate about his "innocence." He seeks "peace" by confession. He is agonized by Munn Short's story of his spiritual death and his recovery by faith. In fact, with his early conversion establishing the pattern, Jerry has always led a kind of pseudoreligious life: he needs an all-embracing, peremptory spiritual command, but his way of finding it is to universalize an unidentified cry from within. Nowhere is the falseness of his devotion more apparent than when he finds "peace" and "grace" in the ex-pirate's stinking sanctuary. He is aware that it is a horrible parody of grace and innocence, but he clings to his raw Eden. He reads the New Testament in Greek and falls into drunkenness and debauchery. With a dirty slut he finds "peace" and "communion."

But Jerry cannot rest in irony. Like Everyman, and like the traditional tragic protagonist, he comes to knowledge, not by magic illumination, but as the outcome of prolonged searching. Then he no longer seeks revenge, or pardon, or justification; he knows that "I may not have redemption." He must "flee from innocence and toward my guilt"; he seeks suffering and expiation. This is his ultimate renunciation of the doctrine of self, of the private determination of value; it is the acknowledgment of spiritual reality, the bowing to cosmic discipline.

Jerry is killed before he can complete action in the light of his new knowledge, but not before he can close his journal with a question: "Oh, was I worth nothing, and my agony? Was all for naught?" And the author closes the novel by repeating, "Was all for naught?" At first glimpse this may seem a kind of lady-or-tiger coyness, or an emcee's request for audience participation, or even a romantic preference for the incomplete. Rather, I think, the rhetorical question does two things: it is a kind of "de te, fabula," and it raises the issue of whether such a tragic fable can be meaningful now. The book does not raise a finger to make the answer easy: the excellence of *World Enough and Time* is precisely its difficulty. The dramatic and intellectual texture is dense; nothing is given away. Which is as it should be. The acknowledgment of the crime of self and the acceptance of guilt are hardly likely to seem pleasantly familiar to us unskilled in tragic perception. Which is as it must be. Our bent is to look for causes, and to find something, or someone, to blame.

IV

PLACE AGAIN: The Region

IV. 16

The South Falls In

(1947)

i

To speak of "The South" is to commit oneself to a special, almost eso-
teric, subject, as if one's materials are of a uniqueness that exacts quite
particular microscopic equipment and a carefully sandpapered awareness that old saws don't hold here. To talk about some other region
might mean that one would have to be alert only for variations in
stress, for reshufflings of the old familiar sociological deck, with about
the same number of cards and the same promise or shadiness as the
game at home. But for the South, no; here one crosses frontiers, con-
tends with forces subtly alien, and measures a human spirit not-quite-
accountably transmuted. That, at any rate, is the conditioning assumption, perhaps hardly articulated, of onlookers hard and soft.

It is ironic, of course, that the different being has so often been
readily defined even by observers who insist upon the difference. The
sense of difference often fails in its duty of warning them that if they
are to achieve their objective they at least need special instruments to
detect the concealed emotional drift that can at length effect a shocking deviation from course. But the ready definers sail ahead, and in
them we can see the sense of difference operating in two ways: when it
goes only skindeep, it means novelty, the stimulus of an exotic which is
not too demanding, the charms of a change of scenery; when it cuts
deeper, its meaning can quickly range from condescension to fear and
hostility. At both levels the definitions have, most of them, the deceptive simplicity that comes from businesslike despatch in making difference intellectually and morally manageable.

There is the simple popular South, the tourist South, the South of movie and melody—the "romantic" South of moon and magnolia, of colonel and julep, of devoted black and easy living, of a lush amorousness in which the passionately pulsating and the fiercely gentle are refreshingly compounded, all against a backdrop of ordered terraces culminating in a tenderized super-Monticello. To count the grains of sand framing this calendar-art mirage is beside the point. For in its relations the mirage takes on a measurable reality. In its purely practical function it is the secularized Venus couched languidly above the bar—the aphrodisiac which catalyzes the profitable commerce between the Pilgrimage Week ladies and the prodigal tourist lusting for the lovely that can be hired for the weekend. It is a phenomenon, of course, which has its parallels from Carlsbad to a thousand beds where Caesar slept. The mirage says next to nothing about the South; on the other hand, it does say something about the optical equipment 1) of those who assert its reality and 2) of those who recognize it as mirage but are indignantly sure that southern critics are themselves taken in by it.

The latter provide interesting research materials. They are the ones who really cannot make head or tail of modern southerners who feel that pre-1861 southern life was given form by values whose loss is serious for all of us; by what they cannot understand they are outraged; they define the outrage, and restore a sense of understanding, by the embarrassingly simple theory that the apologists for the earlier South are mirage-struck—colonels *manqué,* a bit thirsty, yearning to lounge languidly through decadence, and occasionally up to the mild exercise of beating on blacks. Perhaps no other adverse judgment could so obtusely miss the tough realism of the best contemporary southern minds—a realism that, as it appears in fiction, for instance, produces odd responses in the very people who cry "Mirage!" Now they are shocked by the sense of reality, as if idyll-mongers could also practice a horrid coprophagy. And not only to miss the realism—which is nothing more than an unflinching search for durable values, especially in what by the general consent of any given moment is an unlikely place—but to mistake it for escapism: this is a considerable obstinacy. What this tells us about the distant observers is that their modes of judgment are dangerously inflexible, so much so that they find it more congenial to rely on doctrinaire preconceptions than to risk the revisions which consideration of an unforeseen argument may demand.

They have long known what the Old South was; he who sees something different has hallucinations.

Again, the romantic mirage-South is meaningful insofar as it is a widespread American dream, widespread enough to be persistently nourished by outsize doses of visual marijuana from Hollywood and the fiction-millers. What it does is show the country at sentimental reverie: and what we see is degraded contemplation and phony spirituality. "If we can nourish so beautiful a vision, we aren't so bad after all." This fostering of a papier-mâché Paradise may also, insofar as it is a nonsouthern phenomenon, have at its core certain elements of the expiatory, though it is an easy and corrupting penance to pay off the defeated in such neon glory. The South seems, at times, to be moving toward the role of a Troy that had, until the seventeenth century, a special seat in European imagination; but only a burlesque can be produced by a public consciousness that will take Rhett for its Hector— any day. Actually, potential expiation dwindles into defense mechanism, and a hard trader may very well try, without recognizing the process, to ward off petrifaction by cherishing a few soft spots—such as apparent affection for the charming and easygoing and really not very dependable South.

ii

These are some of the considerations called forth by the popular, one-dimensional picture of the South. When the sense of difference sinks in to where it really bites, the resultant portraits appear in harder lights. The "scientific" spirit assumes that climate produces some special brand of morality, with stagnant bloodstreams that quite remold character. But climate is one thing that it is safe to be relativistic about. At the other extreme from such determinism we find the voluntarism which proposes that the South renovate itself by act of will, instituting this or that improvement that the neighbors regard as beneficent. Let it forget the past and live in the present; let it pull itself together, work harder, and get over being poor; let it take a good deep breath of modern air and get rid of poll taxes, sharecropping, and race prejudice— for the past, indolence, indigence, and sociological circumstance are the sole bars to the universal pursuit and probable achievement of happiness. Well, voluntaristic proposals for someone else's reform are rarely acted upon with the despatch that a wholly rational state of affairs might call for, and, failing to demonstrate its free will by following alien prescriptions for soul saving, the South has had its difference constantly described in quite uncompromising terms.

By millions of readers of Westbrook Pegler it is regarded as prejudiced. By millions of customers of the manufacturers of labor-saving devices it is regarded as lazy. By millions of residents of states where unemployment is unknown only in wartime, it is regarded as lamentably poor. By the most solidly Republican sections it is regarded as having a wholly senseless devotion to the Democratic party; by the most solidly Republican sections it is also regarded as having sold out to the Democratic party for a mess of pottage of incredible depth and diameter. By millions of constituents of legislators who voted funds for the use of Martin Dies, and millions of neighbors of the gentry who encourage the useful public services of Pappy O'Daniel and Theodore Bilbo, the South is excoriated for sending demagogues to Congress. By millions of readers of the *Saturday Evening Post* it is regarded as intellectually and esthetically sluggish. By readers of the liberal press it is regarded as doctrinaire, hyperemotional, and unintelligibly satisfied with itself. By millions of readers of best sellers and subscribers to book clubs, it is regarded as unsophisticated, at best quaint and at worst susceptible to dictators. By millions of graduates and foster children of Columbia Teachers College it is regarded as spiritually backward. By those who have found God out, the Bible Belt is regarded as gothically addicted to enthusiasm and, still worse, as being the uncurious slave of illusion. By those to whom fate has entrusted the norm, the South is known to be regrettably abnormal. As two untraveled nonsoutherners, members of the intelligentsia—of different ages, sexes, and points of view—have said, with easy assurance of immunity to the graver human perils, "The South does things to people."

What is worse is that people are doing things to the South: it has at last begun to overhear its critics and to nibble at the apple of conformity.

iii

To the new knowledge into which the South has bitten we shall return after a brief search for likelier images of the present reality. The standard brands of criticism, it is clear, are no more applicable to the South than to other sections, or are beside the point, or dissolve in the light of fact. Take the legend that the southerner is touchy, inordinately sensitive to criticism, aggressively defensive about everything southern. We might argue that any section which has been the recipient of as much adverse criticism from self-satisfied neighbors as has come to the South could only become touchy. We might argue that sensitiveness expresses an awareness of imperfection which is spiritually safer than a complacent conviction that one has come justly and triumphantly into Canaan. But the compelling fact is that outside the South one finds everywhere an equal sensitiveness, often growing into a vast, though unrecognized, self-distrust: "boosters" are saints, "knockers" accurst; Chambers of Commerce and "public relations" experts shout the glories of Megalopolis and Freedom Corners; in these forms of praise we hear not merely the voice of uncertainty but a positive dread of reality, an effort to drown out whispers that possibly all is not well. Finally, with regard to the blanket defensiveness attributed to southerners: they pull the blanket over themselves only at levels where it is not critically significant. What the outsider might observe, if he were less sure of how things go, is that the sharpest critics of the South are southerners—sharpest because they are concerned with the fundamental spiritual well-being in which outside critics rarely show any interest at all, and because they must face not only incomprehension abroad but the hostility of ignorance and privilege at home. In them one finds neither flabby local pride, nor laziness, nor sentimentality—nor faith in socio-political panaceas.

Another rather common allegation is that southerners are clannish, stick together defiantly, hate outsiders. But anyone who has observed a mixed southern community can see that where choices are possible it is not geography but intelligence and character that determine associations. The outsider bent on profits does not fight a solid South; he is soon bosomed among the homegrown entrepreneurs. The minority concerned with ideas and arts are not slow in finding common ground that transcends latitude. But the most fascinating phenomenon is the speed and the minimal margin of error with which the carpetbagger mentality and the Ku-Klux mentality, whether in business or education, identify each other and forge a strong bond. It works like a chemical reaction, and out of it arises, as a by-product, a dislike for individuals of courage and distinction, an antipathy which is far more vigorous than most intersectional dislikes and suspicions.

It is not our business, however, to compile a new Pseudodoxia Epidemica. This brief notice of conventional judgments suggests a paradoxical truth: that the devoted southerner is not at all devoted to everything and everybody southern, and that his devotion may express itself—and prove itself—by the severest criticism. Here we have a clue to an understanding of the South: that it must be sought in the paradoxes in which, in the end, human identity is rooted. Perhaps the general sense of the differentness of the South signifies merely that the essential paradoxes are closer to the surface and more visible to the common eye than those of other sections where a less broken historical continuity has made possible a morphological leveling-off, a handier suppression of the contradictions, the counterturns, the eruptions which are humanity's answer to professional simplifiers with easy generalities.

Of the paradoxes which the South offers to the observer, perhaps the most fundamental is that observed by Donald Davidson: that the South keeps a nostalgic eye on its birthright but at the same time hankers after the fleshpots. It faces, indeed, the perplexing problem of trying to harmonize the fleshpots and the Lares and Penates in one master scheme of interior decoration. Unlike aspiring householders who add antiques to their basic Grand Rapids equipment, the South starts with antiques, to which it is indeed devoted; but it is today finding the Grand Rapids finish more and more seductive. Again, there is on the one hand an almost Oriental ancestor-worship, so compelling that it seems at times to let the present exist only as an echo of a dominant past; and on the other there is a sheer love of the up-to-date which must be very encouraging to exporters of the up-to-date. The one part of the country that is conscious of a specific past longs for the "modern" and goes consciously after a streamlined industrialization that elsewhere was not quite so expressly planned. On the right there are the various material and emotional phenomena popularly summarized under the easy term *backwardness* (a state which may or may not be of spiritual advantage); on the left, an expanding devotion to "progress," which of all the intangibles receives the most explicit, insistent acclaim—at, for instance, the Conference of Southern Governors. Beside a triumphant "progressive" education which progresses

even faster than in the North and which has been rushing school systems off into a life of worldly accommodation as fast as they are born,
there are the Bible Belt's obduracies with respect to secular knowledge
(it is worth noting that the Belt has compensatory psychological immunities which most of the outer world apparently lacks: its suicide
rate must be the lowest in the nation). Sectarian schools with rigidly
delimited curricula flourish across the street from booming colleges
of commerce and engineering. But a general weakening of piety and
spirituality is partly camouflaged by an energetic, bustling ecclesiasticism which must be the envy of clergymen closer to Greenland's icy
mountains.

Again, there is on the one hand a degree of illiteracy greater than
that of any other part of the country; on the other, a highly disciplined
literacy from which springs some of the most complex and subtle of
modern American literature. The South produces a Margaret Mitchell
and a Robert Penn Warren, a Dorothy Dix and a William Faulkner.
Various southern states make relatively generous—some even lavish—
grants for education; yet often they commit the funds to gentlemen of
such inappropriate talents that their antics give one the impression of
watching parvenu poor whites on a gaudy holiday. Perhaps where nature is prodigal, even a continuously talked-of poverty cannot inspire
thrift with its hard corners; looking at evidence of a minor but possibly
symbolic kind, one sees in the South few of the out-of-date but carefully shined and preserved and long-used cars that are fairly abundant
elsewhere in America, but instead either bright new cars or else not-
old cars that have been worn hard and are ready to die young. Perhaps
a healthy indifference to the materialities of existence? Perhaps a habit
of living hard, keeping nothing back, running through capital when it
is available? Perhaps some not consciously recognized incapacity for
restraint? Southern undergraduate bodies show a marked inhospitality
to restraints, and especially to subtler forms of discipline; yet against
this there is a special southern passion for military training and for
military schools hardly equaled elsewhere. The same undergraduate
bodies exhibit a collegiate languor of notable amplitude—"southern
laziness," no doubt; yet against this there must be set, as a distinguishing quality of certain students, scientists, intellectuals, and writers, an
exceptional capacity for and devotion to intense, unremitting work.
The offspring of laborers can hardly be made to work; the apologists

of an old leisure-order hardly rest from work. Among the undergraduate bodies as already described—the products of bad schools and the victims of fuddled educators who treat students like political constituents—the educational problem is well-nigh hopeless; yet from just these bodies come saving individuals of extraordinary abilities who, without being wide-eyed, have an intense desire to know and master and produce that carries them beyond the conventional borders accessible to the youth of more sophisticated areas where the general level of academic achievement is higher. John Peale Bishop has remarked that once in the South old men customarily laid down their Horace beside their bourbon. To judge from the universities, most of their grandchildren lay down their comics book beside their Coca-Cola. Yet somewhere among them may be our best hopes for another Catullus or Juvenal or Lucretius.

In "southern pride" there is another nucleus of contradictions. At its finest it means an awareness of an achieved way of life, of beliefs courageously fought for, of old forms defended against new modes— that is, of an aristocratic stability in the best sense of the words; but that pride has been contorted by a century of exacerbation, and perhaps even more by the late Faustian corruptions which stop at no regional boundaries. With rare exceptions the modern self-esteem misses wholly the best justifications for solid pride—the distinguished work of artists, writers, and thinkers who include some of the best critics in the country. In fact, that South has such a habit of casually exporting talent like raw materials that it is as difficult to find a southern intellectual or poet at work on his native soil as it is to buy choice strawberries in Louisiana or choice peaches in Georgia. Nor is the man of insight who sticks to the native soil likely to have much attention paid to his insights; he is the archetypal prophet ignored; he finds that his fellow-southerners in need of prophecy turn to local moneybags or to newcomers who, drifting in from elsewhere to teach or administer or make money, seem hardly to sustain an export-import balance in human quality. Losing sight of its proper nourishment, pride feeds itself on material things—roads, buildings, increases of population. To change the terms somewhat: beside or beneath a self-assurance often considered characteristically southern there are evidences of diffidence and uncertainty. The diffident and the uncertain, not heeding the guidance of men of talent, seek firm foundations in the most obvious, and hence most deceptive, places. They admire office and tend to believe that the office makes the man. They worship bigness. Universities—and even their graduate schools—keep counting enrollments and measuring the size of the "plant." There is insufficient discrimination among bignesses.

A perverse pride is that of the southerner who scarifies southern indolence, lauds northern energy, debunks the Old South, and welcomes Progress with the enthusiasm of a hotel-greeter. Bobbing equally anchorless across the bay of opinion is the anxious neosoutherner, *né* elsewhere, who is in a loyal fever about "southern problems," announces his devotion to the life graceful and charming, and laments the loss of faithful "country blacks." One such convert, scarcely dry from his sacramental immersion in a S'wanee-Jordan, has proposed that southern libraries should be such that southerners can do all their graduate work in the South because only thus can they be adequately fitted to lead in the solution of southern problems. He forgets, then, to refrain from leading; and he ignores certain southerners who have a pretty good grip on southern problems despite the disadvantage of having been educated, not only not in the South, but not even in America. In the academic analogue of such enthusiasm we find the paradox of southern history: though in the South there is, inevitably, an exceptional, sensitive awareness of the past, the formal study of that past seems in some universities to be almost the private scholastic vocation of midwesterners.

iv

Of such contradictions as these, which are far from exhaustive, he who would define the differentness of the South must take account. The closeness of paradox to the surface evidences a considerable spontaneity and unselfconsciousness. What is happening now, however, is the replacement of spontaneous, even haphazard, existence by a conscious, rational, planned program; and rational management means the flattening out of special modes and features, which contribute to vital contradictions, into a smooth regularity designed by the fashion-sense of the majority.

After long resistance to a barrage of critical club-blows from abroad, the South, as we have said, is now listening to the serpentine voice of its critics, who say, "Be like us, and rejoice"; it has bitten into the apple of conformity; it has become self-conscious and put on the fig leaves of standardization; it has fled its naked individuality. It proposes—the vocal sections, at least—to become modern, progressive, industrial, urban, scientific, rational; and here is something of a problem. In abjuring differentness, perhaps the South leaves little that could be defended as an Earthly Paradise, yet it must depart with far greater misgivings than those which assailed the proto-exiles from Eden. For them, an unchosen proscription was meaningful: nemesis proved the godhead, long penance vindicated the system of beliefs, and ultimate salvation still beckoned. But upon its entry into the World, the South goes by choice (unless, taking a Spenglerian view, we consider it driven by historical necessity); it takes off a hairshirt and bids farewell to antique gods; nothing beckons except the well-to-do neighbors on the North Side. For the first parents, the rough Wanderjahre validated faith; for the South, a swift trip on the best concrete highways means, in the realm of faith and belief, a revolutionary gamble in which nothing is certain.

As a "backward" area by suddenly coming "forward" recapitulates a half-millennium of the cultural cycle, the temporal compression of conflicts heightens the possibilities of explosion or schizophrenia. It may be, of course, that the South has already made so many secret concessions to progress that it will have little nostalgic anguish and internecine struggle. Yet the very paradoxes we have noted imply that not all southerners march expectantly through the gilt archway whose attendant spirit is the Zeitgeist. If they who hold back can keep from being crushed by the leveling-out process, they will illuminate the real problem for the marchers, who otherwise will be a long time in seeing it straight. But it is in the light of that problem that the South will now come to seem more and more familiar, for the problem is embodied in the question that experience asks all of us: what shall we believe? How shall the spirit be nourished? The South is accepting the answer of the majority, and it will have, along with the majority, to make the great pragmatic test.

And having embarked on this perilous adventure, the South may surely expect, from certain distant but attentive observers, a congratulatory pat on the back for having disavowed an apparent failure of nerve.

V

When the South puts on sameness instead of difference, several interesting but perhaps not wholly foreseen consequences may follow. To the outer critics who have long lamented its alien status and who can now in some sort celebrate a triumph, the converted South may, paradoxically enough, bring unsuspected discomfort; and yet at the same time it may do a service more substantial than the flattery of imitation.

For in the standard hostile criticisms of the South there are, we may conjecture, two layers of meaning which rarely show through the familiar surface. In one respect, which is hardly likely to be surmised by the critics, the criticism has elements of the defensive; and conversely the criticized aspects of the South are themselves implied criticisms of a different cultural mode. All nonconformity is a moral judgment, and the South can only have been scourged by the conformity which it did not espouse. The South is lazy, the critics say: laziness is a criticism of puritanical energizing. The South is poor: poverty is a criticism of the profits which have assumed divinity. The South is backward: backwardness is a criticism of the get-ahead-and-devil-take-the-hindmost religion. The South is emotional and violent: emotionality and violence are a criticism of the calculating spirit. And so on.

So then we have had, at least in part, a pleasant irony: northern critics, in their onslaughts on the South, are seen to have been engaging, with the most innocent self-deception, in a bit of extracurricular, but nonetheless sturdy, self-defense. But may there not also be another, more piquantly ironic possibility in their critical fluency? Besides indirectly defending their own *modus vivendi,* have they not also, perhaps, succeeded in keeping their inquiring eyes away from themselves? For any attack on an outside entity or mode of life is often found, upon inspection, to constitute a partial way of avoiding a too-realistic view of oneself.

Xenophobia does, after all, substitute a reassuring telescope for a possibly disturbing microscope. Anti-alienism is like war: it is a boon to a distraught humanity eager to reduce the tragedy of life to melodrama. War comforts man by deluding him with the conviction that he is facing reality when in fact it permits him to get by with the facing of a simpler, secondary reality—that of physical survival. It validates the easy psychology of melodrama, by which all evil is across the water, and all is sound at home. This is no inconsiderable benevolence. Then peace relentlessly brings back the tragic burden of facing the primary reality, that of spiritual survival; here man cannot escape looking directly at himself. As long as the South was all different, and therefore inferior, and in need of reform, it was pretty comforting: it had the essential virtue of every No. 1 Problem—that of permitting the student to assume that all is well with himself and that to create a general, free-for-all Paradise he need only export, possibly at profitable rates, a modicum of that wellness. Problem No. 1 was, ironically, a double boon.

But when the South declares peace, gives up difference, and decides to be like the North, the North—or at least some quite articulate segments of it—may have, alas, to step out of a zestful and tonic melodrama, however well-meaning, as hero, it may have been. To change the figure: the South tells its physician, in effect, that it has a complete supply of all his pills. All that may be left for him to do is to heal himself—an awesome assignment. Perhaps the South, with ironic graciousness, will hold onto the race problem long enough to save the doctor from an immediate plunge into total introspection. But in the main the South is solidly in the World; it will not long be poor and lazy and backward; to the critic who risks travel, it will soon make things seem like home, all right—with better stores, hotels, services, and the like. But all the soothing and flattery will have their price. For will not the most convenient scapegoat be gone? Will not the reforming spirit, though nostalgic for foreign lands, have to undergo all the rigors of repatriation?

This is the ironically unsuspected discomfort that the New South may bring to the North: depriving it of the reassurance of a distant, unmistakable, and surely inferior enemy, and making it face—unless it can find another whipping boy—a subtler and more elusive and ever-present foe who will never surrender. But the discomfort bitter-coats an essential service: for it is surely a needed good to have to face oneself instead of turning one's reforming instinct loose among safely foreign corruptions and failures.

It is possible that even in the scapegoat stage the South has caused some of the missiles fired at it to ricochet and perhaps hit vulnerable spots in the triggermen. One thinks of the dismay aroused by the recent use, here and there, of the concept of original sin or radical evil;

Irwin Edman, for instance, indicates his persuasion that we face not evil but medicable evils—slums, dictators, wars, worms—a position rather typical of the anti-absolutism of our era. But do not the doctrinaire pluralists, those tireless pursuers of the evils that beset us all, prescribe a single good for the South? And do they not think, after all, that original sin is about the only way to account for the unregenerate state of the South? For slavery? For post-slavery negrophobia? If these are simply misdirected goods, or simple ailments, one sees few signs of medication; the southerner is simply beaten over the head—as if, oddly enough, even moderns were trying to scare out the devils of which he is possessed. And the tougher-minded southern fiction, according to some of its reviewers, springs, if not from original sin, at least from original nastiness or radical disagreeableness.

One must suppose, too, that the prescription of modern improvements for the South is rather illiberally dogmatic, and that there is a quite unpragmatic petulance in the attacks on southerners who have their hesitancies about the improvements. One must suppose further that the proponents of the rational mastery of life do not altogether rationally master these hesitancies about improvements. It ought not to be needful to argue that the hesitancy does not mean a positive love for, let us say, outside lavatories. Probably no southern conservative will feud against inside plumbing. But he is rather likely to insist that it will not save souls. He and a few of his fellows, who are suspected of radical intransigence, have a vestigial concern with souls and hope not to see standard amenities mistaken for agencies of salvation. They will not seriously object to sanitation, which Mr. Edman, we may assume, believes will put down quite a number of manageable evils; but it is not, they suspect, of sacramental efficacy.

We are, however, going to have a vast amount of sanitation, and other improvements. The main reasons for the exhorting or contemning of the South are on the way out, and we may anticipate, surely, a proportionate rise of neighborly viewing with pride. Yet even such new kindliness, if it come, may warm the heart of neither giver nor receiver: there is, after all, an ironic irrelevance in either scorn or admiration for the new cultural voyage. For there are no first-class passages in the boat in which we are all traveling through the not wholly trustworthy waters of our century.

IV. 17

The Southern Temper

(1953)

The Southern temper is marked by the coincidence of a sense of the concrete, a sense of the elemental, a sense of the ornamental, a sense of the representative, and a sense of totality. No one of these endowments is unshared; but their concurrency is not frequent. This concurrency is *a* condition of major art and mature thought. The endowments, like most endowments, are not possessed in entire freedom, without price. If you buy an endowment, you don't buy something else. To live with an endowment runs risks, and even the concurrency of several endowments does not guarantee a funding of the counterdeficiency which may accompany the possession of any single one.

The Southern temper is not the temper of all southerners, who, for all of the predeterminations of northerners from Portland, Maine, to Portland, Oregon, are as various as dwellers in other regions. The South generally—the politico-economic-social South, the problem South, the South in need of precept and reprimand—is not my business. It is after all so much like so much of the rest of the country that there is not much to say. The temper I will try to describe is that of certain novelists, poets, and critics who have now, for some twenty or twenty-five years, been at least in the corner of the literate public's eye.

The sense of the concrete, as an attribute of the fiction writer, is so emphatically apparent in Faulkner, Warren, Wolfe, so subtly and variously apparent in Porter, Welty, and Gordon, and so flamboyantly so in someone like Capote (who hardly belongs here at all) that everybody knows it's there. It is there, too, in the poetry of Ransom, Tate, and Warren. In fact, the lesson that fiction and poetry must be grounded in the sensory world, and the dramatic situation, has been learned very thoroughly in our day; everybody—even the students in writing courses whose goal is an abstraction, the omnipurchasing formula—knows how to go out and record the broken eggshells on the pavement, the smell of armpits and violets, the feel of chewing gum, the sound and fury, the synesthetic confluences. Most experts in sensography do not know what to do with their bursting haul, for they have not inherited or been provided with an adequate way of thinking about it or with it, and hence are likely to stop short with a record as lush as a seed catalog, as miscellaneously hard as hooves on concrete, and as variously pungent as a city market toward the end of the day. In the transcendence of aesthetic audio-visual aids, as we shall see, the Southerners are better off.

In criticism, the Southern sense of the concrete takes the form of a preoccupation with the individual work and the precise means by which its author goes about his business. Eliot, Richards, and Empson were predecessors in this critical mode; in America, Burke has long been working in it; and many successors have learned it, even to providing, at times, an embarrassment of explicatory riches. But in neither country is there any other group which, whatever its differences in opinion, can, because of its common background and its shared allegiances, be thought of as a group and which has so much sheer talent in all its parts as Ransom, Tate, Brooks, and Warren. Instinctively they move always to the individual poem; in answering challenges they incline not to linger in the realm of theory as such but to hurry on to the exemplary case. The concretist method extends over into their textbooks and is perhaps more conspicuous there than anywhere else. In the vast influence of these textbooks, imitated almost as widely as they are used (an influence gloomily and often suspiciously complained of), we see the spontaneous welcome of a method of literary study which has put adequate substance where not enough of it had been before. The critical analysis of concrete works by first-rate minds has been the chief influence in getting literary study out of the doldrums of the first three decades of the century, in giving it intellectual respectability, and in making it as attractive to gifted students as physics, mathematics, and medicine. The older schools of literary study gravely lacked intellectual distinction; the neohumanists, while at least they did offer the excitement of ideas and therefore some maturity of appeal, were deficient in the reading of the concrete work; but the literary historians, interested neither in ideas nor in the concrete work, lavished an essentially clerical perseverance and ingenuity upon matters in the main external to literature. As students of literature, they too often chose the realm of the "pseudoconcrete."

In one direction the more recent type of literary study, to which the chief impetus in this country has been given by Southerners, has tended to create a new order of teacher-critics; in another direction it has tended to create—a fact not yet noted, I believe—a more competent general reader. In this respect these critics, sometimes called "reactionary," have done a considerable service to democracy. The older historical mode of study had little to offer the general reader except occasional dashes of extracurricular enthusiasm but of its nature was concerned largely with training a rather narrow professional class—a technocracy of the humanities. Often the literature was forgotten entirely, with serious loss to the community.

The extraordinary competence in dealing with the concrete work is not matched at the level of theory; on the whole I suspect—and this may seem disputable—that Southern critics have not found the most effective theoretical formulations for their insights. Perhaps I should say "have not yet found"; or perhaps they have a deep suspiciousness of abstraction which inhibits the formulatory aspect of thought. In contrast with their enormous influence in focusing attention upon the individual work and its organic relations and in gaining adherents for the single theoretical position implied in their practice, namely that the individual work and its structure are the ultimate concern of literary study, the Southerners have had relatively little influence in other matters of theory—concepts of genre, stylistic and structural modes, etc. This is perhaps less true of Tate, though his intellectual impact is more marked in nonliterary matters. The Southerners have broken trail for Wellek and Warren, and for some very effective generalizations by Wimsatt. But in the specifications of literary form and function, in the extension of theory into new domains and problems, they have been much less influential, say, than Burke. Yet the true counterpoint to the Southerners is not Burke but the Chicagoans, elaborating dogmatic theory, providing a valuable center of speculation but living predeterminedly, monastically, away from the concrete work, remaining therefore almost without influence, seeming content to issue caveats and Everlasting No's and to ambush those who are affirming the living literature and enlarging its status. If their peculiarly arid rationalist plateau could be irrigated by a fresh flow of the literary works themselves, freely submitted to and spontaneously experienced, they might find a more fruitful role than that of erecting such inexorable proofs and carrying so little conviction. In their high abstractionism they are at the opposite extreme from the pseudoconcretism of the old-line scholars.

In their social criticism the Southerners are led, by their sense of the concrete, to suspect the fashionable abstraction, the clichés and slogans, which to the unperceiving may seem the very embodiment of truth but which on inspection are found to ignore many realities of the actual human being. Progress? The concrete evidence of the human being is that he does not change much, that he may actually be harmed by the material phenomena usually implied by *progress,* and that in any case his liability to moral difficulty remains constant. The mechanized life? The concrete evidence is that man is up to it only within limits, that its exactions are more damaging than those of a slower and more laborious mode of life, that he needs regular work in an individualized context, and that few human beings are capable of making leisure fruitful rather than destructive. Political utopias? Man is perfectly capable of making certain improvements in social and political order, but to assume that the millennium is here or will ever come is to ignore the concrete facts of the nature of man. In such realizations the Southerners are by no means alone. Yet it is worthwhile rehearsing such points, though they are neither unique nor unfamiliar, to suggest the relationship between the creative writing, the criticism, and the social thought, and to call attention to the extreme concreteness of the regionalist and Agrarian aspects of Southern thought, which have been felt to be very unfashionable and "unpractical." What about the American ideal of the "practical"? May not practicality itself be, paradoxically, an abstraction from reality, that is, another instance of the "pseudoconcrete"? This is certainly what is implied in Warren's persistent concern, from his own fiction to his essay on Conrad, with the problem of the "idea" (or even the "illusion")—the ideal or meaning or value which establishes the quality of the deed or "redeems" it. In terms of man's need for spiritual grounding we have "the idea as concrete." This rejection of a moral positivism implies a similar objection to philosophical positivism as another mode of addiction to the pseudoconcrete. But that attitude, which is expressed recurrently by Tate, carries us into another aspect of the Southern temper, with which we must deal later.

The sense of the elemental and the sense of the ornamental are roughly complementary phases of the Southern temper—complementary at least to the extent that in our historical context an awareness of the elements is likely to lead to a rejection of ornament, and a devotion to ornament may make the elements seem unacknowledgeable. Fifty years ago, of course, ornament was in the lead, whereas now—not always without self-deception—we tender greater devotion to the elements. In architecture the shift from Victorian Gothic to "modern," with its utilitarian aesthetics, is one symbol of the change in emphasis. But the dramatic version of the elements is still a pretty polite thing, and the mid-century modernist is often left very uncomfortable by the amount of violence in Faulkner and Warren, by their sense of the furious drives that contort and distort men, by the crazy transformations of personality in people under stress, by the unornamented varieties of sex, by all the passions unamenable to sentimentalizing diminuendo. And equally, we should add, by the juxtaposing of life and death in Porter, the insistent awareness of death in Porter and Gordon, and by a certain mystery of being inseparable from the closest factuality in Elizabeth Madox Roberts and Welty. These are only for the mature. For the others, there will be satisfaction with Wolfe, with whom the elemental is not very much more than an orchestral wind soughing through the pines with a kind of calculated unhappiness (there are occasional such accents in Randall Jarrell, too)—an enchanting tune for young men, who thus, with little imaginative commitment or risk, are permitted to enjoy the sensation of being torn by force and sorrow. For the others, also, there is Caldwell, who does not disturb but reassures by selecting materials which elevate almost any reader to an Olympian eminence. But his appropriate marriage of the libidinous and the farcical reduces the elemental to the elementary. Another way of saying this is that he is not sufficiently concrete; just as one may be concrete without being elemental—as in the standard "realistic" novel, or in the work of a satirist like Mary McCarthy—so one may strive for the elements and end in an abstraction: with Caldwell, lust is almost a paradigm or an idea, withdrawn from a concrete human complexness. For these others, who like the elements easy, there will be difficulty in the conception of man as linked to nature, in Ransom's idea that man must make peace with nature. This kind of elementalism is hardly welcome to an age given to two other forms of naturalism—the literary sort in which man is a victim of nature and naturelike forces and can feel sorry for himself, and the scientific sort in which man is a victor over nature and can feel proud of himself. The man of the age who may be puzzled by Ransom may find it easier going with Hemingway, who is inclined to view nature as conquerable, and who, furthermore, for all of his feeling for death and deathliness, is hampered—and not quite willingly—by a fastidiousness that constricts his presentation of the elemental.

As a society we oscillate uneasily between bareness and overstuffed elegance; Hollywood plays it stark one minute, lush the next. Either extreme is hostile to true grace, social or spiritual. If we are uncomfortable with the elemental, we also shy at the true ornament, that of manner and mind (though we are rather tolerant of the spurious kinds). For that reason, the Southern sense of both is distinctive. To speak of the Southern sense of the ornamental is in one way rather startling, for the literary criticism of Southerners has been marked by the severity of its functionalism (with some exceptions, perhaps, for Ransom); yet I am by no means sure that the formal perfection which is the implied standard of judgment in many of the Southerners' literary analyses is not itself the essence of ornament. For by ornament I do not mean superfluous or distracting embellishment; rather I mean nonutilitarian values; whatever comes from the feeling for rhythm, the sense of the incantatory, the awareness of style as integral in all kinds of communication; the intangible goods that lie beyond necessity; grace. A political reflection of the sense of the ornamental is "southern oratory"—in most of its present manifestations debased, parodistic, really pseudo-ornamental. A social reflection is "southern manners," a reality which has virtually been blotted out by promotional facsimiles—the unhappy fate of any virtue that is popularized and made the object of public self-congratulation. Something more than a social reflection appears in contemporary Southerners' assertions of the grace of antebellum life; the very assertion attests to the sense of which I speak. These assertions, which are a way of affirming a value, raise an important issue—the counterattack charges that the social cost of the achievement was prohibitive. Though we may acknowledge that the cost was too high, we must also face the counterproblem of the cost of doing without the value—a problem of which the Southerners at least serve to remind us. To return to literature: the critical manner of the Southerners, even in vigorous controversy, is on the whole urbane, indeed strikingly so compared with such others as the scholarly cumbersome style, the *Partisan* truculent, and the Chicago opaque. The sense of nuance, refinement, the special communication by tone and color, is conspicuously acute. Finally, the sense of ornament appears in the rhetorical bent of Warren and Faulkner—not that with either of them style itself is a substance, open to decorative arrangement on the surface of another substance (characters, ideas, etc.), but that there is a special awareness of the verbal medium, a disposition to elaborate and amplify as a fundamental mode of communication, a willingness to utilize the rich and the rhythmical, an instinctive exploration of the stylistic instrument to the ultimate point at which one senses something of the supererogatory but not yet the excessive or obtrusive. At least in its application to Faulkner, this statement will run into objections. But even in most cases where Faulkner apparently lays himself open to the charge of mannerism or sheer lack of control I believe it demonstrable that his main devices—length of sentence and frequency of parenthesis—are meaningful as formal equivalents of a central imaginative impulse: to view experience as inclusively as possible, to mold-together-into-one, to secure a godlike view of present and past as one. But this brings us to a point for which we are not yet ready—the Southern sense of totality.

If the sense of the ornamental and the sense of the elemental at least in part complement each other, so the sense of the concrete and the sense of the representative may interact fruitfully. To have, as a writer, a sense of the concrete but not a sense of the representative is to exemplify in one way the modern dilemma—to have the concrete world, apparently controlled more or less, at one's fingertips and not to know what it means. To have a sense of the representative alone is to be in danger of falling into hollow allegory. The Southerners, we have seen, always cling to the concrete—in fiction and poetry, in literary and social criticism—but they are not chained to the concrete. The best fictional characters are always individuals, but something more than individuals too: Willie Stark is Willie Stark, but his career embodies a philosophical issue; the Snopeses are so representative as to have become a byword; in Welty's work we see Everyman as salesman, in Gordon's as sportsman, in Porter's as a soul lost in the currents of time. Warren and Faulkner both dig into the past, not for the past's sake, but because of a sense of the immanence of past in present, and for the sake of finding or creating tales of mythic value. It is presumably for some success in this endeavor that the Southerners have won a substantial audience. They certainly cannot appeal either to hunters of the trivial exotic or to the devotees of the stereotype or "pseudorepresentative"—that product of an imagination weak at the general or universal (and for that matter, at the concrete too). Under sense of the representative we can include Warren's preoccupation with the "idea"—a significant reaction against American anti-Platonism. Again, if Southern criticism is marked by its devotion to the concrete work and to the concrete structural elements, it is equally marked by a sensitivity to the symbolic, to the work as symbolic of the writer, or more particularly to the meanings and values symbolically present. It boldly assumes as axiomatic the symbolic quality of all works, and finds in the explication of the symbolic content a basic means of distinguishing the trivial and the important. And to give one final instance of the sense of the representative, this one from the social criticism: if regionalism is on the one hand marked by a sense of the concrete necessities of immediate living and has emphasized the specificities of local place and manner, it is also true that regionalism has been said to provide a sound base for internationalism. From this point of view regionalism has not been a vain separatism or a sterile cult of uniqueness, but at once a rejection of the abstract "differentness" implied by nationalism and a search for a mode of embodying the representative human values on which both individual life and a sound internationalism must rest.

Finally, the sense of totality: it is a sense of time, of the extent of human need and possibility, of world and of spirit. It appears in

Faulkner's style; in the critical focusing on the organic whole; in the antinominalism which has been most explicitly formulated by Richard Weaver; in Tate's emphasis on mythic or nonscientific values; in the conjunction, in numerous pieces of fiction, of violence and spiritual awareness—a conjunction disturbing to readers who are used to taking one part of the whole at a time; in the penumbra of mystery—a mystery to be accepted, not solved—always bordering the clear light of Welty's characters and scenes; in the nostalgia, so frequent in Porter, for the reality felt behind the stage of action; in the questioning of nostrums and panaceas which can exist only by treating a part of human truth as if it were the whole; in suspecting our inclination to separate the present from all the rest of time, to exhaust all devotion in the religion of humanity, and to consider scientific inquiry as the only avenue to truth.

Whereas Hemingway's most reliable talent is that for seizing upon the lyric moment, Warren's enveloping mind can hardly work in short stories but needs the room to be found in the novel (or the long poem); Faulkner is impelled to invent whole sagas; Gordon's stories expand into the myth of a recurrent character. In their instinct for inclusiveness, these and others, in both fiction and social criticism, dig into and rely upon the past. For the past is in the present; we do not live alone in time, thrust into eminence, and into finality, by what went before, servile and unentangling. With their sense of the whole, the Southerners keep reminding us that we are not altogether free agents in the here and now, and that the past is part master. The past also provides allegiance and perspective—not as an object of sentimental devotion but as a storehouse of values which may be seen in perspective and at the same time provide us an entirely necessary perspective on our own times. Through a sense of the past we may escape provincialism in time, which is one mark of the failure of a sense of totality.

With a comparable unwillingness to be uncritically content inside fashionable limits, the Southerners apparently find the religion of humanity inadequate. Not that any of them do not value the human; the question is whether the obligation to be humane can be secured by a secular religion, and whether humanity alone can adequately engage the religious imagination. Inclined to question whether suffering is totally eliminatable or univocally evil, the Southerners are most aware that, as Tate has put it, man is incurably religious and that the critical problem is not one of skeptically analyzing the religious impulse or of thinking as if religion did not exist for a mature individual and culture, but of distinguishing the real thing and the surrogates. They have a large enough sense of reality not to exclude all enlightenment that is not laboratory-tested. For them, totality is more than the sum of the sensory and the rational. The invention of gods is a mark, not of a passion for unreality, but of a high sense of reality; is not a regrettable flight from science, but a more accurate approach to the problem of being. The Southerners utilize and invoke reason no less than, let us say, any follower of John Dewey; but also they suspect an excessive rationalism which mistakes the ailerons for the power plant and fosters the illusion that all nonrationalities have been, or can be, discarded.

This kind of evidence of the sense of totality is plain enough in Southern criticism and the fiction (though the latter, as yet, has difficulty in finding a dramatic form for the sense). I am inclined to add that the whole man is really not very fashionable right now, and that the sense of totality is likely to get one into disrepute as a kind of willful and fanciful archaist, for we are supposed to have got man properly trimmed down to a true, *i.e.,* naturalistic, dimension. Aside from this intellectual majority-pressure, there is another difficulty in that institutions that historically stand for the sense of totality have suffered from loss of belief in their role and from an addiction to organizational politics, so that to be believed to be unreservedly *en rapport* with them may lead to misconceptions of one's role. But the Southerners have been content to take their chances, with very little effort at self-protection by evasive movement.

The Southerners, indeed, have a surprisingly "liberal" complexion; they are in the classical American tradition of "protest." Their agrarianism could be read as a protest against both capitalist giantism and Marxism, their regionalism as a protest against abstract nationalism and uniformitarianism, their essential critical habits as a protest against the relativist antiquarianism of literary study (their fondness for "paradox" a protest against an exaggerated view of the straightforwardness of literature; for symbolism, a protest against the hampering limitations of realism, which had assumed a normative role). And their sense of totality, we have seen, leads to overt or implied protests against the

restrictions of secular rationalism. There is, of course, protest and protest. In its most familiar manifestations, protest is topical; a social or
political injustice brings it forth, often in a historical context that may
require great bravery and sacrifice of the protestant—and is alleviated.
Yet this context may so mold the style of the liberal protestantism that
it may go on like a habit, the old slogans becoming platitudes, the old
courage replaced by fluency and complacency, the old vitality declin-
ing into sheer forgetfulness of the calendar. Thus standard liberalism
of the 1950s seems at times to be still living in the 1920s. Then there is
another protest, the protest exemplified by the Southerners—what I
should call a radical protestantism because it is rooted in the sense of
totality. It is a philosophical protest against lack of wholeness, against
exclusions that restrict human potentiality, against the naturalist clo-
sure of other avenues to wisdom. Though it is nowadays a minority
operation, we may perhaps risk calling it, according to its actual nature, catholic. If Mr. Tate, who has exhibited it with particular force,
becomes, as we must expect, the most protestant of Catholics, his
fellow-Southerners, we may predict, will become no less catholic in
their protestantism.

I want to reemphasize my earlier statement that it is in the strength
and the *combination* of the qualities enumerated that the Southern
temper is distinctive. No trait is distinctively southern, of course, and
all of them may be found to some extent in other American literature
and thought, *i.e.*, in the American temper. As a people we doubtless
have a considerable sense for the concrete, yet we often take up with
abstractions that will not bear much critical inspection—*e.g.*, freedom
as an absolute. We like to be at once "down to earth" and up to the
amenities, but we are perhaps too Victorian to feel at ease with the
elemental, and too anti-Victorian to trust the ornamental. As for a
sense of the representative: we have produced Hawthorne and Melville
and James, though it is only lately that we have begun to estimate them
seriously; and we are inclined to take a rather particularistic view of
ourselves. We have enjoyed special immunities, and they tend to seem
an inalienable grace. And though we like the phrase "the whole man,"
it is perhaps the sense of totality which is least widely possessed among
us. On the philosophical side, it is our bent to take the naturalist part

for the whole; and since those who would argue for a larger view seem contrary, out of line, unwilling to "advance" with the rest, and even prone to the last sin against the times—invoking the past—we are honestly ready to regard them as in headlong retreat. This view must often have tried the Southern temper, and have seemed to invite a reply in the words of Agatha in *The Family Reunion:*

> In a world of fugitives
> The person taking the opposite direction
> Will appear to run away.

Acknowledgments

The author and the publisher express gratitude to copyright-holders and original publishers for permission to reprint:

To *Four Quarters* for "*Ship of Fools*: Notes on Style" (1962); to the *Kentucky Review* for "RPW at LSU: Some Reminiscences" (1981); to the *Louisiana English Journal* for "The Past: Fact, Fancy, and Luck" (1974); to the editor of *Shenandoah:* The Washington and Lee University Review, for "Salesmen's Deaths: Documentary and Myth," copyright 1969 by Washington and Lee University;

To George Core, editor of the *Sewanee Review*, for articles first published in the *Sewanee Review:* "Melpomene as Wallflower; or, The Reading of Tragedy," LV (1947), copyright by the University of the South, 1947, 1975; "Tangled Web," LIX (1951), copyright by the University of the South, 1951, 1979; "Baton Rouge and LSU Forty Years After," LXXXVIII (1980), copyright 1980 by Robert B. Heilman; "Cleanth Brooks and *The Well Wrought Urn*," XCI (1983), copyright 1983 by Robert B. Heilman; and "The Story of the *Southern Review*," XCIII (1985), copyright 1985 by Robert B. Heilman;

To the *Southern Review* for "Williams on Long: The Story Itself," n.s., VI (1970), copyright 1970 by Robert B. Heilman;

To the Louisiana State University Press for "Cleanth Brooks: Some Snapshots, Mostly from an Old Album," from *The Possibilities of Order: Cleanth Brooks and His Work*, edited by Lewis P. Simpson, copyright © 1976 by Louisiana State University Press; for "Spokesman and Seer: The Agrarian Movement and European Culture," from *A Band of Prophets: The Vanderbilt Agrarians After Fifty Years*, edited by William C. Havard and Walter Sullivan, copyright © 1982 by Louisiana State University Press; and for "Some Aspects of LSU Then," from *The "Southern Review" and Modern Literature, 1935–1985,* edited by Lewis P. Simpson, James Olney, and Jo Gulledge, copyright © 1988 by Louisiana State University Press;

To the University Press of Mississippi for "*Losing Battles* and Winning the War," from *Eudora Welty: Critical Essays,* edited by Peggy Whitman Prenshaw, copyright 1979 by the University Press of Mississippi;

To Louis D. Rubin, Jr., and Robert D. Jacobs (eds.), *Southern Renascence: The Literature of the Modern South,* The Johns Hopkins University Press (Baltimore and London, 1953), for "The Southern Temper";

To the Flora Levy Humanities Series, which published "Mrs. Cleanth Brooks: Reminiscences" along with Cleanth Brooks's lecture, "*All the King's Men:* The Local and the Universal" (1989).

"The South Falls In" originally appeared in *A Southern Vanguard,* edited by Allen Tate (New York, 1947).

Full bibliographical details on all of these essays and reviews are provided in the following "Bibliography: Writings on Southern Subjects by Robert Bechtold Heilman."

Bibliography: Writings on Southern Subjects by Robert Bechtold Heilman

CONTRIBUTIONS TO BOOKS

"The South Falls In." In *A Southern Vanguard: The John Peale Bishop Memorial Volume,* edited by Allen Tate. New York, 1947.

"The Southern Temper." In *Southern Renascence: The Literature of the Modern South,* edited by Louis D. Rubin, Jr., and Robert D. Jacobs. Baltimore and London, 1953.

"Cleanth Brooks: Some Snapshots, Mostly from an Old Album." In *The Possibilities of Order: Cleanth Brooks and His Work,* edited by Lewis P. Simpson. Baton Rouge, 1976.

"*Losing Battles* and Winning the War." In *Eudora Welty: Critical Essays,* edited by Peggy W. Prenshaw. Jackson, Miss., 1979.

"Spokesman and Seer: The Agrarian Movement and European Culture." In *A Band of Prophets: The Vanderbilt Agrarians After Fifty Years,* edited by William C. Havard and Walter Sullivan. Baton Rouge, 1982.

"Some Aspects of LSU Then." In *The "Southern Review" and Modern Literature 1935–1985,* edited by Lewis P. Simpson, James Olney, and Jo Gulledge. Baton Rouge, 1988.

JOURNAL ARTICLES

"*Ship of Fools:* Notes on Style." *Four Quarters,* XII (November, 1962), 46–55.

"Tennessee Williams: Approaches to Tragedy." *Southern Review,* n.s., I (October, 1965), 770–90.

"Salesmen's Deaths: Documentary and Myth." *Shenandoah Review,* XX (Spring, 1969), 20–28.

"The Past: Fact, Fancy, and Luck." *Louisiana English Journal*, XIV (Fall, 1974), 7–15.

"Baton Rouge and LSU Forty Years After." *Sewanee Review*, LXXXVIII (Winter, 1980), 126–43.

"RPW at LSU: Some Reminiscences." *Kentucky Review*, II (Spring, 1981), 31–46.

"Cleanth Brooks and *The Well Wrought Urn*" ("The Critics Who Made Us" series). *Sewanee Review*, XCI (Spring, 1983), 322–34.

REVIEWS

"Melpomene as Wallflower; or, The Reading of Tragedy." *Sewanee Review*, LV (Winter, 1947), 154–66. (Robert Penn Warren, *All the King's Men*)

"Tangled Web." *Sewanee Review*, LIX (Winter, 1951), 107–19. (Robert Penn Warren, *World Enough and Time*)

"Schools for Girls." *Sewanee Review*, LX (Spring, 1952), 299–309. (William Faulkner, *Requiem for a Nun*; Caroline Gordon, *The Strange Children*; Shirley Jackson, *Hangsaman*)

"Williams on Long: The Story Itself." *Southern Review*, n.s., VI (October, 1970), 935–53. (T. Harry Williams, *Huey Long*)

"Ty Cobb: The Hero and His Warts." *American Scholar*, LIII (Autumn, 1984), 541–46. (Charles C. Alexander, *Ty Cobb*)

"The Story of the *Southern Review*." *Sewanee Review*, XCIII (Spring, 1985), 330–33. (Thomas W. Cutrer, *Parnassus on the Mississippi: The "Southern Review" and the Baton Rouge Literary Community, 1935–1985*)

"Mr. Tate and the Biographical Idiom." *Sewanee Review*, XCVII (Spring, 1989), 289–93. (Walter Sullivan, *Allen Tate: A Recollection*)

"*Robert Penn Warren and American Idealism*" by John Burt. *Journal of English and Germanic Philology*, LXXXVIII (July, 1989), 459–62.

Brief reviews in the *United States Quarterly Book List*:

Flannery O'Connor, *Wise Blood*, September, 1952, p. 256.

Robert Penn Warren, *Brother to Dragons*, March, 1954, p. 57.

Flannery O'Connor, *A Good Man Is Hard To Find*, December, 1955, p. 472.

Robert Penn Warren, *Band of Angels*, December, 1955, pp. 472–73.

OTHER

"Mrs. Cleanth Brooks: Reminiscences." Published with Cleanth Brooks, *"All the King's Men": The Local and the Universal*. Lafayette, La., 1989.

Index

273